**SAGE ANNUAL REVIEWS OF
STUDIES IN DEVIANCE**
Volume 2

SAGE ANNUAL REVIEWS OF STUDIES IN DEVIANCE ➤

Series Editors: EDWARD SAGARIN
CHARLES WINICK
The City College of the City University of New York

Deviance is one of the most important, exciting and stimulating areas in sociology. It covers the entire spectrum of activities and people who are disvalued, denigrated, punished, ostracized, and in other ways made to feel undesired and undesirable in society—whether this be for something that was done (as the commission of a crime), or for some peculiar stigmatic status. It extends into criminology, social problems, social pathology, and numerous other areas. Despite many texts, readers, and countless journal articles, there has never been a serial publication devoted exclusively to deviance. It is to fill this gap that this annual series is being launched.

Volumes in this series: ━━━━━━━━━━━━━━━━━━━━➤

DEVIANCE
and
MASS
MEDIA

Edited by
CHARLES WINICK

 **SAGE PUBLICATIONS**   Beverly Hills   London

For information address:

SAGE PUBLICATIONS, INC.
275 South Beverly Drive
Beverly Hills, California 90212

SAGE PUBLICATIONS LTD
28 Banner Street
London ECIY 8QE

Printed in the United States of America

Library of Congress Cataloging in Publication Data

Main entry under title:
Deviance and mass media.

(Sage annual reviews of studies in deviance; v. 2)
Includes bibliographical references.
1. Deviant behavior in mass media—Addresses, essays, lectures. 2. Mass media—Social aspects—United States—Addresses, essays, lectures. 3. Mass media—Psychological aspects—United States—Addresses, essays, lectures. I. WINICK, Charles, 1922-
HN90.M3D48   301.6'2   78-16024
ISBN O-8039-1040-1
ISBN O-839-1041-X pbk.

FIRST PRINTING

CONTENTS

DEVIANCE AND MASS MEDIA
Introducing a Volume

CHARLES WINICK

For a good part of this century, many different kinds of deviance were attributed to the regnant mass medium of the time. In turn, movies, magazines, radio, fiction, comic books, popular music, television, advertising, and rock music have been said to share responsibility for such problems as robbery, burglary, poor grades at school, antisocial fantasies, drug abuse, the "youth revolution," declining college entrance examination scores, decline of moral standards, poor diet, fostering passivity, the amotivational syndrome, wasting time, desensitization, amorality, and even war, rape, and murder.

Media themselves have been said to be deviant in a variety of ways. Obscenity and blasphemy are crimes which may be committed by a specific media modality, and the perpetrators of those crimes may go to prison. A mass medium can act as a vehicle for the dissemination of ideas about a particular kind of deviant behavior.

Heavy exposure to one or another medium may be implicated in the gestation of destructive activity. In a 1977 Florida trial, the defense maintained that

7

15-year old Ronney Zamora, who admitted killing an 82-year old woman, had become a sociopath by virtue of "television intoxication," or a heavy diet of action-adventure and policy programs. Although a jury convicted Zamora, the court permitted his lawyer to make the argument.

The Supreme Court has ruled in a 1978 decision in the "Born Innocent" television case that First Amendment rights of a mass medium may not prevent it from being sued for its possible role in contributing to the genesis of a specific crime. No matter how this case is ultimately decided in the courts, the principle of possible media liability for aftereffects of a communication is a new element in the continuing debate over the effects of media. At issue here are the central considerations of content and effects of media and how they are perceived by audiences.

The 14 reports that appear in this volume grapple with the relationships between deviance and the media in a number of exciting and original ways. The chapters are grouped into four categories: content oriented studies, a report on deviant media behavior, comparative studies, and analysis of the role of media in contributing to deviance.

George Gerbner's content analysis of much comic book and "anti-drug abuse" literature suggests how media use stigmatization as a form of social control and a way of exerting political power. Philip Leonhard-Spark's article on the ways in which obesity is presented in the media shows how an ideal is formulated and disseminated. Charles Winick traces the concept of mental illness and psychiatrists through a half century of movies. The presentation of illness on television is documented by Joan Liebmann-Smith and Sharon L. Rosen. Death in condolence cards is the focus of a content study by Abigail Stahl Woods and Robert G. DeLisle. A synthesis of how crime and law enforcement are portrayed in newspapers and television is set forth by Joseph R. Dominick.

An unusual case study of media deviance is documented by Karl Erik Rosengren, Peter Arvidsson, and Dahn Sturesson, writing from Sweden.

Two comparative studies help to broaden perspectives. On the basis of field work in England and America, Gilbert Geis identifies differences in the two country's media coverage of rape. Andrew Karmen scrutinizes differences in coverage of an actual event which also became a major media event.

Public policy is often believed to be influenced by the role of media in contributing to deviance. Sanform Sherizen underscores how newspaper images of crime are based on very limited forms of reporting. Writing from Israel, Gerald Cromer sets forth a model for character assassination in the press. The extent to which transsexualism is a mass media creation is documented by Edward Sagarin. Nonvoting as a special kind of deviant behavior is explored in terms of motivations and media use by Garrett J. O'Keefe and Harold Mendelsohn. A British perspective on the crucial issue of how media relate to violence as one kind of deviant behavior is provided by James D. Halloran.

The contributors to this volume focus on a number of major issues. They have raised central questions and collected groundbreaking data. They have helped us in understanding one of the most complex and vexing issues of our time: the relationships between deviance and mass media.

Mass Treatments
of Deviance:
Some
Contemporary
Examples

Part 1

1

DEVIANCE AND POWER
Symbolic Functions of "Drug Abuse"

GEORGE GERBNER

AUTHOR'S NOTE: *An earlier version of this chapter appeared as "Symbolic Functions of 'Drug Abuse': A Mass Communications Approach," studies in the Anthropology of Visual Communication, 1974 (1): 27-34.*

Modern culture power means mass communication. Mass communication is the mass production of images and their discharge into the mainstream of the common symbolic environment (Gerbner, 1972). The ability to print the Book (Bible) and distribute it to laymen was necessary to break up a rigidly land-based religious order. The ability to mass-produce and disseminate the symbolic link that binds far-flung communities together has loosened the hold of *all* traditional religions on mental life and has created a new religion out of the merger of technology and culture. The chief cultural nexus of modern governance is no longer church and state; it is mass media and state (Gerbner, 1977).

Symbolic functions are the way things actually work in mass-produced culture rather than the way they are supposed to work. The symbolic function of deviance as a cultural concept is to define the norm and delineate that which is beyond the scope of normal behavior. That function is of course at the heart of the process of socialization and acculturation, i.e., the process of making us behave voluntarily and normally or "naturally" in socially functional ways.

The critical question is "functional for whom?" Much as we would like to share the benefits of society as broadly as possible, conflicts of interest prevent many values from being equitably shared. If a rich person's dog gets the milk needed to save a poor person's child from the rickets, that is how a purely objective market mechanism is "normally" supposed to work; from each according to ability, to each according to pocketbook. Social welfare, from that "objective" point of view, is a deviation from the norm. Objectivity itself is a cultural concept which arose in the 19th century to make it possible to manipulate symbolic functions, particularly by the press, and to hide their dysfunctions behind a facade of impersonality (Schiller, 1978).

Much of what is reported and depicted as deviant purports to describe some abnormal state of affairs or persons. The symbolic function of the depiction, however, is to make it easier to behave toward the subject of the depiction in "abnormal" but (to the symbol manipulators, at least) highly functional ways.

Social behavior that is misanthropic, prejudicial, and often murderous is made "normal" through the effective use of a series of images of some abhorrent "reality" or implacable "enemy." We can behave barbarically toward a group of people best if we can call them barbarians and thus appear only to be defending our more civilized norms. Large-scale terror must be sustained by vivid images of horror that would be visited upon us if we did not keep "them" under control. The symbolic function of violence is to demonstrate power and cultivate fear of power. Criminals are those who can be dealt with by legitimately suspending normal rules of humanity and decency. We tend to call a group of people insane if we want to suspend normal rules of rationality and reason in managing them.

When a certain type of practice crosses class lines it may become vulgar or illegal or otherwise deviant and thus usable for stigmatization and control. Obscenity is Saxon peasant idiom intruding into the speech of Norman nobles. Crime is the ruled trying to act like rulers.

These and other definitions of deviance function as instruments of social control and mechanisms of social stability and maintenance. That is not to say that there are no "real" barbarians or criminals or mentally ill people, but that the reality of these terms is inextricably mixed with their projective use to deal with threats to the social order or, if needed, to enhance the structure of power within the social order against invented threats.

The image of the "drug abuser," quite independently from the reality behind that image, has been a useful instrument of such power. Not so long ago, narcotics in the U.S. were a luxury for the idle rich to enjoy in relative obscurity. It was only after World War II that the ghettos of America reached the level of becoming lucrative markets for a commodity that helps enslave its customers.

Congress made the sentencing of federal narcotics offenders mandatory in 1951. The number of arrests doubled within 10 years. The largest outbreaks continued to occur in low-income neighborhoods even if suburbs and campuses were to get the most publicity. Stiffer penalties speeded the process. By the mid-sixties it took only four years to double the rate of arrests. Most of them were—and still are—made in the areas where most of all arrests are made: the "underprivileged" neighborhoods. In July 1972 it was reported that President Nixon ordered arrests doubled in *one year (Philadelphia Inquirer,* 1972):

> During a meeting in his Oval Office, Mr. Nixon pointed to a chart showing 16,144 arrests in fiscal 1972—compared with the 1969 figure of 8,465—and said, "I'd like to see this number doubled next year." "We very likely may do that," responded Myles Ambrose, special consultant to the President and director of the Office of Drug Abuse Law Enforcement.

The same week, long-suppressed government reports revealed that narcotics investigators saw "no prospect" of halting smuggling into the U.S. Despite daily reports of "record" seizures, less than one percent of the heroin flow was intercepted. "It's nonsense to me to keep reading these stories about how we're going to stop it from growing," said Mr. Ambrose. "The fact of the matter is that we're not thinking so much about the addicts as the 10 million other people they might infect," he added *(New York Times,* 1972).

Conjuring up the vision of 10 million addicts when, in fact, even one-twentieth was an artificially inflated number was part of one of the most extraordinary power plays in American history. Its White House cast included John D. Ehrlichman, Egil Krogh, Jr., E. Howard Hunt, G. Gorden Liddy, Robert Mardian and John Dean. The scenario, as documented by Edward Jay Epstein (1977b:51), assumed that:

> if Americans could be persuaded that their lives and the lives of their children were being threatened by a rampant epidemic of narcotics addiction, they would not object to decisive government actions, such as no-knock warrants, pretrial detention, wiretaps, and unorthodox strike

forces—even if the emergency measures had to cross or circumvent the traditional rights of a suspect. To achieve this state of fear required transforming a relatively small heroin addiction problem—which even according to the most exaggerated estimates directly affected only a minute fraction of the population in 1971—into a plague that threatened all. This in turn required the artful use of the media to propagate a simple but terrifying set of stereotypes.

THE CULTURAL SCENARIO

The underlying cultural scenario has much deeper roots. The history of drugs intermingles with that of global and—wherever it took hold—domestic imperialism. Tough little wars were fought to open China to Western fortunes through control of the opium trade. Making the trade illegal did not stop it. On the contrary, it gave the police vast powers to use at their discretion.

Our own culture has also defined the problem in a way that helps sustain a multi-billion dollar international industry largely on money siphoned off from the poorest sector of society. To make things even more "functional," enough terror has been generated to enable private and public "security" agencies to greatly strengthen the total surveillance and repression machinery available to cope with any opposition. The underlying cultural scenario is no more likely to achieve its purported aims than was prohibition or the Cold War. But, as in those symbolic crusades, it may be a powerful if costly mechanism of social control.

The evidence available to me suggests a pincer-movement. Act I of the scenario comes from that section of our mass culture in which the rituals of society are spelled out in unmistakable forms—the comics. It is a Faustian ploy, displaying a world of winners and losers and a *rite de passage* into the winners' circle. Delicious power, sweet immortality, astounding insight, and the ability to right all wrongs—yours but for one bold deed of defiance and daring.

Act II starts in agony and ends in hell. You fell for the oldest trick in the cultural repertory and are now trapped by the forces you set out to conquer. Captivity provides another opportunity for basic training in the socio-sexual-political lesson of deviance that animates the scenario. Its form is that of "drug abuse" literature, and our case in point will be a widely distributed booklet appropriately entitled "Teen-age Booby Trap."

Act I: Potent Potions Of Pleasure, Power, and Profit

Of all the symbolic quests that test human frailty few are as persistent as the lure of potent potions of pleasure, power, and profit. Over the last 100 years or so, this venerable motif has been finessed by the peddlers of drugs and nostrums who have subsidized so much of our emergent mass culture, and then by virtually the entire myth-making apparatus of the new populist commercialism. The cult of instant individual gratification made into an article of democratic faith suggests and supports drug use (or "abuse") as the ideal style of life for the dutiful consumer literally addicted to his purchasing habits.

The nearest outright promises of magic transformation from scrawny youngsters to dashing musclemen and Amazons are the elixir and health-gadget ads in comic books and similar materials. The more subtle attractions of sophisticated advertising are not too different. The clearest expressions of the basic appeal come from those ideal types of mass-produced culture heroes described in Jules Feiffer's book on *The Great Comic Book Heroes* (1965):

> That strange bubbly world of test tubes and gobbledy-gook which had, in the past, done such great work in bringing the dead back to life in the form of monsters—why couldn't it also make men super. Thus Joe Higgins went into his laboratory and came out as the Shield; and John Sterling went into his laboratory and came out as Steel Sterling; and Steve Rogers went in the laboratory of kindly Professor Reinsten and came out as Captain America; and kindly Professor Horton went into his laboratory and came out with a synthetic man, named, illogically, the Human Torch.

The creation of Captain America is prophetic. In the first issue of the comic, the scientist examines a youthful "98 pound weakling." "Observe this young man closely," he says. "Today he volunteered for army service and was refused because of his unfit condition! His chance to serve his country seemed gone!!"

The next frame is a close-up of the scientist lifting up a giant hypodermic needle, and the caption: "Don't be afraid son . . . you are about to become one of America's saviors!" Then the narration: "Calmly the young man allows himself to be innoculated with the strange seething liquid. Little does he realize that the serum coursing through his blood is rapidly building his body and brain tissues, until his stature and intelligence increase to an amazing degree!" (Feiffer, 1965).

Frederick Leaman, a member of my graduate communications research seminar, conducted an informal study of the hidden message of comic books. He visited three large drugstores in different sections of Philadelphia and asked for their best-selling comics. From a list of 204 titles, he selected all stories that depicted different casts of characters in order to diversify the sample and avoid having the same heroes in most books. From this group of 26 stories and 87 characters, he constructed a composite image of the world of popular (mostly action-adventure type) comics.

The world he found is a world of conflict and contest. Its stories endlessly reiterate brutal lessons of transgression and sin. Of all the main themes contained in every 10 stories, eight depict the foul deeds of criminals, seven show the magic of science, six demonstrate how the forces of righteousness smash criminals or evil scientists, five present miraculous transformations through drugs, and four relate some hair-raising lesson about "power-hungry" politicians.

The fictional population is male 4 to 1 (the usual representation of the sexes in the mass media), and predominantly young, white, middle-majority. Of every 10 characters, seven commit some crime, the same number fall victim of violence, and six inflict violence. Killers represent 13% of the population and their fatal victims 7%.

Virtually all stories present problems of life and death, but the real name of the social-symbolic game is power. It takes super-power and super-consciousness to wrest the world about. In more than half (54%) of the stories, the key to super-status is the consumption of some chemical substance that can affect a drastic transformation.

On the whole, one out of every five characters uses drugs to seek super-power, ultra-intelligence, or eternal life. Scientists, as a group, are heavy users; some of them become (or try to become) super-heroes. Scientists *administer* the drugs even more frequently. While 28% of all scientists take drugs, 36% administer drugs. By comparison, 21% of all super-heroes use but only 4% give drugs. Here we begin to see a role differentiation between those who can bestow and those who may use the gift of superhuman insight and power. Of all *users,* 33% are super-heroes, 28% are scientists, and the rest are divided among other characters. Of all those who administer drugs, 56% are scientists and 33% are super-heroes.

Positive, active, violent characters use drugs most. The heroes of the comic book world comprise 67% of all drug-takers. Only 17% of their antagonists, the villains of the comic book world, use drugs.

When it comes to administering drugs, heroes are less important (but still in the majority), while villains double their representation. In other words, 67 % of all drug users but only 56% of drug givers are heroes, while only 17% of all drug users but 33% of drug givers are villains.

The role of the drug user is thus relatively untainted by villainy. Heroes use drugs in a good cause. The drug giver is more likely to be evil, and also more likely to be a scientist.

Personality ratings provide a further clue to the dynamics of comic book power. Figure 1 shows the mean ratings of all 87 comic book characters on a series of personality traits. The broken line (marked "A" for "Administers drugs") shows the aggregate personality profile of all characters who dispense or inject the drugs in comparison with those who ingest them (dotted line) and those who neither give nor take them (solid line). The givers are relatively intelligent, but also relatively weak, effeminate, elderly, and peaceful. The takers as a group are (or become)

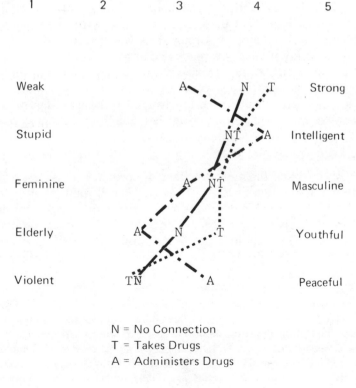

N = No Connection
T = Takes Drugs
A = Administers Drugs

Figure 1
Personality Profiles of All Comic Book Characters

more youthful and strong, and demonstrate through violence the power that flows from the potent potion, power, or serum. The independent intellect—sand in the gears of any consciousness industry—is neutralized by showing scientists or teachers as generally benign but impotent except to serve others. When they move outside of the reach of responsible corporate service and control, and grab the powers they should bestow on others, they usually turn vicious or go mad.

For example, in one comic book story of our sample the "left-leaning professor of biochemistry," Derek Willden, neglects his attractive wife Sylvia to spend all his time in the laboratory working on a serum of eternal life. Scholarly but athletic professor Ross Cochran is named head of the department, but Derek does not care. "They're FOOLS!" . . . he snorts, as he tells Sylvia his secret. "Oh, really!" she retorts. "If you know the secret of the Universe, Derek, then why did Ross get promoted?" "This bourgeois materialistic thinking doesn't become you dear," he replies. "Soon . . . I shall be VINDICATED! Then . . . just you and me, Sylvia! Together FOREVER!" But the elixir lacks one ingredient, a human gland, which Derek obtains by killing Ross who had by now become Sylvia's lover. The potion is now ready and he gulps it down—only to be arrested and sentenced to life imprisonment—forever!

Act I of the scenario is for everyone. Although comics spell it out most clearly, it is implicit in much general news, advertisement, fiction, and drama. It is the promise of power through individual acts of consumption.

Act II: "Teen-age Booby Trap"

Act II is for those—the most disaffected, uprooted, powerless—who yield to the siren song that enthralls so many. "Try it, you'll like it"—and now you are trapped. Our case in point is the widely used anti-drug booklet appropriately entitled "Teen-Age Booby Trap." It was produced in comic book style by Commercial Comics, Inc., of Washington D.C., whose President, Malcolm W. Ater, describes the effort in these words (Ater, 1972):

> To be sure we produced the right kind of brochure—one which would be well received by the intended audience of children of junior and high school age—we sought the support and helpful guidance of experts in this field. I do not mean "self-styled" experts, but authorities whose counseling I could depend on for the best kind of evaluation. Major contributors in an editorial way were the Bureau of Narcotics and Dangerous Drugs, the Senate Judiciary Sub-committee on Juvenile Delinquency and the U.S. Department of Defense (Education) and we also had editorial approval of the

American Pharmaceutical Association and the National Coordinating Council on Drug Abuse and Education. All the above named approved the copy before the magazines were first printed. The Bureau of Narcotics and Dangerous Drugs ordered a substantial quantity twice and the Department of Defense purchased 625,000 copies only after they had made an evaluation study of a cross-section of 18-25 year olds representative of their troops. The study was made by an independent organization outside the government and showed overwhelming acceptance of both the technique and the contents. I repeat, it was only because of this very high approval of the brochure that DOD made its purchase.

We have sold millions of copies and have filled orders for as low as 250 copies for school systems. The praise has not stopped coming in for this brochure.

Let us examine this widely praised and well-tested work, approved by the highest authorities (except for a few "self-styled" experts). Again we shall probe for the lessons implicit in the world of people and events that the booklet reveals to its readers.

On the 32 pages and 57 frames of the booklet, about 142 persons are portrayed. More than half are males, and 13% are nonwhite. Active professional help or service comes mostly from males, nearly all white. Even nurses and hospital attendants are mostly male and all white. In fact, practically all work is performed by males; men are shown as scientists, teachers, doctors, farmers, firemen, and drivers. Women and nonwhites are portrayed only as drug addicts, or as listening to white males give lectures or orders.

Although in the booklet male and female drug addicts number the same, they differ in their respective proportions of their own sex. Half of all women, but only 35% of the men are shown as victims of drugs despite the fact that real-life drug addiction is much more prevalent among males. The male addicts are somber, tragic figures engaged in serious business. The women—mostly blond and scantily clad—are just hysterical. Blacks and whites are also different in ways we shall see as we examine some of the illustrations.

The cover reveals the shadowy world of drug abuse. A bushy haired young man smirks contentedly as he is about to puff on a joint. A demure blond reaches for a syringe about the size of a short bicycle pump. An equally oversized bottle of pills rests on the table between them. Through the window we can see the sunlit campus scene, supporting popular assumptions about the prevalence of drug use on campus. In fact, however, Johnston's (1972) survey of drugs and american youth found *less* drug abuse on campus than off. The highest rate of conversion to

Figure 2

Figure 3

drugs occurred after leaving high school and among the groups most likely to enter military service rather than college.

A few pages later our eyes fall on three faces of Blondie (Figure 3). She goes into wide-eyed, full-lipped hysterics, and then hallucinates with eyes closed, mouth wide open. The male user, on the other hand, is doing a man's work. He is a truck driver in work clothes, union buttons on his cap, using stimulants to keep awake at night on the road.

Next comes a lesson in comic-book history (Figure 4). It begins with the Western fantasy of exotic oriental religious ceremonies complete with monster-gods, inscrutable faces, and gyrating belly-dancers. Dipping even farther back into the mists of prehistory, we see a "nomadic tribe in Southern Russia" sniff poppy seed around the campfire. (For the edification of Boy Scouts?).

On the next page we come upon the drug-crazed hordes of Southeast Asia, so hopped-up on hashish that they rush headlong into their deaths (Figure 5). The story served the British Empire and the Foreign Legion even before American troops (with *their* drug problems) fought and killed Southeast Asians on their own native soil. These ape-like creatures, and the two ceremonial dancing girls on the previous page, are the only nonwhite drug users portrayed in the book. A favored media "solution" to the delicate problem of overtly unfavorable portrayal is to take nonwhites back into "history"where they can be shown as naturally savage fanatics and primitives. Contrast the savegery on top of Figure 5 with the nobility in the bottom frame. Cannons and guns (in white hands) indicate that we are now in civilized times. Here drugs are used not to send ape-men into mindless slaughter, but to "relieve suffering." Unfortunately, explains the caption, many of the soldiers thus treated returned to civilian life as addicts. *They* were considered sick men.

But not for long. The next headline (Figure 6) marks the transition from sickness to crime. The picture supplies what illustrated manuals call the "how-to-do-it," showing the well-aimed shot being self-administered into the powerful fisted arm.

Soon addicts become criminals in the cultural as well as the legal sense. The cultural function of this category is to stigmatize a variety of presumably associated transgressions. The bottom frame of Figure 6 illustrates that function. A glassy-eyed, bearded hippie addict wearing a peace symbol is shown panhandling a well-dressed young woman. The tendency to piggyback an overtly political message onto the drug education story recurs a few pages later.

After some frames showing pushers, an anxiety-ridden female addict, policemen grabbing a hopped-up bank robber, a white male teacher

The use and misuse of drugs is probably as old as civilization itself. Primitive people knew about opium and sometimes used it to produce a state of intoxication during religious ceremonies.

As early as 500 B.C. the Scythians, a nomadic tribe in Southern Russia, also had learned about opium. . .

By burning dried poppy plants and inhaling the smoke they were able to experience the intoxicating effects of the opium narcotic.

Figure 4

In Southeast Asia, young warriors were sometimes keyed up for battle to the point where they rushed headlong to their deaths due to the psychoactive effects of hashish, a concentrated preparation of marijuana.

By the time of the Civil War, opium was used as a pain killer. Wounded soldiers were treated with morphine, the major constituent of opium, to relieve suffering. . .

. . .Unfortunately, many of them returned to civilian life with an addiction not then understood, but commonly referred to as "Soldier's Disease."

Figure 5

lecturing to a mixed audience, marijuana plants, and how to roll a joint, we come to a pot party. This time Blondie wears the peace symbol (Figure 7). As the caption speaks of "impairment of judgement and confusion," she passes the joint to two intellectual types as other sophisticates cavort in the background. The bottom frame gives examples of further hazards of marijuana smoking, some of them misleading.

The next page below introduces a sequence of frames in horror-comic style (Figure 8). A chief social function of horror as a cultural ritual is the scaring of women to (and with) death. The ultimate sexual put-down, rape by a beast, is usually part of the fun. Here we see all faces of Blondie shrieking in psychodelic horror as monsters fall upon her. A giant bird descends with claws ready and long sharp beak and tongue poised for action. A death head puts a bony finger on her curly locks.

The sex-role message is further developed through frames (not shown here) depicting one woman raging and two others buying and using amphetamines while a male druggist looks worried and a male scientist is engaged in laboratory research.

Next we see Blondie green with terror (Figure 9). She is caught in an imaginary cobweb, with fantasy insects crawling over her curvaceous body. She is clad in a negligee and is writhing on a sofa, agonizing over how best to scratch the itch. Underneath that scene, the Male Thinker sits in a torn workshirt, silhouetted against a beam of light, contemplating suicide. To be or not to be, that is *his* question.

After frames of another male scientist, two male doctors, two female nurses, and "drug abusers" of both sexes (not shown), we come to Blondie again (Figure 10). She has shed her negligee and moved from the sofa into bed, alluring as ever, still itching and twitching in horror. The insects, skeleton, and long-beaked bird now become a giant snake-dragon with fangs and a forked tongue, literally enveloping and ready to rape the terrified woman victim. "The torture of one horrible withdrawal," states the bottom caption "far outweighs any possible pleasure."

Next are frames (not shown here) depicting a poppy field, another male physician, three firemen, three male underworld characters, and another hysterical woman. Later, as if one snake would not have been enough, we see six slimy tentacles of a hairy monster grab Blondie in the arms, legs, and thigh (Figure 11).

In the lower half of the page, the male figure is doing difficult, dangerous work. The sadistic imagery of the female victim again contrasts with the male self-image engaged in serious (if illicit) business. While furry tentacles wrap around her body, he reaches for pearls and precious stones "to feed his ugly habit."

Figure 6

IS DRUG ABUSE A SICKNESS OR A CRIME?

When heroin, a derivative of morphine, was introduced late in the 19th century it was believed that injection of the drug into a vein rather than having it ingested through the stomach would prevent people from becoming "enslaved by the habit."

At first, heroin was even believed to be a cure for addiction to morphine. It turned out that heroin produced an even stronger addiction.

With the nature of addiction poorly understood, public opinion accused the drug rather than the user. Perhaps this attitude stemmed from the fact that so many had unwittingly become dependent upon drugs. As a result, addicts at that time were pitied more than they were condemned.

Figure 7

A marijuana cigarette burns rapidly and is often shared by several persons. It produces varying effects such as hilarity, distortion of sensations and perception, impairment of judgment and confusion.

The fogging up of a marijuana user's concepts of time and space is similar to that of a person who misuses alcohol. But where an excess of alcohol can cause a person to "pass out" and remove himself as a social hazard, heavy use of marijuana simply further distorts the senses and allows the abuser to become a greater hazard to himself and others.

Amphetamine use, when carried to the point of dependence, offers many hazards. As with barbiturates, there is an increasing demand by the body for larger doses to produce a "high." When drugs are not available, unpleasant reactions usually follow. . . .

. . . A feeling that insects are crawling over one's body is often the unhappy reward of users of amphetamines and other stimulants such as METHAMPHETAMINE and COCAINE.

A common reaction to amphetamine abuse is a form of paranoia where the abuser imagines he is being persecuted. Despondency, severe depression and other mental disorders which sometimes lead to suicide are associated with the abuse of amphetamines.

Figure 9

LSD, nicknamed "acid", is a chemical in the family of hallucinogens. Like other hallucinogens, LSD brings to the user an escape from realism.

LSD users imagine all sorts of weird things—like thinking they are birds . . . or vicious animals . . . or even other people. The impact on the mind is great and sometimes of long duration.

LSD "trips" produce not only varying reactions among different users, but different results from time to time with repeat users. No one, even on a planned repeat trip, can foretell what will happen. The reaction might range anywhere from euphoria to terror.

Figure 8

Soon we come to the first and only picture in which Blondie is not an alluring, if hysterical, sex-symbol (Figure 12). The potent potions worked their magic too well. She is sitting on a park bench suggestively near a trash can, looking poor, sloppy, stupid, and pregnant.

Woman's fate is biology; man's is society. She is sentenced for life and more; "she knows," claims the caption, that "the baby may be born an addict." The Male Thinker pays for his mistake in jail and risks "chances for employment and promotion." Culture sets each his or her own "booby trap."

The implicit lesson recalls the paradox of commodity culture preaching salvation through the consumption of illusions for a price. The tragic hero of that culture is the dutiful consumer chained to his purchasing habits, including the ultimate delusion of liberation through potent potions for pleasure, power, and profit.

This way of dealing with "drug abuse" can only generate increasing misery and conflict until its cultural sources and social uses are recognized and altered. That will not be easy or painless, because the sources run deep and the uses benefit powerful groups in our society. A counter-scenario is needed that would be of sufficient sweep and scope to begin to turn the tide.

First, all advertising, and not only patent medicine and other drug commercials, would have to be scrutinized to avoid promising spurious values and unrealistic expectations of the achievement of feelings of mastery and power. Similarly, teachers, parents, and critics should oppose the celebration of irrationality and the attribution of magic or superhuman virtues to be derived from any mechanical or chemical intervention. And, finally, the implicit social content and covert communication of all types of imagery, especially "drug abuse" literature, must be examined for the unwitting reinforcement of the very pressures that make dangerous drugs so attractive a risk to so many. The projective and instrumental portrayals of deviance for purposes of repression as well as of control pose a challenge to analyst and citizen alike.

Users of heroin get "hooked" and have a compelling physical dependence on the drug. With repeated use, a person develops a tolerance, meaning that increased dosages are required to meet the demands of dependence. If the heroin supply is cut off, "withdrawal" results.

Narcotics withdrawal, or detoxification, is a torture hard to endure. An addict begins to feel a sense of desperation for a "fix" to calm him about 8 to 12 hours after the last dose. . .

If unable to obtain the fix, and in order to avoid going through the painful withdrawal, the addict is all too often driven to crime to get money to feed his ugly habit.

Figure 11

Detoxification (withdrawal) from barbiturates is even more dangerous than from heroin and should be done gradually. ALWAYS under the supervision of a physician.

As with heroin, there is nervousness, muscle twitching, tremor and a sudden drop in blood pressure. After about 24 hours from the last dose, the abuser becomes desperate for more drugs. After 36 to 72 hours, agonizing convulsions begin.

These convulsions, which often lead to death, may last up to eight days. Even if there are no convulsions, the patient suffers delirium and frightening hallucinations similar to the DT's of alcoholism.

The torture of one horrible withdrawal far outweighs any possible pleasure derived from the abuse.

Figure 10

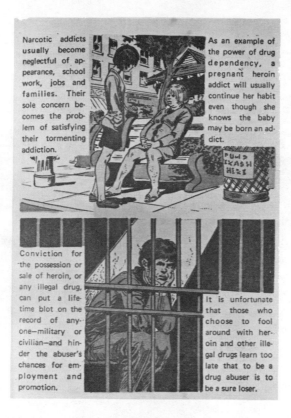

Figure 12

REFERENCES

ATER, M. W. (May 3, 1972). Personal communication.

EPSTEIN, E. J. (1977a). Agency of fear: Opiates and political power in America. New York: G. P. Putnam and Sons.

_____ (1977b). "Peddling a drug scare." Columbia Journalism Review, November-December, 1977:51-56.

FEIFFER, J. (ed.) (1965). The great comic book heroes. New York: Bonanza Books.

GERBNER, G. (1972). "Communication and social environment." Scientific American, 227:153-160.

_____ (1977). "Television: The new state religion." Etcetera, June 1977:145-150.

JOHNSTON, L. (1972). Drugs and American Youth. Ann Arbor: Institute of Social Research.

New York Times (July 25, 1972).

Philadelphia Inquirer (July 25, 1972).

SCHILLER, D. T. (1978). "Professionalism, public community and objectivity in nineteenth century American newsgathering." Journal of Communication (forthcoming).

OBESITY AND THE POPULAR ARTS

PHILIP J. LEONHARD-SPARK

AUTHOR'S NOTE: *This paper is partly an outgrowth of an interest developed in the sociological aspects of obesity while team-teaching a course in "Nutrition and Behavior Change"with my wife, Arlene Leonhard-Spark, during the summer, 1977 in the Program in Nutrition at Teachers College, Columbia University. Special thanks go to her and to my colleagues, Edward Sagarin and Saul Brody at City College, for helpful comments and editorial help on early drafts.*

Over the past decade, and with increasing persistence and alarm, doctors and public health professionals have used the mass media to make the American people aware of a new epidemic in their midst. This epidemic, by varying estimates, may afflict one in every three adult Americans, causing considerable suffering for many and contributing to early deaths for others. Among health professionals, this form of malnutrition is known as obesity, or too much fat.

The identification of obesity as a major American health problem has had widespread repercussions on our society over the last several decades. Today and here, a degree of leanness which in other places might be taken as a sign of poverty or illness is regarded as an indication of potential good health and fashionable acceptability. The most common of the numerous ills associated in one way or another with obesity include diabetes, hypertension, and atherosclerosis. In addition, the obese are high risks for many types of surgical procedures (cf., Mayer, 1968; Kannel et al, 1969; Dairy Council Digest, 1975).

physiological condition. Yet, at the same time, it is a culturally disvalued physical attribute whose possessors are subject to various types of humiliating and discrediting incidents. On the basis of moral, aesthetic, and medical criteria, fatness has been considered a social deviance as well as a physical disability and a social as well as a health problem (Cahnman, 1968; Maddox and Liederman, 1969; Allon, 1973).

A central theme of this study is that the mass media are important mechanisms by which various changes have led to an increased prevalence of obesity in American society and concern with its consequences for people's health and well-being. Media influence has been indirect and operates in combination with several social trends: changes in family food consumption practices, the sedentary nature of work, the entrance of large numbers of women into the labor force, and more passive leisure activities.

THE FAT OF THE LAND

There are actually only some arbitrary guidelines available for the purpose of classifying people as overweight or obese by physical size alone. Even in everyday conversation, there exists vagueness in the use of such terms as fat, stout, chubby, stocky, overweight, chunky, pudgy, etc. Some people refer to themselves in relation to these ambiguous terms in ways which almost verge on the pathological, as when a "normal"-sized woman goes on a diet or a large-sized male argues that his bulging stomach area is just a "beer belly."

Who Is Obese? Actuarial Criteria

Most data on the weight distribution of the adult American population are available from actuarial statistics gathered under the sponsorship in insurance companies or from periodic surveys conducted through the National Center for Health Statistics (U.S. Department of Heath, Education, and Welfare, 1966).

Typically, people who are at least 20-30% over the "best weight" standard for their category are classified as obese. Those classified in any of these studies as *overweight* (from 14% to 19% over "best weight standard") and *obese* (from 15% to 25% or more above) are generally assumed to have excess body fat, rather than lean body mass (musculature). A third category, that of the *morbidly obese,* includes those who are 100% or more above their "best weight" standard.

Prevalence of Obesity in the Population

Depending on which criterion is used, from 10% to 40% of the older children and from 15% to 40% of the adult populations of the United States can be classified as obese today.

THE CASE OF THE DISAPPEARING OBESE

The 1960s witnessed major changes in concern about the consequences of weight control. There was a substantial decline in the number of visibly overweight characters presented on television and in the movies, along with fewer fat performers in music. There are also indications that the visibly overweight performers being presented in the mass entertainment media are now subject to less negative stereotyping.

Popular Music; From Kate Smith to Cher

There is a shift in popular music themes which reflect more on people's individual qualities and their range of emotional expression, in contrast to earlier emphasis on outward appearances and attractiveness. There has been a corresponding decrease in the number of popular fat performers in all areas of musical expression.

For example, among popular song stylists, the Kate Smiths of the 1940s and 1950s have been slowly, though steadily replaced by the Chers of the 1960s and 1970s. Few contemporary rock stars are visibly obese.

The massive Wagnerian heroine attired in breastplate and horned helmet has been replaced by a new crop of sensuously lithe sopranos with slim figures. Even Luciano Pavarotti is dieting and Beverly Sills is as likely to discuss her weight loss as her music. Some artists have been media sensations as much for their weight control success as for performance abilities. Opera stars' new slimness is remarkable because of the long-held belief that weight reduction might damage the voice.

The popular song has come a long way from the explicit emphasis placed on leanness in so many rock and roll songs popular in the 1950s, when songs often contained lyrics which stressed outward appearance (especially clothing) and slim women (e.g., "Long Tall Sally" and "Boney Marone").

Thin is in, not so much because ugly bodies are out, but because this is less distracting than fat when inner qualities are the focal point. This ambivalency has much to do with the inconsistent elements that comprise the stereotypes of the obese that have persisted for so long in American society. The negative stereotype of the fat person includes disvaluing assesments of their bodies as awkward and ugly along with assumptions about their selves as people lacking in self-control, lazy, and unconcerned with their health as well as their appearance. Fat people are stigmatized for their physical size and for their lack of ascetic self-discipline in eating.

Fat is ugly, not so much in its contrast to our ideals of beauty, but in its making us aware of the fact that the act of eating can have as its consequence, an uncontrolled expansion of the physical self to the point where the person no longer "fits" into the world.

To be a fat performer is to have a physical quality which is necessarily distracting from other aspects of the performance because it clashes with the themes that our music now expresses. "Red hot mamas" can sing the blues and overweight divas can portray tragic heroines, but the emotive dimensions of contemporary musical taste create images of a world with which the meanings given to the obese performer's own body are at grating variance.

Fat Men as Motion Picture Character Types

There is a long standing belief that when the movies first appeared as a form of mass entertainment, many stars of the stage were unable to make the transition because the camera's lens flattens out the human body, so that only the very thin appeared attractive. American film stars have been cast into two main camps on the basis if body size. In the first camp are the thin waisted, but otherwise well endowed heroines and the broad shouldered heroes with hairless chests and, often, muscles that rippled during movement. In the second camp are a vast collection of "other" types, of which the most interesting to us are the visibly overweight who played at being jolly fat men and villainous heavies.

The Comic Fat Man. Funny fat men have been fixtures in American movies from the very beginning when John Bunny established and largely defined the comic fat man as a type from 1910 to 1915. For the comic fat men, the visual cue was the stimulus for laughter in the audience. This visual element is as important as their stereotyped roles as bumbling public servants (sheriffs, firemen, mayors, etc.) good hearted but naive travellers away from home and, finally, sly and ever so daringly risque partners to either a much smarter, but staighter wife or male friend.

From John Bunny, Mark Swain, and Fatty Arbuckle during the silent years up to 1920 and from then on down through Jack Oakie, Peter Ustinov, Jackie Gleason, and Zero Mostel, the fat man as comedian has used his body to transmit a visual message that provoked laughter.

These lessons in body language taught so well by the comic fat men of the movies are best seen in the performances of those like Jack Oakie's Mussolini style character in the "Great Dictator" (1941), by Victor Moore's bumbling antics in "Louisianna Purchase" (1941) and Peter Ustinov's slyness, so vivid in "Spartacus" (1960) and "Topkapi" (1964).

The fat member of Laurel and Hardy, Abbott and Costello, and Art Carney and Jackie Gleason in the "Honeymooners" on television were combative but ever faithful friends and/or sidekicks of their partners. By using his size to communicate, the comic fat man was able to define himself as having a set of exaggerated disabilities which were comic in their displays of awkwardness, indulgence, and disruptiveness against a protagonist who could then, with relative impunity, violate the rules governing social intercourse with both strangers and friends.

We have developed such a tolerance and/or indifference to nonconformity that rule breaking for the purpose of eliciting laughter is today a poor strategy for a comedian. Where Lenny Bruce might shock his audiences into laughter by making public their often shared resentment of the hypocrisies inherent in sacred private acts and institutions, by the time his biographical movie was released, even Dustin Hoffman was unable to elicit laughs from the same material.

There are fat comedians today, but few are funny fat men in the mold of the motion picture comics who worked through the 1950s. Jackie Vernon, Buddy Hacket, Dom DeLuise and Jonathan Winters are overweight, but for these newer comics, the aural overwhelms the visual in the emphasis on impressions, dialects, sex, and barbs directed at the powerful.

The Heavy. The fat man "heavy" in dramatic mysteries and adventure stories is a character type most common from the early 1940s through the 1960s. The "heavy" type was represented by Sidney Greenstreet ("The Maltese Falcon," 1941) and the domineering patriarchs and plutocrats brought to life by Orson Welles in "Citizen Kane" (1941). The powerful and malevolent fat men and the villainous outsiders whose personal strength challenged heroes of hundreds of movies through the 1950s have also gone the way of the fat comic.

Television's Waist Land

Today television is no land of vast waists. From its early days onward, there has been a trend toward an increasingly smaller number of visibly overweight actors. In the early 1950s, Charles Laughton had a show in which he gave dramatic readings, while on other nights the portly Paul

Whiteman directed music and Arthur Godfrey presented new talent. From 1952 onward, Jackie Gleason developed many memorable comic characters whose charm in part rested on his ability to use his large body as a vehicle for humorous gestures. In the mornings since 1955 through the present, children have been watching Bob Keeshan in the role of a well rounded Captain Kangaroo.

If their parents allowed them to watch again after dinner, from 1953 they might tune in to one of the ever present family comedy series starring visibly overweight men (William Bendix in the "Life of Riley"; Private Doberman on the "Phil Silvers' Show"). Finally, during an evening of watching mystery or adventure programing, there were few children or adults who could not immediately recognize Alfred Hitchcock's distinctively rounded profile at the start of his suspense shows. Such an evening might also involve watching a Western series with a chubby sidekick for the fast drawing hero. Today, in television as in the movies, the visibly overweight have all but disappeared.

Among today's television shows, the visibly obese are found with any regularity only on children's shows, comedy programs, and as mothers. Captain Kangaroo has remained in the current decade. An occasional fat cartoon character such as the popular Fred Flintstone or Fat Albert can be seen. The friendly and stocky grocer on Sesame Street has been a stable character. To some extent, the obese have been characterized as having friendly and nurturant qualities. Despite our cultural emphasis on thinness, nursemaids, indulgent grandparents, playful uncles and Santa Claus are best when at least a little on the hefty side.

While the thin mother still predominates, in some households she is likely to be older and large. Such a woman was seen in early television on the "Molly Goldberg Show," and, more recently, on "Maude," "Family," "Good Times," and "That's My Mama." Shirley Booth as the maid in "Hazel," Ethel Waters in "Beulah," and the Black maid on "Make Room for Daddy" were nurturant, yet also strong and self-reliant in meeting the personal needs of members of their television families. Rarely deferential to male authority, they were also from a lower social class or minority ethnic background when contrasted with their WASPish and lean counterparts.

By comparison, the few visibly overweight men now represented on television appear most frequently on comedy and variety shows, e.g., Jonathan Winters, Don Rickles, Tim O'Connor, and Carroll O'Connor. Apart from these comedians, only William Conrad, in "Cannon," stands apart from other heroes by virtue of girth.

Stereotypes of the obese are often explained by making reference to the more general disvaluation placed on people with obvious physical disabilities. However, at least on 1970s television, physical disabilities are not themselves matters of concern among the producers of adventure shows.

While the overweight themselves are given only limited coverage in television programing, there has occurred over the years at least some depiction of characters' efforts at weight reduction. There is the association of successful weight reduction with increased attractiveness and a more positive self-image.

The latter factor figured in an instance in which a weight control theme was given a central place in a television series. The theme was introduced in the popular "Mary Tyler Moore Show" and carried over to one of its several spin-off series, "Rhoda." Valerie Harper played the character of Rhoda on the first show as a single New Yorker living in Mary Tyler Moore's apartment house. After Valerie Harper lost a noticeable amount of weight, the producers focussed one episode around Rhoda's weight loss and her subsequent victory in a local beauty contest. Later, Rhoda was transformed into an apparently happier and more sexually attractive person.

This public dieting was given further publicity in a cover story article in *Weight Watcher's Magazine* and repeated as a theme over several episodes on Valerie Harper's own show in which her initially chubby and unhappily unattractive kid sister was featured. After the sister loses weight, she no longer has problems finding boyfriends. The characters derive from their weight losses rewards like happiness, popularity, and success.

Selling Slimness

For the advertisers selling to obese Americans, there seems to be a recognition that in the packaging and promotion of diet books and weight control aids they must tread a narrow path between enticement to purchase and affront to dignity. The advertiser rarely gives overt recognition to the condition of the obese. Advertising projects themes of increased attractiveness (especially for women) and longer life through better health. Low calorie beverages and foods are promoted through recreational and social activities. In ads for health spas, muscular men and well-endowed women frolic together in pools; while gracefully moving ballerinas appear in reducing salons. The goals of weight reduction are to "take off inches" when purchasing exercise equipment or by joining a health club. While ads promise to help their users "lose pounds," a lean model appears in the ads.

There has grown up a vocabulary of euphemisms: fashions for overweight women are "Queen size" and for men "husky." Foundation garments "firm you up" and "flatter" your figure. *Weight Watchers Magazine* claims to be for "attractive people."

DIETING, MEDICINE AND THE MEDIA

In many respects, for health-related matters of all types, the mass media have replaced the family doctor. The news media have publicized new medical discoveries and warnings of the dangers that modern life poses for health. "Howtoism" has entered into matters related to ways of overcoming personal disabilities and interpersonal liabilities.

Obesity and the Medical Profession

Medical professionals tend to regard obesity from the perspective of clinical criteria which differ from actuarial criteria. Medical researchers increasingly consider obesity "as a heterogeneous group of disorders" (Salans, 1977:764). While people gain, maintain, and lose weight according to their levels of caloric intake and energy expenditure, why they do so reflects genetic background, endocrinologic functions, pharmacological state, psychological makeup and socio-cultural environment.

Few medical practitioners treat patients who are less than morbidly obese.

This avoidance of medical professionals by the obese is made even more intriguing when, by law in most states, weight control groups require prospective members to consult with their doctors before starting a dietary program and when the authors of most magazine articles and books about dieting strongly advise their readers to do so. Relatively few dieters are under supervision by physicians (Food and Drug Administration, 1976).

Medical Stigmatization of the Obese

Maddox and Leiderman (1969) report that most physicians have little desire to treat obese patients, viewing them in stereotypical terms as both physically unattractive and lacking in self-control. It is widely know that "success rates" for weight reduction methods used by medical practitioners are uniformly low, perhaps partially because diet "experts" tend to stigmatize obesity. Theodore Rubin, in *Forever Thin* (1970) and Alvin Eden, in *Growing Up Thin* (1975), make considerable use of comments and case studies which characterize the obese as unhappy and unpleasant companions, responsible for their own state of ill health. Such unflattering descriptions may come from a conscious attempt to prod readers into changing their ways of eating. Laslett and Warren (1975:75) argue that, "the use of stigma as a strategy for individual behavioral change constructs a foolproof ideology; success comes from following the organization's program, while failure is the responsibility of the individual member reflecting his or her essential identity."

The Diet Book: Do-It-Yourself Weight Reduction

Advice on how to lose weight has found its way into books for years. From about 1955, many new diet books argued that the overweight could eat almost all they desired and still show a noticeable weight loss within just a few short weeks.

With titles like *Eat Your Troubles Away* (1955) and *Stop Dieting! Start Losing!* (1956), this new type of diet strategy gained popularity until, in 1961, the book *Calories Don't Count* by Dr. Herman Taller sold 1,000,000 copies. In 1967, Irwin Stillman published the *Quick Weight Loss Diet,* which sold over 5,000,000 copies. Again, in 1972, still another doctor published the *Dr. Atkin's Diet Revolution* which sold over 2,000,000 copies in various editions, as well as boosting sales for *Vogue* magazine. Dozens of imitators offered weight conscious American men and women the promise of a quick, easy, inexpensive and medically approved way of losing weight. The twin threats of personal failure and fraud had seemed to be dispelled as millions tried, often with varying degrees of success, the diet regimens these books proposed.

These three diet books were media events in their own right. In large part this was due to their astoundingly high sales for health-oriented material, the excerpted selections presented in women's consumer magazines, and the celebrity status that television and radio interviews gave to their authors. But, most importantly, there was the controversy each book generated. In the case of Taller, the charges focused around the over-the-counter sale of a dietary aid from which the doctor was claimed to derive profit. Exposé style articles by other medical professionals put Stillman under attack in the news media and in the pages of women's consumer magazines. The battles between Atkins and the American Medical Association were also well covered and created a groundswell of disapproval and denunciation for the diet plan's deleterious effects and exaggerated claims of effectiveness.

Newspapers and Magazines

While newpapers and weekly news magazines have covered new dieting fads and frauds, they also increased reporting on health-related topics of all kinds. Today, many papers have "lifestyle" sections, with materials on new exercise plans, active leisure activities, fashion, and personal health.

Where in the not so distant past, showing concern about the health benefits of exercise and dieting was largely a matter confined to upper middle class females, the range of concern within the population has expanded considerably in many directions. Male-oriented periodicals like *Field and Stream, Sports Illustrated,* and *Mechanix Illustrated* reflect and reinforce this new concern with articles about the benefits of exercising and dieting.

Stuart and Davis (1972:15) suggest that one reason why the lower income segments of the population were more frequently overweight was that thinness as an aesthetic/cosmetic value was most significant to the white middle class. This factor, coupled with differential access to nutritional knowledge related to weight and occupational discrimination against the overweight, may have created a larger prevalence of obesity among lower economic groups. However, a process of embourgeoisement seems at work today among magazines designed for all classes of women. There is an extensive and almost constant array of articles dealing with body size.

There are now a handful of magazines devoted exclusively to exercise and weight control, the most popular of which is sponsored by the Weight Watchers corporation. Entitled *Weight Watchers: Magazine for Attractive People,* it presents articles which reflect the broader spectrum of periodical pieces on matters of weight control: weight loss success stories by celebrities or those who have gone into glamorous jobs (Playboy bunny, photographic model, etc.), articles on the psychological and interpersonal aspects of dieting, and short pieces about fashions and cosmetics for overweight women.

During the 1970s, several women's magazines established special sections devoted to weight control and dieting (e.g., *McCalls'* "Diet of the Month," *Seventeen*'s "Dieter's Clipboard," and *Good Housekeeping*'s "You and Your Diet"). Each of these sections and their imitators presented monthly advice and commentary on such topics. Many diets that enjoyed popularity were often introduced first in these women's magazines.

An examination of magazine articles on obesity, dieting, and weight control listed in the *Reader's Guide to Periodical Literature* from 1960 through 1977 brings to light some details on two significant trends in such articles for the most popular and widely read women's consumer magazines. Such articles were more likely to appear during the early 1960s, then they drop off somewhat until they steadily increase their frequency of appearance again from the early 1970s onward. During the middle and late 1960s, there was what appears to be a proportionately greater emphasis on educating the reader about the causes and health consequences of obesity. One might also refer to this period as one in which there was as great a concern with taking pounds off as with taking inches off, i.e., with the health as well as the cosmetic benefits of weight reduction.

Among the womens's magazines, there exists a class hierarchy of readership with the elite consisting of *Vogue, Harper's Bazaar,* and *Mademoiselle* on down to *McCalls* and *Ladies Home Journal* for the middle class reader, with such supermarket items as *Woman's Day* and *Family Circle* aimed more directly at lower middle and working class housewives. While readers at all class levels are presented with articles which stress the health and cosmetic benefits of being weight conscious, strategies proposed for losing weight vary considerably among classes. Those magazines with predominantly lower middle and working class readerships focus almost exclusively on dieting and fashion. Articles which recommend formal exercise regimens, sports, and health spas are most often found in the magazines aimed at a more affluent audience of readers. Again, in contrast, the advertising found in magazines directed at the less affluent was seen to promote weight reduction aids such as appetite suppressing candies, easy exercise equipment for home use, various types of belts, girdles and inflatable pants as well as putting a greater editorial emphasis on clothing styles which help conceal the more obvious attributes of those with ample figures.

These magazines, along with their more sexually sophisticated counterparts for men and women alike, have mirrored and to some extent reinforced a number of ambivalencies Americans have about health, the aesthetics of body size and the appropriateness of various means of weight control in a society which stresses passive leisure pursuits and has redefined food to a degree where its nutritive aspects are the least important.

Changing Patterns of Food Choice

In most human societies, the wife/mother has been the food "gate-keeper" for her family. It was she who had the primary responsibility for selecting foods for home consumption, preparing them, and serving such meals to husband and children. Today, with many women working outside the home and still responsible for domestic chores as well, there has been a decrease in effectiveness of this "gatekeeping" function. While in the 1930s, American families took only about one meal in eight outside the home, by some estimates the rate is now one in three (Parrish, 1971). Nearly 40% of family food dollars is spent in restaurants, with much of the remainder going for purchases of calorically dense and highly processed convenience foods for home consumption.

The best selling diet books described above, food advertisements in general, and popular women's magazines in particular have all served to reshape what Americans choose to eat and their beliefs about the relation between food and obesity. The diet books severely undermined a previously taken for granted assumption that how much one eats affects how much one weighs. By promising that a person can lose weight without discomfort or superhuman will power, these books place the locus of blame for obesity on *what* one eats, not how much is eaten or the extent to which calories taken into the body are expended through physical activity. Food advertisements give little mention to the nutritive qualities of their products, promoting instead associations with the "good life" based on the product's taste, convenience, and ability to produce grateful comments from family and friends. Public denunciations and defenses of various diets appearing in the news media and magazines have generated considerable confusion about the nature of the relationship between food, calories, and body fat as well meaning doctors with promising "cures" for obesity are challenged in print by well meaning doctors with no such promises, although they have the expertise in nutritional biochemistry to provide an adequate explanation.

We can see in these changes the source of much of the ambiguity and ambivalence we have noted throughout as to the nature of obesity as a deviance within the context of contemporary American society and its notions about health, food, and attractiveness. Obesity is defined as a health problem, yet the obese are denied access to the sick role, falling back instead on do-it-yourself methods of treatment. Modern food merchandising practices have redefined eating from a deadly sin to a pleasure in which all are encouraged to indulge, because food is no longer seen as a temptation from the ascetic path or even a cause of obesity. The fat are no longer sinners, having been redefined in the modern psychological vogue as people lacking in the self-control necessary for losing weight, not gluttonous sinners who had strayed into a state of sin for which the worldly punishment was social exclusion and the threat of early death.

CONCLUDING COMMENTS

The study of obesity reveals much about the forces shaping contemporary American society. As examined here, it reveals some of the ways in which a form of deviance is generated in both prevalence and definition by the interplay of structural changes and the mass media. The changes in family patterns, work activities, and the use of discretionary time have produced a population with many members at high risk for obesity and its related disabilities. At the same time, mass entertainment media altered attitudes toward food, eating, and body size in ways which create and reinforce ambivalencies in such attitudes.

The consequence is that the obese are people in a quandary. Each society typically provides its oppressed with some form of ideological rationalization for their condition which may justify their lot and offer them hope of eventual redemption. Yet, there is little the obese have to construct such an ideology. The media have built up around this health problem a cloak of invisibility and semantic denial and a veil of confusion through the inconsistencies and contradictions that arise whenever some new hope of redemption comes to their attention.

Understanding obesity within its social and cultural setting and for its consequences in the form of ill-health and stigmatization as well presents a challenge to those interested in both the nature of deviance and the role of mass communications in its creation and control. It is a problem in process—a matter in which public concern and personal troubles meet in a complex interplay among the forces producing change in modern societies.

REFERENCES

ALLON, N. (1973). "The stigma of overweight in everyday life." Pp. 83-102 in G. A.
    Bray (ed.), Obesity in perspective (vol. 2, part 1). Washington, D.C.: U.S. Government
    Printing Office (Proceedings of the Fogarty International Center Series on Preventative
    Medicine).
_____ (1974). "Fat as a sociological and social problem: Fat as an example of socio-
    logical ambivalence." Paper presented at the 69th annual meetings of the American
    Sociological Association, Montreal, Canada, August 29.
BRODY, J. (1973). "Findings of research promise hope to 70 million overweight
    Americans." New York Times, December 27:30.
CAHNMAN, W. J. (1968). "The stigma of obesity." Sociological Quarterly, 9 (Summer):
    283-299.
Dairy Council Digest (1975). "Current concepts of obesity." 46 (July-August):19-22.
Food and Drug Administration (1976). Consumer nutrition knowledge survey, report II,
    1975. Washington, D.C.: U.S. Government Printing Office (U.S. Department of
    Health, Education and Welfare).
KANNEL, W. B., PEARSON, B., and McNAMARA, P. M. (1969). "Obesity as a force
    of morbidity and mortality in adolescence." Pp. 51-71 in F. P. Heald (ed.), Adolescent
    nutrition and growth. New York: Appleton-Century-Crofts.
LASLETT, B., and WARREN, C.A.B. (1975). "Losing Weight: The organizational
    promotion of behavior change." Social Problems, 32(Summer):69-80.
MADDOX, G. L., and LIEDERMAN, V. (1969). "Overweight as a social disability
    with medical implications." Journal of Medical Education, 44 (March):214-220.
_____ , and BACK, K. W. (1969). "Overweight as social deviance and disability."
    Journal of Health and Social Behavior, 9 (December):287-298.
MAYER, J. (1968). Overweight: Causes, cost, and control. Englewood Cliffs, N.J.:
    Prentice-Hall.
PARRISH, J. B. (1971). "Implications of changing food habits for nutrition educators."
    Journal of Nutrition Education, 2 (Spring):140-146.
SALANS, L. (1977). "Obesity: An approach to its evaluation and management." Journal
    of Family Practice, 4 (April):761-767, 773-775.
STUART, R. B., and DAVIS, B. (1972). Fat chance in a slim world. Champaign, Ill.:
    Research Press.
U.S. Department of Health, Education and Welfare (1966). Obesity and health.
    Washington, D.C.: U.S. Government Printing Office (U.S. Public Health Service
    Publication No. 1485).

MENTAL ILLNESS AND PSYCHIATRISTS IN MOVIES

CHARLES WINICK

This is a report on the manner in which mental illness and psychiatrists have been presented in motion pictures from 1919 through the present. How they figure in this medium is important because many Americans may form their impressions of mental illness, and those who treat it, from movies. From the 1920s through the 1940s, the typical American went to the movies every week. Young people today are seeing older films on television as well as seeing recent movies in the theaters. Films may give worldwide currency to material that had a more limited audience as a play or book.

A successful film about mental illness or psychotherapists may be seen by 25 or 30 million persons in contrast to the much smaller number of people who may come into contact with the treatment system for mental illness. Perhaps one million people see a psychiatrist each year and around 11,000 persons are undergoing psychoanalysis at any one time (Rogow, 1971).

Since movies represent the most important leisure mass medium of the pre-television era, it is reasonable to expect that

AUTHOR'S NOTE: *This is part of a larger investigation into the presentation of deviance in the mass media.*

their attitudes toward mental illness and psychiatry would reflect the same kinds of attitudes as popular fiction and orally communicated jokes, each of which devotes much attention to mental illness (Winick, 1963, 1976).

There is little doubt that one contributor to the reasons for which many persons decide to become patients of psychiatrists is the manner in which mental illness and the helping professions are presented in movies, which have so long provided food for popular fantasy needs. How psychiatry has been shown in cinema may have other implications for the profession itself, in terms of young physicians' interest in it. Many people may form their impressions of various kinds of mental illness from movies, which carry special emotional freight because they feature famous stars.

Patients in real life may use movie material on mental illness as reinforcement for resistances. It is also possible that such content could have some positive effects on the doctor-patient relationship by providing a question, a topic of conversation, or some other content that may be turned to therapeutic advantage.

One reason for the interest of Hollywood in themes of mental illness could be the unique ability of the camera to capture and represent fantasy, dreams, the unconscious, thought processes, ambiguity, juxtapositions of images, and of past, present, and future, and similar content that would seem to be germane to mental illness. The film provides an unusual opportunity to communicate the "primary process" or world of the nonrational (Winick, 1977). The social context of moviegoing, in which a decision is made to see a film, a trip is made to a theater where other people are also paying to share an experience in a large darkened room, and there is a return trip home, provides a "set" with special expectancies and readiness.

Another reason for Hollywood's interest in movies about mental illness and its treatment would be the role of psychoanalysis in the private lives of Hollywood film people. Psychoanalysis achieved greater success in America than in any European country and of all the communities in America, there are proportionately more psychoanalysts (67) in Beverly Hills, which has a population of 33,400 and where many movie people live, than in any other city. Movie executives and performers are thus relatively more likely to be patients than are most other kinds of workers. They can afford to pay for treatment and, by the nature of their work, are continually aware of their sensibilities. Psychoanalysts are so accepted in Hollywood that one of their number, Dr. Aaron Stern, was appointed director of the movie industry's Rating Administration in 1971.

Films about analysts or mental illness could be made for many reasons, in addition to the desire to make money. They might represent an informed piety, a way for a patient who is a movie functionary to try to please his analyst. They could also be an indirect way of learning more about one's symptoms, as well as an approach to undermining the treatment process, or toward acting out feelings about the therapist. For example, the author of "Lover Come Back" and "That Touch of Mink" has said that although he had six years as an analysand, his treatment would continue until the psychoanalyst completed building a swimming pool (Crowther, 1962). This attitude toward the psychoanalyst may be responsible for the startlingly negative representation of the profession in these two films, in which even the doctors' names are silly.

An actor's experience with mental illness may add texture to a part he is playing. It is probable that Robert Walker's extended stay in a mental hospital contributed to his dazzling performance as sympathetic murderer Bruno Anthony in Alfred Hitchcock's "Strangers on a Train" (1951) and his last role in Leo McCarey's "My Son John" (1952), as a secret Communist agent.

Dissonances may occur, however, between the actor's real life condition and a film role. Some distinguished actors who have played the role of a psychiatrist or patient have turned in extraordinarily bad performances, perhaps because they were too involved as in real life roles as patients. The same considerations may apply to directors or producers whose decision to make a film on mental illness may be affected by latent factors of which they are not conscious.

Psychiatrists and the mentally ill may, however, be presented in films by some artists who are quite aware of the effects they are creating. Fritz Lang (1962), who has directed "The Ministry of Fear" and four Dr. Mabuse films, said that "My profession makes me like a psychoanalyst." Less self-aware artists may be using psychiatrist or mentally ill characters because of demands of the plot or the availability of a specific actor. Even where the decision to have a particular kind of therapist or mentally ill person in a film was overt, the group nature of film making is such that it is very difficult even to infer the decisions that resulted in a specific portrayal.

PREVIOUS STUDIES

There are few previous relevant studies. One article presents an overview of the psychiatrist in fiction (Winick, 1963) while the manner in which mental illness content is regulated in movies and television has

been surveyed (Gerbner and Tannenbaum, 1960). A French fan magazine has dealt with mental illness in American films (Taconet, 1974)

METHOD

The study was conducted by taking every film with mental illness or a
psychiatrist or other psychotherapist released in this country since 1919,
which enjoyed some commercial success, on the assumption that such
films were meeting some needs of their audiences. Commercial success
was determined by reports in trade papers and other industry sources. In
spite of indices and lists published by the American Film Institute (1976)
and others, there are serious difficulties in attempting to determine which
films are concerned with such a subject. Even after a film has been
identified, viewing is necessary and may not be possible. Another and
serious problem is that the relevant content may be in a short scene which
would not figure in a plot summary, even though it is important, e.g.,
Elwood P. Dowd's visit to psychiatrist Cecil Kellaway in Henry Koster's
"Harvey" (1950), to discuss the invisible rabbit whom he claims to see.

The films were viewed and coded in terms of content categories, which
had been established on the basis of preliminary scrutiny of representative films.

Psychiatrists and other psychotherapists were generally clearly identifiable in terms of their function and "doctor" title. Mental illness was
either so identified in the film or else the character's behavior was
psychotic, extremely neurotic, psychopathic, or otherwise extremely
disturbed. Eccentric or odd behavior which merely added texture to a
film, like the character actors of early films who represented "humors"or
types, was not counted as mental illness (Winick, 1965).

Even major stars may play eccentric or odd people who are not
mentally ill. W.C. Fields' misogyny and dubious habits as Egbert Souse in
"The Bank Dick" (1940), the softcore transvestism of Jack Benny in
"Charley's Aunt" (1941), the raffish gamblers in such Damon Runyon
stories as "Guys and Dolls" (1955) or "Pocketful of Miracles" (1961),
the extravagant characters in "You Can't Take It With You" (1938), and
Judy Holiday's acting out her fantasies in "It Should Happen to You"
(1954), are examples of stars playing bizarre or off-centered parts, which
are not classified as mental illness. In spite of the film's title, Katherine
Hepburn as "The Madwoman of Chaillot" (1969) is sane, even if she was
opposed to modern corporate life, and acted out ancient memories,
behaved oddly, and wore strange outfits.

In the discussion that follows, the date for both domestic and foreign films is the date of their release in America. Each film cited is identified by its director. Since the actors who play patient and psychotherapist may contribute to the audience's perceptions, the actors' names are included where they appear to be relevant. Table 1 gives the films by the year of release.

Table 1. FILMS DEALING WITH MENTAL ILLNESS OR PSYCHIATRY BY DATE OF AMERICAN RELEASE

Year	Title
1919	Cabinet of Dr. Caligari
1926	Secrets of a Soul
1931	Front Page
1932	M
1933	Freaks; Reunion in Vienna
1934	Dr. Mabuse; Flame Within; Private Worlds
1936	Desire; Eternal Mask
1938	Amazing Dr. Clitterhouse; Bringing up Baby; Carefree
1939	Blind Alley
1940	My Favorite Wife
1941	Mad Doctor; Suspicion; Testament of Dr. Mabuse; Woman's Face
1942	Astonished Heart; Calling Dr. Gillespie; Kings Row; Lady in a Jam; Now Voyager
1943	Crime Doctor; Dr. Ordway's Strangest Case
1944	Arsenic and Old Lace; Lady in the Dark
1945	Bewitched; Ministry of Fear; Seventh Veil; Spellbound
1946	Bedlam; Dark Mirror; Dead of Night; Undercurrent
1947	Locket; Nightmare Alley; Possessed; Trouble with Women
1948	Dark Past; High Wall; Let's Live a Little
1949	Home of the Brave; Mine Own Executioner; Snake Pit; White Heat; You Can't Sleep Here
1950	Harvey; Whirlpool
1951	Europa 1951; M; Scarf; Tony Draws a Horse
1952	Strangers on a Train
1954	Caine Mutiny; Knock on Wood; Love Lottery; Sleeping Tiger
1955	Cobweb; Seven Year Itch; Shrike
1957	Lizzie; Three Faces of Eve; Oh Men, Oh Women
1958	Blood of the Vampires; Vertigo
1959	Girl of the Night; Glass Tower; Suddenly Last Summer; Three Strange Loves
1960	From the Terrace; Lover Come Back; Psycho; Subterraneans
1961	Full Treatment; Mark; Millionairess; Tender is the Night; West Side Story; Wild in the Country
1962	Cabinet of Dr. Caligari ; David and Lisa; Freud; Hell is for Heroes; Lolita; Lovers and Thieves; Manchurian Candidate; Pressure Point; That Touch of Mink
1963	Caretakers; Diary of a Madman; Dr. Strangelove; Shock Corridor

Table 1. FILMS DEALING WITH MENTAL ILLNESS OR PSYCHIATRY BY DATE OF AMERICAN RELEASE

Year	Title
1964	Captain Newman, M.D.; Disorderly Orderly; Lilith; Marnie; Third Secret; What a Way to Go
1965	Collector; Life Upside Down; Mirage; Night Walker; Repulsion; Thirty-Six Hours; Very Special Favor
1966	Fine Madness; Lord Love a Duck; Morgan; Persona; Promise Her Anything; Three on a Couch
1967	Cul de Sac; Fists in the Pocket; President's Analyst
1968	Hour of the Wolf; Impossible Years; Secret Ceremony
1969	Bob and Carol and Ted and Alice; Rosemary's Baby
1970	Catch 22; Diary of a Mad Housewife; Puzzle of a Downfall Child; Trash
1971	Harold and Maude; Klute; Little Murders; Made for Each Other; They Might be Giants
1972	Frenzy; Images; Hospital; The Other
1973	Blume in Love; Pink Flamingo
1974	Exorcist
1975	One Flew Over the Cuckoo's Nest; Return of the Pink Panther
1976	Face to Face; Seven-Per-Cent Solution; Taxi Driver
1977	Annie Hall; Equus; High Anxiety; I Never Promised You a Rose Garden; Outrageous; Semi-Tough
1978	An Unmarried Woman; Fingers

It is reasonable to expect that larger social forces contribute to the number and type of films about mental illness and psychiatry. Psychiatric ideas had begun to take hold in America in the 1920s, but it was not until the Depression of the 1930s and around the time of World War II, when people presumably needed reassurance, that there was a steady stream of movies about psychiatrists. Of the 151 movies in Table 1, only 11% were released from 1919 through the 1930s. Twenty-one percent were made during the war decade of the 1940s. The presumably bland Fifties produced only 15% of the total.

The many problems of the 1960s were concomitant with a massive increase in these movies, to 33% of all the titles. These problems included racial confrontation, disillusion resulting from the Cold War, Vietnam, anxieties over the Cuban missile crisis and Berlin blockade, and withdrawal of many citizens from public life after the assassination of President John Kennedy, Senator Robert Kennedy, and Dr. Martin Luther King. A parallel development in other mass media was the decline of the solo cowboy and detective hero. They were replaced by heroes who had such difficulties in coping that they functioned as vigilantes (James Bond, Mike Hammer), or as members of a group (Bonanza). Small wonder that the decade of the Sixties welcomed the movie psychiatrist, who might promise understanding for problems (Winick, 1968).

Although the current decade is not even 80% over, it already accounts for 19% of all the titles. The preparation of films presenting mental illness rather than psychiatrists has been increasing with time. The number of films dealing with psychiatry and mental illness must be interpreted as a proportion of the total Hollywood output, which was around 500 films annually in the "Golden Age" of movies, the 1930s and 1940s, but has dropped to around 100 per year now.

One reason for the comparatively high proportion of movies dealing with mental illness and psychiatry is that many have already generated interest as successful plays (12%) or novels (31%) so that there is lessened risk that they will be commercial failures. Plays like "Lady in the Dark" and "Equus" and books like *Lolita, The Snake Pit, From the Terrace, Diary of a Mad Housewife,* and *Tender Is the Night* are recognizable "brand name" titles. The moviegoer is likely to know about the titles' success in the previous medium and have an imagery transfer of positive expectations to the movie.

MOTION PICTURE PRODUCTION CODE

The motion picture Production Code, which was in effect from 1930 through 1968 and effectively controlled the content of Hollywood film until the advent of the rating system, made no reference to mental illness. An attorney who codified Code decisions concluded, however, that "insanity is a dangerous and unpleasant subject for screen presentations" (Gerbner and Tannenbaum, 1960). In movies, one way of presenting a person as evil or repellent, e.g., a murderer, was to present him as being "insane." Because a film without a Production Code seal could not expect general distribution, it was unlikely that mentally ill persons would be the foci of Hollywood movies, up to 1968. One result of the existence of the Code was that very few films could be made, before 1968, with mental illness as the main theme. Rather, such material was presented via the psychiatrist or other psychotherapist who usually became the key figure in the film.

After 1968, the Code became less important and a film now receives a rating (X, R, PG, G) to indicate its degree of suitability for children. Such ratings presumably permit movie makers greater latitude in making films, since "adult" content can be identified as such and there is no longer a need for the movie's problem to be resolved happily by the final frame.

Themes of mental illness can now be presented without a moral dimension, and with the sick person as the main character.

THE FILMS

Of the films listed in Table 1, over four fifths are American. It is noteworthy that several important film-making countries are poorly represented, notably Italy, India, Sweden, and France.

Italy's film industry is famous for the sophistication of writers and directors like De Sica, Rossellini, Antonioni, and Fellini. The comparative lack of mental illness and psychiatry in the country's films is probably partly a function of the central place of the confession as an Italian institution. It may also be a result of the large number of characters playing onlookers, who perform the function of interpreting others' actions. A director in Italian films also exercises many of the traditional functions of a novelist, making the psychiatrist even less necessary. Scriptwriters may feel that it would be reductionist to introduce psychiatric concepts into the dramatic colors of Italian life.

The country's relative paucity of psychiatrists is probably responsible for the lack of psychiatric films from India, which is the world's most active movie-making country. Sweden had also made few psychiatric films in spite of its film leadership. The Swedes' relative lack of interest in such films may reflect their feeling that the kind of psychological problems with which psychiatrists are concerned are adequately handled in the religious and mystical themes that characterize much Scandinavian screen output.

France, with a well-established psychotherapeutic profession, has produced very few films involving mental illness or its treatment. Possibly, the writers of French films, like French novelists and playwrights, regard themselves as such authorities on human behavior that there is no need for a psychotherapist or the concept of mental illness. It may also reflect the well-established French tradition of satirizing the medical profession.

One of the very few French films about mental illness is Sacha Guitry's "Lovers and Thieves" (1962). A psychiatrist who is the director of a mental hospital speaks at a machine-gun rate, in a kind of burbling manic manner. An example of this psychiatrist's tone is a remark he makes about why he likes to save women from drowning: "It is the only way that I can ask a woman to put her arms around my neck and spread her legs."

Inasmuch as films that are popular in their country of origin are likely to be those that are exported to America, we can probably make some generalizations about foreign psychiatric films on the basis of those that have been released and achieved popularity in this country. Most European films with psychiatrist characters usually present them as serious persons, and seldom as caricatures. In Europe, psychiatry has not been as ubiquitous as it has in America, nor has it had the same degree of popularization and vulgarization. Such factors contribute to the prestige of the psychiatrist in European films that have been released in America. Foreign countries are even less likely than Hollywood to make a film about mental illness rather than psychotherapy, as they may prefer not to export films which present their residents' problems.

Some Directors

Many directors who specialize in supernatural, melodrama, and horror movies have used a psychiatric or mental illness theme because it lends itself to mystery and dramatic climaxes. Almost every noted Hollywood director has made a psychiatrist or mental illness film, perhaps because the theme permits so much latitude. One additional reason for the subject's attractions is that it is one of the few medical themes in which the integrity and effectiveness of doctors may be criticized. Eleven directors have made two or more such films.

Some Actors

The conventional handsome leading man is unlikely to be presented as either psychiatrist or patient, because such a role would be contrary to audience expectations. Perhaps the only time a matinee idol star appeared in such a film was Tyrone Power in Edmund Goulding's "Nightmare Alley" (1947), which was a commercial failure. Ironically, Power had sought the role because he was tired of the romantic costume dramas he had been playing and thought "Nightmare Alley" would be the beginning of a new career. Because psychotherapist and patient represent illness and the irrational, audiences evidently cannot accept someone with whom they identify strongly in such a role, because it is out of character.

Gregory Peck, the only major star to appear in three films concerned with mental illness ("Spellbound," "Captain Newman, M.D.," "Mirage") conveys a sense of probity and dullness, which probably makes his good looks more acceptable to audiences. Lee J. Cobb, who comes across as a self-assured, square-jawed and humorless person, appeared as a psychiatrist in two films: "Three Faces of Eve" and "Dark Past."

Another character star who played a psychiatrist twice is Ralph Bellamy, who is attractive, cool, and serious in "Blind Alley" and "Lady in a Jam."

Debonair David Niven plays a famous movie star seeking psycho-analytic help for his "power fixation" in Charles Crichton's "The Love Lottery" (1954). Niven becomes a suburban psychiatrist, barely able to cope with life, in Michael Gordon's "The Impossible Years" (1968). Also working both sides of the couch is Joanne Woodward, who won an Academy Award for being a multiple personality in "Three Faces of Eve" (1957). Her most impressive performances, however, have been as an overwrought slattern, so that her casting as the psychiatrist in "They Might Be Giants" (1971) had some peculiar resonances.

The most eccentric resonances of a movie psychiatrist were communi-cated by Montgomery Clift, who had previously played a handsome young leading man but was obsessive and suffering in two such roles, perhaps because of serious injuries he had sustained in 1957 in an automobile accident. One of the most bizarre films ever made in America is Joseph L. Mankiewicz's "Suddenly Last Summer" (1959). It stars Elizabeth Taylor as a wealthy patient whose aunt (Katherine Hepburn) offers a million dollars to the Louisiana mental hospital of psychiatrist Dr. Cukrowicz (Montgomery Clift) for his performing a lobotomy on Miss Taylor. The doctor agrees, but first administers a "truth serum"to her. He discovers that she was traumatized by the death of her cousin Sebastian, "suddenly, last summer."

The cousin was a homosexual who had been using Miss Taylor and his mother as bait in his quest for young men. Some of the young men had torn off Sebastian's flesh and eaten him. Sebastian's mother cannot face the truth and becomes psychotic, thinking that the doctor is Sebastian. Clift, as the psychiatrist, plays his part with twitches rather than movement and seems very depressed and withdrawn.

Susannah York plays a Viennese invalid who is lovely and young and is treated by young Sigmund Freud, played by Clift, in John Huston's "Freud" (1962). Several of the case histories actually described by Freud were combined for the representation of patient Cecily Koertner. Dream sequences are presented in almost a baroque manner. The film presents Freud's self-awareness developing coterminously with the growing insight of his patient, which he encourages. Frau Freud calls her husband "Siggy." He is shown in many discussions with Dr. Breuer (Larry Parks) and an unfriendly physician (Eric Portman), but although Freud is presented as a symbolic hero who has helped the world, he comes across as more of a patient than a healer. Charles Boyer's brooding sensuality has also been seen in two different psychiatric roles, each involving an institution where things were going very badly.

Psychiatrists

In general, the tendency over time has been for the psychiatrist or other psychotherapist to move from a heroic and major character in movies to a characterization. In the early films of the 1920s and 1930s he may have been a hero or a monster, but he was a significant figure, as in films like "Reunion in Vienna," or "Private Worlds," with the role played by an important leading man (Charles Boyer, Fred Astaire). During this period, the great pioneers of psychiatry and psychoanalysis were getting much attention in other mass media. Their importance, and the novelty of their ideas at the time, are reflected in the importance of psychiatrists in the first few decades of motion pictures.

The last few decades, however, have seen a greater demystification and acceptance of psychiatrists in real life and in movies. They tend to be presented as characterizations, played by character actors, in the more recent films. These latter-day psychiatrists are often not given an opportunity to develop as characters or persons in their own right, but may be identified by cliches of behavior or mannerism.

Around 1961-1962, movies began to present what might be called the post-analytic analyst. Rod Steiger in "The Mark" (1961), is charming and warm in his work with patient Stuart Whitman. The doctor in "David and Lisa"(1962) is intelligent but less effective than the institution's therapeutic environment. David Niven as a psychiatrist in "The Impossible Years" (1968) is told by his 17-year-old daughter that he deals in "psychological poop."

The matter-of-fact approach of the modern therapist can be seen in the cool interaction between Jane Fonda and her therapist in Alan Pakula's "Klute" (1971). Like many recent movie patients, Fonda sits rather than lies on a couch while she chats about her career problems. In Woody Allen's "Annie Hall" (1977), there are split screen shots of Allen and Diane Keaton, each talking to their sensible, but only moderately helpful, therapists. In Robert Bean's "Made For Each Other" (1971), a man and woman meet at an emergency therapy group session but their therapist cannot do much about his patients' "self-destructive patterns."

Since the early 1960s, minority group members have been shown as psychotherapists. A Black psychiatrist is played by Sidney Poitier in John Frankenheimer's "Pressure Point" (1962). Bobby Darin is a Nazi psychopath prisoner who hates Jews even more than he hates Blacks. He is being treated by Poitier, who is very analytically oriented. The doctor's patience and forbearance are tested daily by the prisoner's rabble-rousing goading. Poitier works with his patient's dreams, whose problems he relates to a sadistic father.

Another Black psychiatrist in John Frankenheimer's "The Manchurian Candidate" (1962) is in a sufficiently exalted position in the federal government to be a member of a special panel that meets to interview Major Marco (Frank Sinatra), who has a peculiar dream. The psychiatrist has an Ivy League manner and an impressive command of psychiatric jargon.

Although the real-life role of Jews as both psychoanalysts and their patients has been widely accepted as quite important, it is curious that they seldom figure in movies about mental illness or its treatment. Even in books that have a significant Jewish dimension in either a patient or psychiatrist, the ethnic aspect is minimal when the book is made into a movie, as in "I Never Promised You a Rose Garden" (1977). Perhaps the movie makers wanted to avoid reinforcing stereotypes, or otherwise wanted to present a "bleached"impression of patients and doctors,in order to maximize audience appeal.

THE PSYCHOTHERAPISTS

There are about five male psychotherapists to every female in the movies. This ratio has remained fairly constant, although as women stars become more influential, more may appear as therapists. Jane Fonda, for example, is said to have insisted that the therapist in "Klute" (1971) be female. Most of the female psychotherapists, prior to the 1960s, seem to have been themselves involved in emotional difficulties.

Typical of the kind of emotional intern formerly represented by the female psychotherapist is Dr. J. O. Loring, played by Hedy Lamarr in Richard Wallaces's "Let's Live a Little" (1948). Lamarr, who was then probably the world's most famous beauty after having appeared nude in the Czech film "Ecstasy" (1932), is a psychoanalyst who has written a novel that advertising executive Robert Cummings is assigned to exploit for publicity purposes, until Dr. Loring decides that he could profit from treatment. Dr. Loring is about to marry another doctor, but becomes involved with Cummings. Most of the other female psychiatrists in early movies tend, like Lamarr, to be beautiful leading ladies. More recently, perhaps because of the women's movement, they seem to be more detached and professional, but also less likely to have central roles.

The male psychiatrist as lover or husband is often a ludicrous figure. Either he does not get the woman he is seeking, or, if he is married, something strange or pathetic may characterize the marriage or spouse.

Victor Hanbury's "The Sleeping Tiger" (1954) is what is seething within the wife of psychiatrist Clive Esmond (Alexander Knox). Dr. Esmond permits a young criminal to live with him as a houseguest as a method of treatment. Esmond, busy working, neglects his beautiful wife (Alexis Smith). She stubs out cigarettes after a few puffs, drives cars at high speed, and bites her lips so sharply that blood comes. The criminal, who is a thief by day, spends his nights seducing Mrs. Esmond, whom he describes as a "tight wire" who is "empty inside." When the criminal decides to leave, Mrs. Esmond follows him. The doctor's treatment method and marriage both collapse at the same time.

The growing public visibility of psychiatrists is probably related to their increasing movie appearance as lovers or spouses. There is a considerable number of movie psychiatrists who fall in love with their patients and enter into various extra-therapeutic relationships with them. When a psychiatrist's private life is part of a film, it is generally quite troublesome and disturbed. A typical situation is presented in Otto Preminger's "Whirlpool" (1950), the story of a psychiatrist (Richard Conte) whose wife is a shoplifter. She is apprehended by a charlatan, who hypnotizes her and implicates her in a murder.

Seducing patients appears to be common. Patrick Neal is a villainous psychiatrist in Mark Robson's "From the Terrace" (1960). He seems to spend much of his time seducing patients and their friends, while treating not only their husbands but also the husbands' girl friends.

The psychiatrist in Ingmar Bergman's Swedish "Three Strange Loves" (1959) wears a pencil-thin moustache and an untrustworthy expression. When an attractive woman comes for a consultation, the doctor tries to seduce the patient, but his attempt to do so is foiled by a window washer. The patient, fleeing from the doctor's Freudian jargon and his advances, is so distraught that she is an easy prey for a lesbian who accosts her.

Psychiatrist Dr. Diver (Jason Robards, Jr.) in Henry King's "Tender Is the Night" (1961) is a pathetic figure of wistful moods and halting charm who gives up his career and self-respect in order to become completely dependent on the psychotic patient (Jennifer Jones) whom he marries. Both he and his career are ruined by this marriage.

Some movie therapists tend to engage in unusually active therapy, like Dr. Enright (Ralph Bellamy), the psychiatrist hero of Gregory La Cava's "Lady in a Jam" (1942). A young lady who poses serious problems to her guardian is sent to Enright for treatment. He decides that the best treatment for her would be to reestablish her roots in the West, and that it would be good if he accompanied her. The doctor accompanies his flibbertigibbet patient to her grandmother's abandoned gold mine in the West. All of Dr. Enright's sensitivity training has apparently blinded him to his patient's having fallen in love with him.

The psychiatrist as parent is usually a failure. A woman psychiatrist married to a Harley Street physician is the focus of John P. Carstairs' "Tony Draws a Horse" (1951), a British film. Their son likes to draw lewd pictures on walls, but the doctor believes that her son should be encouraged to express himself freely: "I will not have my son put into a psychological straightjacket." The psychiatrist is pompous and seemingly unable to use her professional knowledge in her role as a mother.

Psychotherapists are psychiatrist in over nine tenths of the titles, perhaps because an M.D. carries substantial prestige as well as the physician's control over life and death, and has considerable potential for drama. The films present only a few psychologists, and social workers who are engaging in psychotherapy, whereas the reverse is true in the "real" world. Although more people in "real" life consult a minister, priest, or rabbi for emotional problems than any other professional, pastoral psychology is hardly to be found in movies.

Of the various forms of treatment, psychoanalytic is the most frequent (41%). An eclectic approach is also popular (27%), while directive techniques (15%) and drug/physical therapy (5%) are less likely. About a sixth (12%) of the contacts involve diagnosis rather than treatment. Some significant treatment techniques, like biofeedback, existential psychotherapy, and behavior modification, are hardly represented at all, perhaps because of problems in their film visualization. Another reason for their underpresentation is that an average of two years elapses from the beginning of movie project to its completion. Movie makers may feel that if their theme is built around a fad, the fad could have run its course by the time the movie is ready for release.

Inasmuch as less than a tenth of the members of American psychiatrists are also psychoanalysts, the proportion of psychoanalysts would seem to be extremely high. Movie psychoanalysts usually interpret dreams in a literal manner, so that the audience may believe that a patient reports a dream and the analyst promptly interprets it to the patient. The more the audience admires the effects of a dream, the more outside the dream it is likely to be.

Psychoanalysis itself is generally presented as a series of dramatic climaxes of dream interpretation. Such a dream interpretation figures in Rudolph Mate's "The Dark Past" (1949), a remake of "Blind Alley"

(1939). A psychoanalyst and his weekend guests are visited by escaped murderer Al Walker and his girl friend. Analyst Lee J. Cobb, a thoughtful pipe smoker, gets the murderer to recount a recurrent dream, and to free associate to each aspect of it. Walker realizes that the thought of his father's blood being on his hands has led him to kill every man who stood in his way, as an acting out of the Oedipus complex. Once he understands the dream, Dr. Collins assures Walker, he will not be able to kill anymore. When police surround the house and Walker raises his rifle to his shoulder and sqeezes the trigger, he cannot do so, even to protect himself.

Usually, a character's work as a psychiatrist is so salient that it becomes important for the development of the plot. It is rare that, as in Sam Wood's "Kings Row" (1942), a character's vocation as a psychiatrist is almost incidental to the plot.

It is possible to classify all the psychotherapists presented in movies into one of several categories, as set forth in Table 2. Some examples of each category are indicated below.

Table 2. MOVIE PSYCHOTHERAPISTS CLASSIFICATIONS IN %

Kind of Psychotherapist	%
Serious, effective	48
Eccentric, whimsical, lighthearted	10
Ludicrous, comic	10
Miracle worker	10
Personally troubled	8
Evil, destructive	8
Foolish	6
	100

The Serious Effective Doctor (48%)

The serious and effective doctor is an experienced professional who communicates competence. In Fritz Lang's German film "M" (1932), a psychiatrist attempts to describe M, who kills little girls and takes their shoes. On the basis of some scattered clues and bits of information provided by the police, the psychiatrist correctly diagnoses M as a paranoid schizophrenic. The psychiatrist conveys a feeling of expertise and quiet knowledge.

The Swiss production, Werner Hochbaum's "The Eternal Mask" (1936), presents a young psychoanalyst trying to reconstruct the past of Dr. DuMartin, a physician, whose guilt over the death of a patient leads to his developing an acute schizophrenic psychosis. A series of flash-backs and dream sequences relies very heavily on Freudian symbolism. In the final scene, the dark room in which the patient has been resting becomes lighter, symbolizing his recovery. The psychoanalyst is a very capable, low-key professional.

Psychoanalyst Dr. Alexander Brooks (Barry Sullivan) is treating a magazine editor played by Ginger Rogers in Mitchell Leisen's "Lady in the Dark" (1944). Miss Rogers' treatment is unusual in that many of her dreams are acted out with music, with very literal symbols. Thus, she dreams of being at a wedding, and the doctor helps her to see that she would like it to be her wedding. Dr. Brooks, although a classical analyst, also engages in considerable questioning of the patient. This film was made from the famous 1941 musical comedy of the same name, starring Gertrude Lawrence, with the lyrics by Ira Gershwin and Kurt Weill's best American score.

In Anatole Litvak's "The Snake Pit" (1949), adapted from Mary Jane Ward's exposé novel, Dr. Mark Kik (Leo Genn) is on the staff of a state mental hospital and uses shock, hydrotherapy, and psychotherapy on patient Virginia Cunningham. He has a picture of Freud in his office, as well as a leather couch. Dr. Kik interprets Mrs. Cunningham's illness to her as being a result of her fantasy of having killed her father. Although other psychiatrists at the hospital are shown as ignorant, Dr. Kik is a real healer whose commitment is made to appear a function of his European background. "The Snake Pit" was the fourth most successful film at the box office for 1949 and its title has entered the language.

For movie characters to obtain professional treatment for mental illness or for problems in living has recently become so accepted that Paul Mazursky, a director who has made six films about upward mobile middle-class people since 1969, has had characters consulting a psychiatrist in half the films ("Bob and Carol and Ted and Alice," "Blume in Love," and "An Unmarried Woman"). In each of these films, the character was effectively played by a real psychotherapist, just as the hospital director in "One Flew Over the Cuckoo's Nest" actually has the job in real life. In two of the films, the psychiatrist was played by Mazursky's own therapist, suggesting how closely movie psychiatrists may reflect movie creators' actual lives.

Eccentric, Whimsical, Lighthearted Doctors

Another group of practitioners was either eccentric, whimsical, or lighthearted. Oscar Homolka's eccentricities are exaggerated by his shambling gate, beetling brows, and mannerisms, as the psychiatrist who tries to help a publisher overcome the affliction called "The Seven Year Itch" (Billy Wilder, 1955).

Dr Tony Flagg is a casual and jolly psychoanalyst, played by Fred Astaire, in Mark Sandrich's "Carefree" (1938). Dr. Flagg accepts his best friend's fiancee (Ginger Rogers) as a patient, whose problem is her reluctance to get married. The doctor not only dances astonishingly well, including a sword dance, the symbolism of which does not seem to concern him, but also prescribes special diets like seafood with whipped cream for his patient. In this film, which could be described as the story of quirk and Flagg, the doctor uses the concept of the unconscious in his "treatment," as well as drugs and hypnosis.

Ludicrous, Comic Doctors

The ludicrous comic doctor is a preposterous figure, presented in caricature. One of the most memorable movie psychiatrists is the police alienist played by Gustav Von Seyffertitz in Lewis Milestone's "The Front Page" (1931). A hobo who has shot and killed a policeman is taken for diagnosis to a cadaverous doctor who speaks with a heavy accent. He tells the prisoner to reenact the crime. The prisoner says, "I got frightened and shot him." The doctor says, "We need more realism here—Sheriff, lend him your gun." When the prisoner reluctantly takes the gun, the doctor says, "Well . . . ?" The prisoner points it at the doctor and pulls the trigger. The blood spurts out of the doctor, who falls to the floor crying, "Dementia Praecox!"

Two generations later, a similar scene occurs in Blake Edwards' "Return of the Pink Panther" (1975). The chief inspector who supervises bumbling Inspector Clouseau (Peter Sellers) has dreams of killing Clouseau. When the chief inspector's analyst tries to get him to illustrate the dreams, he strangles the analyst.

Howard Hawk's "Bringing up Baby" (1938) has a monocled European psychiatrist as a foil for the "madcap comedy" antics of Cary Grant and Katherine Hepburn. The doctor is vain, naive, and completely enchanted with his own jargon and cliche interpretations. In the final scene of the film, the doctor ("you have probably heard me lecture on love") is completely fooled by Katherine Hepburn's rather transparent attempt to claim that she is a gun moll.

The ease with which even juvenile delinquents can poke fun at psychiatrists and their methods is shown in Robert Wise and Jerome Robbins' "West Side Story" (1961). Several delinquents are singing about the difficulties of their lives. One lies on the step of a slum building and another simulates puffing on a pipe, to represent an analyst. When the "patient" reports his difficult family situation, the "analyst" says that he cannot help the "patient" because he has a "social disease." The "analyst" therefore refers him to a social worker. The scene vividly illustrates the delinquents' command of psychiatric jargon and the inadequacies of the psychiatrist in coping with reality problems.

Miracle Worker

These doctors are insightful and brilliant, achieving very successful results. The first movie to present a psychoanalyst was G.W. Pabst's "Secrets of a Soul" (1926), made in Germany. The film was supervised by famous analysts Nicholas Kaufmann, Hanns Sachs, and Karl Abraham. A still photograph of Freud is shown at its beginning. A chemist loses his house keys in a coffee house, and is followed home by psychoanalyst Dr. Charles Orth, who tells the chemist that he has reasons for not wishing to enter his home. The chemist becomes a patient, and is shown free associating on a couch as Dr. Orth animatedly smokes.

The analyst helps the patient, via a dream and repressed memories, to deal with his fantasies of killing his young wife with a knife. Good use is made of the dream sequences, which are loaded with symbols: e.g., "That water in your dream is impending birth." After a few sessions, the patient's cure is complete.

Arch Oboler's "Bewitched" (1945) centers around Dr. Bergson (Edmund Gwenn), psychiatrist who gets the state governor to agree to see Joan Ellis, a woman who is to be executed for murder, on the morning of her execution. Dr. Bergson hypnotizes Joan and forces her to talk about Karen, another woman who is living "inside" her and who committed the murder. The camera shows Karen actually leaving Joan's body. The governor pardons Joan and we know that Karen will die but Joan will live and be free.

Psychiatrist Dr. Luther (Lee J. Cobb) almost magically cures a woman with three different identities (Joanne Woodward) in Nunnally Johnson's "The Three Faces of Eve" (1957). The woman switches back and forth among her personalities so rapidly that the psychiatrist almost seems to be turning the personalities on and off at will; "Let's have Eve Black; now, we'll see Miss White." The psychiatrist discovers that Eve's being forced by her mother to kiss her dead grandmother was the genesis of her current problem.

Personally Troubled Doctors

Some practitioners are so heavily involved in their own serious interpersonal difficulties that their professional work is secondary. A psychiatric staff that is almost as troubled as the patients is the subject of Gregory La Cava's "Private Worlds" (1934). Dr. Charles Monet (Charles Boyer) is the new director of a mental hospital where Dr. Jane Everest (Claudette Colbert) works. Monet's sister has an affair with Dr. MacGregor, another staff psychiatrist, who is married. Mrs. MacGregor becomes psychotic, Monet finds it impossible to conceal his sister's lurid past, and many other complications ensue. The complications underscore how human, all too human, the hospital's psychiatrists are in their own interpersonal relations.

"The Flame Within" (1934) is waiting to be fanned to life in Dr. Mary White (Ann Harding), a calm and clear-eyed psychiatrist in Edmund Goulding's film. She falls in love with an alcoholic patient who is 15 years her junior and who is married to a dipsomaniac heiress. Dr. White entertains the idea of marrying the patient (Louis Hayward), but decides against it because his wife, who is also her patient, will commit suicide if her husband leaves her.

A fashionable psychoanalyst in Nunnally Johnson's "Oh Men, Oh Women" (1957), is treating a patient who used to be in love with the analyst's fiancee. Franchot Tone, the analyst, is amiable, but is so bedeviled by this situation that he returns to his own analyst, who reminds him that, "You must remember that there is an enormous distance between the library and the bedroom." The analyst's theories are upset by his personal difficulties.

Evil and Destructive Doctors

A number of practitioners do great harm and destruction. In Robert Wiene's famous German film, "The Cabinet of Dr. Caligari" (1919), the doctor uses witchcraft to exercise power over a somnambulist, whom he commands to commit murders. Caligari, who is the personification of evil, is the head of a mental hospital. Caligari is myopic, even when wearing his spectacles. Caligari's face is pasty white with ghoulishly framed eyes and white hair askew. The sets convey a visual sensation of disorientation and unbalance. Caligari's appearance is that of a madman, and few films have captured the world of madness so effectively. The film's use of expressionist photography techniques made it a landmark, and helped to give the wide currency to its picture of psychiatry.

One of the most ruthless and depraved psychiatrists on film reappears in Fritz Lang's production of "The Testament of Dr. Mabuse" (1941). This German film deals with the criminal gang that Dr. Mabuse is still directing from the hospital for the criminally insane to which he has been sent and where he has hypnotized another doctor who becomes his medium. The doctor parrots Nazi slogans, and Lang himself subsequently indicates that he deliberately put such slogans into the mouth of a psychotic. Another Lang film, "The Ministry of Fear" (1945), features Dr. Forester, who runs a clinic with a robotized staff and who kills patients.

One of the coldest psychiatrists on film is Dr. Christian Faber (Noel Coward) in Terence Fisher and Anthony Darnborough's "The Astonished Heart" (1942), a British film. Dr. Faber falls violently in love with an old school friend of his wife's and becomes the friend's very jealous and possessive lover. The doctor cannot help himself and commits suicide. The title, from the Bible, refers to a man stricken with madness, blindness, and astonishment of heart.

Dr. Lilith Ritter is a psychologist (Helen Walker) in Edmund Goulding's "Nightmare Alley" (1947). She appears to be professional in her manner and in her considerable private practice—except that she is in league with an unscrupulous "mentalist," with whom she cooperates in blackmailing her patients. The psychologist double-crosses "mentalist" Tyrone Power and convinces him that he is mentally ill, after stealing $150,000 from him.

Foolish Doctors

Some practitioners are not bright and lack common sense. Marlene Dietrich hoodwinks a gullible psychiatrist, played by Alan Mowbray, in Frank Borzage's "Desire" (1936). She asks a jeweler to deliver a brooch to her "husband," Dr. Edouard Pauquet, the famous psychiatrist. She explains that he doesn't like to pay bills. She then visits the doctor as a patient, telling him that her "husband," the jeweler, has the delusion that everybody owes him money. Leaving the consulting room, she meets the jeweler, takes delivery of the brooch, and drives rapidly away. The jeweler is ushered into Dr. Pauquet's office. When he asks the doctor for money for the brooch, the doctor says, "Of course, of course." Both he and the jeweler are fooled by Dietrich.

Psychoanalyst Dr. Gruber provides the plot continuity as well as its climax in Delbert Mann's "That Touch of Mink" (1962). Dr. Gruber (Alan Hewitt), treating an economic adviser (Gig Young) to a millionaire businessman (Cary Grant), invests his money on the basis of the economic adviser's "tips." The doctor displays an uncanny ability to misinterpret what his patient says and to be totally unable to help him in coping with his problems, or even in understanding them.

A Navy psychiatrist who has written a book about the stresses and strains of the executive life but does not seem able to apply his knowledge is the butt of cross-examination by defense counsel in the court-martial scene of Edward Dymtryk's "The Caine Mutiny" (1954). The attorney makes the psychiatrist seem very foolish and naive. The doctor denies that Captain Queeg is paranoid, but admits that Queeg's symptoms are those of paranoia.

Sometimes a psychiatrist is not so much foolish as smugly confident in his rationality. The British film, "Dead of Night" (1946), directed by Cavalcanti, Basil Deardon, and Robert Hamer, is a collection of four strange experiences which blend psychiatry with mysticism. At the beginning of the film, a man is shown walking to a house. He tells a group in the house that he has a recurring dream that he will murder someone who wishes him no ill. He strangles a psychiatrist who is heavy, nearsighted, speaks with an accent, and continually ridicules the previous discussion of ghosts and the supernatural. The psychiatrist is obviously the man of good will. The implication is that the stereotyped psychiatrist was so sure of the power of reason that he lost his life as the result of underestimating the power of the nonrational.

Psychiatrists in movies seldom can cope with the mystical. In William Friedkin's "The Exorcist" (1974), a psychiatrist fails to unearth the hidden personality of a child who has been infested by a demon. The child's schizophrenic breakdown is parallel with her struggle between good and evil.

THE PATIENTS

Just half of the mentally ill persons are male, two fifths are female, and one tenth involve mixed situations with both sexes. Middle class was the most frequent (40%) socioeconomic state encountered among the mentally ill. It is perhaps surprising that almost a third (32%) were upper class and 11% lower class. In the remaining cases (17%), socioeconomic affiliation could not be estimated.

Half the mentally ill persons who were treated by a professional were helped, 32% were not helped, and in 18% of the cases, no determination of degree of symptom relief was possible. This rate of success is higher than obtains in actual pratice and probably reflects the problem of interesting audiences in downbeat themes and the desire to avoid ambiguous endings.

Almost two thirds (63%) of the patients were seen in a private practice setting. About a fifth (19%) were in a clinic, hospital or other institution and almost as many (18%) had some relationship with criminal justice, often as someone involved with a crime. In real life, more patients are seen in an institutional setting than in private practice.

The criminal justice dimension is very varied in these films. Anatole Litvak's "The Amazing Dr. Clitterhouse" (1938) deals with a psychiatrist who becomes the leader of a criminal gang in order to obtain material for a book. Played by Edward G. Robinson, Dr. Clitterhouse kills a gangster who is a blackmailer, and goes on trial for the crime. In a bizarre final courtroom scene, Clitterhouse insists he is sane. The jury finds him not guilty of murder on the ground that he must be insane to claim that he was sane.

Warner Baxter, dapper in double-breasted, pin stripe suit, plays "The Crime Doctor" (1943) in Michael Gordon's film. He is a psychiatrist specializing in criminals, who puts on his slouch hat to do detective work, which is based on the Lombroso approach to criminals. As society has become more aware of the complexities of crime and criminals, movies have become less likely to present a psychiatrist whose knowledge of the "criminal mind" enables him to solve crimes.

Psychiatrist Dr. Constance Peterson (Ingrid Bergman) is a staff member at a private sanitarium in Alfred Hitchcock's "Spellbound" (1945). Gregory Peck, a new doctor at the sanitarium, replaces Dr. Edwards, who has recently died. Peck develops amnesia and thinks he has killed Dr. Edwards and assumed his identity. A recurrent dream (designed by Salvador Dali in color, although the rest of the film is black and white), enables Peck to solve his problems. When Bergman confronts the head of the sanitarium with her awareness that he killed Dr. Edwards, he takes out his revolver to shoot her. However, she "psyches" him and he shoots himself.

Sometimes a particular symptom is "in the air" in one year and appears in several films. Amnesia, for example, hit James Garner in George Seaton's "36 Hours" (1965). Garner is an American officer in World War II who is privy to D-Day secrets and who is captured by Germans and told by a Nazi psychiatrist (Rod Taylor) that the war is over, and that his amnesia will be cured if he recalls the events surrounding D-Day. In the same year, in Edward Dmytryk's "Mirage," scientist Gregory Peck's amnesia blocks his ability to recall his method for eliminating nuclear fallout. Two films about multiple personalities ("Three Faces of Eve" and "Lizzie") were released in 1957. Amnesia and multiple personality are so unusual that their simultaneous appearance in different films is curious.

In one content study of movies of the 1950s, only 56% of mentally ill males had any occupation (Gerbner and Tannenbaum, 1960). Of these, one third were criminals, one third had miscellaneous occupations, and one third were professionals. Half the professionals were "mad" scientists or psychiatrists.

Taking all the patients in the films in the current study, 70% had some recognizable occupation. Each decade, the proportion of patients with some occupation has increased, probably reflecting the decreasing stigmatization of mental illness and declining likelihood that a trade or professional society would complain that its members were being maligned by being associated with mental illness (Winick, 1959).

What are the symptoms or diagnoses of the persons being treated in these films? Table 3 gives the presenting problems, symptoms, and/or diagnoses of the patients, for those symptoms which occurred in more than 2% of the films. It is evident that the symptoms are relatively unusual when compared with the symptoms of real life patients obtaining treatment. For example, in many urban treatment settings, the three most common diagnoses are "character disorder," "borderline," and "passive-aggressive personality," which do not figure in even one movie. Scriptwriters presumably select those conditions that will lend themselves to relatively easy filmic visualization and facilitate conflict situations. Thus, although senile psychosis is also very common in real life, it does not easily lend itself to cinematic treatment and seldom occurs in movies.

Usually, we see the patients already in the sway of their disease. There are relatively few films, like Roger Coggio's "Diary of a Madman" (1963), which actually show the processes of disease and disintegration. In Coggio's film, we see the collapse of a man who is convinced that he is heir to the throne of Spain and is placed in a mental hospital.

One film device for presenting the difference between ordinary and mentally ill people is to present the latter's thought processes in color and ordinary activity in black and white. Thus, in Samuel Fuller's "Shock Corridor" (1963), the film is in black and white but a psychotic's hallucinations are seen in color.

Perhaps the most important movie analyst in terms of his patients is played by James Coburn in Theodore Flicker's "The President's Analyst" (1967). This "hip" psychiatrist is charming and has been

Table 3. SYMPTOMS OR DIAGNOSES OF PATIENTS IN %

Symptom or Diagnosis	% of Total
Schizophrenia	10
Homicide/Psychosis	9
Neurosis	7
Psychopathy	6
Work problems	6
Paranoia	5
Amnesia	5
Phobia	3
Multiple personality	3
Traumatic memory	3
Repression leading to problem	3
Love/Sex difficulties	3
Feigned symptoms	2
Kleptomania	2
Alcoholism	2
Sociopath	2
Hallucinations	2
Depersonalization	2
Acting out conflicts	2
Suicidal	2
	79

recruited to ease the problems of the President of the United States, before spies kidnap him in order to discover his patient's secrets. Coburn, worried, consults his own analyst. That the President would require an analyst suggests how acceptable the notion of analytic treatment has become.

At the same time that such relatively exalted persons are being treated, movies are also concerned with more ordinary people experiencing problems in living. Mental illness as an exhausting and depressing condition that is almost incomprehensible to others figures in Anthony Page's "I Never Promised You a Rose Garden" (1977), made from a famous autobiographical novel by a former schizophrenic. Her psychiatrist (Bibi Andersson) helps the 16-year-old patient to deal with her fantasies. This film is unusually delicate in suggesting that different patients proceed at different rates toward improvement. It is like a number of other films in contrasting the good psychiatrist with other personnel who are incompetent, like nurses who assault patients, patronizing staff members, and foolish doctors.

Until the 1950s, movies often ridiculed some psychiatric disabilities. Thus, in Frank Capra's "Arsenic and Old Lace" (1944), Cary Grant's brother thinks that he is President Theodore Roosevelt, dresses like

Roosevelt, and keeps charging up the stairs to imitate the attack at San Juan Hill. This paranoia is humored by Grant and the other characters. Such laughing *at* a mentally ill person is unlikely in the movies of the last two decades.

Few recent films rely on the presentation of the interaction between patient and therapist. Such "talking heads" are usually "slow" and difficult for and audience to accept. "Pressure Point" (1962) and "The Mark" (1961) are among the latter films showing extended patient-doctor communication.

The current emphasis on patients' rights and "revolt of the patients" was prefigured in Mark Robson's "Bedlam" (1946), in which an actress is sent to an 18th-century hospital, suggested by the Hogarth painting which is the film's opening shot, on trumped-up charges of lunacy. By the film's end, the residents have captured the hospital head and put him on trial for insanity.

Demystification

One reason for the demystification of mental illness and psychiatry in movies around 1962-1963, as well as an increase in the number of such movies, was the popularity of two television psychiatric dramas ("The Eleventh Hour" and "The Breaking Point"), which were each broadcast weekly. These one-hour dramas presented a wide range of human problems, usually handled effectively by the psychiatrists, who were low key and played by solid performers like Wendell Corey and Ralph Bellamy.

Also in the early 1960s, when talk shows became a staple format on television, many actual psychologists, psychiatrists, and psychoanalysts appeared as guests. They often were relatively young, articulate, and attractive persons, like psychiatrist David Reuben and psychologists Joyce Brothers and Haim Ginott, who offered practical advice on a wide range of problems of daily living. Similar guests have been appearing on talk shows, up to the present, and help to facilitate audiences' feeling about the social acceptability of emotional difficulties and the people who treat them.

Another reason for the change in movie attitudes toward psychotherapists was probably the considerable interest expressed in the subject by President Kennedy. By his frequent and favorable references to psychiatry and encouragement of the community mental health center movement, he helped to create a more favorable climate.

Perhaps the most dramatic expression of the more positive attitudes toward treatment of the mentally ill in the early 1960s could be found in Philip Dunne's "Wild In the Country" (1961), in which a character played by Elvis Presley is shown visiting a psychiatrist (Hope Lange). Since Presley was the most famous and important popular singer at the time, his appearance as a patient represented a benchmark.

Kinds of People

In recent years, the kinds of people who seek professional assistance for their personal problems, in movies, have been changing. More middle-class persons are shown obtaining treatment and such involvement with a psychotherapist is less related to the criminal justice system. In Paul Mazursky's "Bob and Carol and Ted and Alice" (1969), a young upper-middle-class woman of 35, married for 10 years, with one child in "Updike Country," living in an attractive house with a pool and barbecue pit, consults a psychiatrist because of problems resulting from her attendance at a sensitivity training session.

More attractive, upscale, and interesting people are presented seeking psychotherapeutic assistance in movies since the 1960s. The world's richest woman (Sophia Loren) consults psychiatrist Adrian Bland in Anthony Asquith's British film, "The Millionairess" (1961), to find out why nobody loves her. Dissatisfied with his answer, she throws him into a river, perhaps reflecting patients' assertiveness during the decade of the Sixties.

Prestigious actress Liv Ullmann played an upper-class psychiatrist who gets help for her own problems in Ingmar Bergman's "Face to Face" (1976), a part for which she received an Academy Award nomination. Even the master of logic and good works, the redoubtable detective Sherlock Holmes, sought assistance for his cocaine habit by treatment from young Dr. Sigmund Freud in Herbert Ross's "The Seven Per Cent Solution" (1976). And the sensitive, brilliant doctor played by George C. Scott in Arthur Hiller's "Hospital" (1972) consults a psychiatric colleague in the hospital for assistance in coping with his anxiety and suicidal tendencies.

Mental illness is shown in high places in a number of films. In Stanley Kubrick's savage "Dr. Strangelove" (1963), General Jack D. Ripper as well as major government officials are clearly mad, although not motivated for treatment. As a result of their madness, the earth is destroyed in an atomic explosion.

CHANGES IN TREATMENT AND PATIENTS

During the 60 years covered by this study, there have been significant changes in treatment methods, demystification of the treatment process, and the kinds of people becoming patients, all of which have been reflected, to some extent, in these movies.

Changes in Treatment

Movies have been somewhat indicative of changes in the form of therapy. The classical analytic technique of the 1920s and 1930s yielded to shock therapy in "The Snake Pit" (1949).

The concept of the therapeutic community appears in Frank Perry's "David and Lisa" (1962). A 17-year-old obsessive boy who is afraid to be touched, and 15-year-old schizophrenic girl who only talks in rhyme, are patients at the institution. The relationship that David and Lisa develop toward each other, and their being in a therapeutic community which has approximately 20 patients, are made to seem more important factors in their recovery than the formal treatment they receive from doctors.

Group therapy figures in "The Mark" (1961) and Esalen-type encounter groups meet in "Bob and Carol and Ted and Alice" (1969). The authoritarian directive "pop" therapies like EST are ridiculed in Michael Ritchie's "Semi-Tough" (1977), in which a superstud football hero gets involved in the BEAT consciousness therapy movement and claims to have found 'it," the solution to the world's problems.

BETTER INSANE THAN SANE?

During the last decade, a number of movies presented the theme that, in the world today, perhaps the only true wisdom and validity are to be found in persons who would ordinarily be classed as psychotic.

One such film, which was built around a presold book title and a high voltage star, is Milos Forman's "One Flew Over the Cuckoo's Nest," which not only won an Academy Award as best picture, but enjoyed the biggest box office success of any film with a mental illness theme. It grossed $56.5 million in 1976, more than twice as much as the year's next most popular film. Its success is probably attributable to a combination of the message, brilliant direction, powerful supporting roles, Jack Nicholson's bravura performance, and an exceptional score. Randle Patrick McMurphy is a fast-talking convict in the film, who is serving time for statutory rape, but decides to feign insanity and get transferred to a psychiatric hospital for observation.

The movie, made from Ken Kesey's nightmare novel which was one of the key youth books of the 1960s, centers around the conflict between iconoclastic, magnetic McMurphy and a dignified nurse who shrewdly controls the ward, in which the solemn doctors are not very important. We see group therapy, with the psychotic participants very real and identifiable. Shock treatments are used as punishment and the nurse is able to authorize lobotomy. As a Broadway play with substantial political allegorical content, "Cuckoo's Nest" failed. As a movie with minimal ulterior meanings, it was a blockbuster. It is a commentary on the caution with which Hollywood approached the theme of mental illness that various previous producers had unsuccessfully tried, over a 15-year period, to get funding for a film to be made from the Kesey book. For the same reason, the British film "Morgan: A Suitable Case for Treatment" (1966) was released in America without its subtitle.

Along with Ken Kesey, author Peter Shaffer, in Sidney Lumet's (1977) movie version of the successful play "Equus," thinks that madness could be a greater virtue than sanity in a sterile modern world. Madness, conceived as the true root of vitality, is represented by a handsome blond youth whose sexual interest in horses leads him to blind them. The youth consults a psychiatrist (Richard Burton) who is sterile, bland, and repressed. Envious of the boy and feeling fraudulent, the doctor says that "passion can be destroyed by an analyst."

A spate of earlier movies, such as "King of Hearts" (1967), "Marat/ Sade" (1967), and "Going Places" (1974), argues that it is more reasonable to be mad than sane in today's world. Such films, reflecting popular philosophers of the 1960s like R. D. Laing, hold that authority is repressive and hostile to the spirit of self-expression.

Richard Benner's "Outrageous" (1977) also presents the sanity versus insanity argument, but is unusual in permitting its "crazies" to cope successfully with their problems. A male homosexual hairdresser shares an apartment with a schizophrenic young woman who has escaped from a mental hospital. The hairdresser, who asks, "Who's insane anyhow?" becomes a successful female impersonator and the woman resumes treatment with a psychiatrist, but on an outpatient basis. Toward the film's end, the hairdresser tells the woman, "You'll never be normal . . . you have a healthy case of craziness, just make it work for you."

Although this approach blossomed in the 1960s, as part of the antiwar, "greening of America" revolutionary movement, it has found its fullest expression in the 1970s. It is probably relevant that the movie audience primarily consists of young adults, with the one third of the population between 13 and 29 accounting for three fourths of all movie ticket sales.

THE PSYCHOTIC OR MENTALLY ILL AS HEROES

Psychosis, or mental illness which is not being treated and for which there is no resolution or treatment, began to figure in movies by the late 1960s, probably as part of the same liberating forces which otherwise characterized the decade's arts. John Waters' "Pink Flamingo" (1973), starring Divine, a 300-pound transvestite who sells kidnapped children to lesbian couples and kills two people because "murder relieves tension" and who eats dog feces, became a national favorite, although it cost only $12,000 to make. Movies, vying with television for audiences, became more and more bold in presenting heroes with aberrations which would be unacceptable for television.

One of the few precursors of the modern cinema of the psychotic was Raoul Walsh's "White Heat" (1949), with James Cagney as a tight-lipped, trigger-happy misfit gangster. In his many previous gangster films, Cagney was somehow admirable although a killer, but in "White Heat," his fits of howling and murderous rages are attributable to a mother fixation. Cagney was one of the few major stars who could have carried off such an unsympathetic role.

Even if an actor were willing to accept such a role, to present a very disturbed psychotic character may create problems in audience identification with behavior that is so out of line with ordinary experience. Prior to the beginning of the rating system in 1968, few movies dealt with psychosis without making it part of a psychiatric situation. More recently, a number of films have presented case histories of psychotics. Such films generally do not have a simple ending or a solution to the situation they expose and most do not present therapy as any solution; it is simply irrelevant.

A number of directors who specialize in presenting disturbed people have achieved major recognition, especially in recent years. It is no accident that Luis Bunuel, the great surrealist Spanish director who has been making movies for a half century, has become a major commerical success since the 1960s. Themes of fetishism, sadism, masochism, and necrophilia are common in Bunuel's films, which used to be heavily censored and had difficulty in getting shown but now are honored with awards and box office recognition.

Alfred Hitchcock, who has been making films about voyeurism for 40 years and is today's most celebrated director, specialized in characters who are psychotic or psychopathic, often juxtaposed with an ordinary, normal person. "Square" James Stuart is playing against a mad Kim Novak in "Vertigo" (1958) and smiling psychopath Robert Walker, in "Strangers on the Train" (1951), is counterpoint to handsome tennis player Farley Granger. "Psycho" (1960) investigates madness and "The Birds" (1963) dramatizes emotional insecurity.

Hitchcock's suspense thrillers seldom have a psychiatrist. One exception is "Psycho" (1960), in which Dr. Richmond appears at the end to sum up the motivations of the murderer and bring together the tangled threads of the story. His desire to explain every tiny detail is almost overwhelming. He explains that the murderer's problems stem from having murdered his mother after finding her in bed with a lover. According to the psychiatrist, the murderer lived both his own life as well as his mother's.

Andy Warhol, who had been a cult figure in the 1960s, became a commercial success in 1970, when a major distributor took over his film "Trash," which deals with an impotent heroin addict being romanced by Holly Woodlawn, a female impersonator. In all his films, the characters tend to be ambulatory schizophrenics or psychopaths who are open to all behavior, and for whom dimensions like "normal" or "right" actions are meaningless.

Some other successful directors, like Roman Polanski, specialize in oddity verging on psychopathy (e.g., "Cul de Sac," 1966). Very disturbed people engage in antisocial acting out in several films by Arthur Penn ("Left Handed Gun," 1958; "Bonnie and Clyde," 1967). Disturbed alienation characterizes most of the films of Nicholas Ray (e.g., "True Story of Jesse James," 1957).

The hero of Karel Reisz's "Morgan" (1966) is an artist attempting to get back his former wife, who is marrying a businessman. Morgan upsets their wedding. Becoming increasingly manic and self-indulgent, he becomes a gorilla and ends up quite mad, his fantasies having blurred into reality.

Although perhaps not psychotic, the 80-year-old woman and 20-year-old man who become lovers and about to marry in Hal Ashby's "Harold and Maude" (1971) are clearly disturbed. The young man continually attempts suicide until he finally succeeds.

During the 1960s, the freak was a frequent symbol for the goals sought by some proponents of cultural revolution. Counterculture underground "comix" like Zap promoted this theme, as did the reemergence and frequent screenings of Todd Browning's famous cult movie, "Freaks" (1933).

Most of the films of Roman Polanski present desperate, highly disturbed people. Thus, the beautiful manicurist in Polanski's "Repulsion" (1965) lives in a private world of reverie, with a progressive psychopathy which involves hallucinations, delusions, and catatonia. This withdrawn woman commits two murders. Her unusual behavior, perhaps because of her beauty, is not perceived to be troubling by others.

Alain Jessua's "Life Upside Down" (1965) presents the onset of schizophrenia in a very intelligent man, who believes that he can see the world in a unique way. Robert Altman's "Images" (1972) shows us the world through the eyes of a woman experiencing a schizophrenic collapse.

In Martin Scorsese's "Taxi Driver" (1976), Robert De Niro is a psychotic Vietnam veteran who cannot relate to others and hates everybody. This "commando for God" is a kind of charming lunatic who decides to achieve recognition by assassinating a presidential candidate. Alan Alda's "Little Murders" had previously (1971) presented a photographer who barricades himself into the apartment of his murdered fiancee and shoots aimlessly at passersby.

DISCUSSION

No survey of mental illness or psychotherapy in movies can assess the impact of these movies, which represent one contributor to the complex of attitudes on the subject. Other media, life experiences, the changing salience of the subject, widely publicized incidents like Senator McGovern's 1972 rejection of Senator Eagleton as a vice-presidential running mate because of previous mental illness, publicity given director Joshua Logan's presentations about how lithium cured his depression, investigation like the 1977 hearings on mental health conducted by President Carter's wife, and scientific breakthroughs are among the developments which provide a background for attitude changes.

Some movies may generate much attention, because of a star or treatment or their appearance at the right time. For different reasons, films like "M," "Lady in the Dark," "Dr. Strangelove," and "Klute" provoke great interest, often lead to a cycle of imitators, and help to legitimate a particular approach to mental illness or its treatment. A film which is reinforced by subsequent films or by related media emphasis is, of course, more likely to communicate its themes than one which is not so reinforced.

A specific scene may register with some members of an audience even though it does not take up much time. The importance of individual scenes, and the selective nature of audience exposure to movies, makes generalizations about these movies' effects very hazardous.

Some clues to Hollywood's sense of what attracts audiences to themes of mental illness emerge from noting those films which have been remade. "Caligari" (1919 and 1962) deals with a psychopathic psychiatrist. "M" (1932 and 1951) is about a murderer who is pedophilic. "Blind Alley" (1939 and 1949) concerns a murderer who is neutralized by a psychiatrist. All three of these films feature unusual forms of mental illness, murder, and a brilliant psychiatrist.

In recent years, such extreme portrayals have been rare and will probably become more rare. The movie psychiatrist is less likely to be concerned with criminals. He or she is also not often presented as an evil manipulater, or as a brilliant surgeon of the soul, as in the early films. There are occasional throwbacks to the older type of film, like the comic doctor who figures in Mel Brooks's "High Anxiety" (1977), in which a Nobel prizewinning psychiatrist directs Los Angeles' Psycho-Neurotic Institute for the Very, Very Nervous. The doctor suffers from acrophobia and is involved in a murder investigation which both debunks psychiatry and tries to spoof Alfred Hitchcock films. "High Anxiety" could only be released now because it is intended as a spoof, which relies on the audience's knowledge of previous films for much of its humorous appeal. As a "straight" film, it would be impossible.

The film dealing with psychiatry and mental illness has generally, accurately reflected its times. When mental illness was an exotic condition, characterized by extreme symptoms, and when psychiatrists were relatively unfamiliar figures on the cultural landscape, movies tended to present symptoms and therapists as larger than life. As mental illness and its treatment have become more accepted, the sick person and his therapist become more human, less magical and frightening and less likely to represent peaks or valleys of behavior.

Because mental illness, or the treatment of the illness, can lend themselves to so many different movie formats—suspense, horror, comedy, drama, satire, *film noir,* social comment, expose—there is reason to suspect that this protean theme will continue to attract film makers.

REFERENCES

American Film Institute Catalog (1976). Feature films 1961-1970. New York: R. R. Bowker.

CROWTHER, B. (1962). "Maestro of sophisticated comedy." New York Times Magazine, November 18:36.

GERBNER, G., and TANNENBAUM, P. H. (1960). "Regulation of mental illness content in motion pictures and television." Gazette, 6(4):365-385.

LANG, F. (1962). "Interview." Film, 32-13.

ROGOW, A. A. (1971). The psychiatrists. New York: Dell.

TACONET, M. (1974). "La theme de la folie dans le cinema Americain." Cinema (Paris), 189:76-95.

WINICK, C. (1959). Taste and the censor on television. New York: Fund for the Republic.

_____ (1963). "The psychiatrist in fiction." Journal of Nervous and mental disease, 163(1):43-57.

_____ (1965). "The face was familiar." Films and Filming, 11(4):19-35.

_____ (1968). The new people. New York: Bobbs-Merrill.

_____ (1976). "The social contexts of humor." Journal of Communication, 26(3):124-128.

_____ (1977). From deviant to normative: Changes in the social acceptability of sexually explicit material. Pp. 219-248 in E. Sagarin (ed.), Deviance and social change. Beverly Hills, Calif.: Sage.

THE PRESENTATION OF ILLNESS ON TELEVISION

JOAN LIEBMANN-SMITH
SHARON L. ROSEN

Illness, as one of the most significant concerns of the American people, has always held a prominent role in popular arts. Television may have various impacts on the attitudes of its audience so that it be may useful to look at television's depiction of illness, doctors, and patients. Each of us is a potential patient whose expectations about his role as patient, the doctor's role a healer, and the subsequent relationship between them will in part be determined by our own experiences, and the experiences of others both in real life and fiction. The manner in which the doctor-patient relationship is portrayed on television could effect those expectations.

This chapter looks at the trends in medical programs on television and in detail at the most successful recent medical show, "Marcus Welby, M.D." We will attempt to demonstrate both the accuracies and inaccuracies of this program and to evaluate the effect these may have on the audience.

ILLNESS AS DEVIANCE

Talcott Parsons, the eminent sociologist, views illness as a form of social deviance that, like other forms of deviance, should be controlled. He believes (1951:430) that "the problem of health is intimately involved in the functional prerequisites of the social system . . . (that) too low a general level of health, too high an incidence of illness, is dysfunctional."

"Disease" may not seem relevant to the concept of deviance because it is biologically determined. "Illness," the individual's reaction to disease, on the other hand, is socially defined. If one has a disease without his or anyone else's knowledge, he is not defined as ill; he is only labelled ill if he or someone else defined him as such. He may, in fact, be labelled ill even though no disease is present. As Eliot Freidson, a contemporary sociologist, explains (1970:207), "illness is a type of deviation or 'deviance' from a set of norms representing health or normality."

SICK ROLE

As opposed to other forms of deviance, one normally does not choose to become ill; in fact, most people take considerable pains to avoid becoming ill. Once illness occurs, the individual is expected to follow certain norms ascribed to the "sick role." If these norms are not adhered to, the individual may be regarded as doubly deviant.

Inherent in the sick role are certain rights and obligations: the sick individual is obligated to want to get well, and since he cannot be expected to do so by himself, he is obligated to seek appropriate medical help and cooperate with the helping agent. Because he is ill, he is exempted from normal social role responsibilities. (Parsons, 1951.)

HISTORICAL TRENDS

Since the advent of television programming, there have been 30 medical entertainment shows from "Medic" in 1954 to the short-lived "Rafferty" series in 1977. The medical shows which ran for five or more years are: "Ben Casey" (1961-1966), "Dr. Kildare" (1961-1965), "The Bold Ones"(1963-1967), "Marcus Welby, M.D." (1969-1976), "Medical Center" (1969-1976), "Emergency" (1972-1976), and "M.A.S.H." (1972 to present). Many of these shows are syndicated and still shown as reruns. Except for "The Bold Ones," which has a medical content only on alternate segments, and "Emergency," which is about a "hotline" health team, most of the successful shows revolve around a generally young, handsome, idealistic and charismatic doctor who is

Table 1. MEDICAL PROGRAMS ON TELEVISION: 1954 to 1977

Program	Years on TV	No. of Shows
Medic (D)	1954-1956	59
Dr. Hudson's Secret Journal (D)	1955-1957	78
Dr. Christian (D)	1956-1957	39
Young Dr. Malone (D)	1958-1961	N.A.
Ben Casey (D)	1960-1966	153
Dr. Kildare (D)	1961-1965	142
Eleventh Hour (PD)	1962-1964	62
The Nurses (D)	1962-1964	103
Breaking Point (PD)	1963-1964	30
The Bold Ones (D)	1963-1967	98
Marcus Welby, M.D. (D)	1969-1976	172
Medical Center (D)	1969-1976	144
Matt Lincoln (D)	1970	16
The Interns (D)	1970-1971	24
Doctor in the House (C)	1970-1973	90
Paul Bernard, Psychiatrist (PD)	1971-1973	50
Doctor Simon Locke (D)	1971	N.A.
Police Surgeon (D)	1972-1974	76
Emergency (D)	1972-1976	84
Temperatures Rising (C)	1972-1973	24
M.A.S.H. (C)	1972- *	96+
The Brian Keith Show (C)	1972-1974	48
Young Dr. Kildare (D)	1972	24
Doc Elliot (D)	1973-1974	15
Doctor at Sea	1974-1975	13
Medical Story (D)	1975	13
Doctors Hospital (D)	1975	13
Doc (C)	1975-1976	13
The Practice (C)	1975-1976	13
Rafferty (D)	1977	N.A.

(D) - Dramatic show
(PD) - Psychiatric drama
(C) - Comedy
N.A. - Not Available
* - Still on in 1978

counterbalanced by an older, more experienced doctor who acts as his mentor. This older doctor acts as a calming influence and provides the knowledge and intuition which the younger doctor has not yet acquired. Dr. Casey and Dr. Kildare have respectively Dr. Zorba and Dr. Gillespie as their role models. More recently, Dr. Gannon in "Medical Center" and Dr. Kiley in "Marcus Welby, M.D." have Dr. Lochner and Dr. Welby for guidance.

Dramatic Content

Generally, all dramatic medical programs over the years follow a basic formula in which the doctor is viewed as a skilled professional striving to alleviate the problems of his patients. In earlier shows such as "Medic," "Doctor Hudson's Secret Journal," and "Doctor Christian," the focus is on the doctor—his skill and his societal role. In the more popular series ("Ben Casey" and "Dr. Kildare") the focus is on the newly practicing doctor's initiation into the uncertainties of medicine and his professional development through subjective relationships with patients. With the advent of "Marcus Welby, M.D.," the emphasis shifts from the young doctor's development to the older doctor's expertise. More than teaching a novice physician the ways of coping with varying complex medical situations, the older doctor is teaching the audience about the causes, symptoms, and treatment of disease.

"Medical Center," which ran concurrently with "Marcus Welby, M.D.," centers on an experienced physician who is a professor of surgery. Yet, like "Ben Casey" and "Dr. Kildare," the doctor frequently becomes emotionally involved with female patients. The highly contrived plots of this series titillate rather than inform.

> Gannon falls in love with a beautiful patient, unaware that she is a European crown princess who is the target of political enemies who murdered her father.
> Dr. Gannon unwittingly places a psychotic patient who is a potential murderer into the same hospital room with one of his close friends.

No medical dramatic series since "Marcus Welby, M.D." and Medical Center" has attracted as much audience appeal. More recent and realistic series such as "Medical Story" and "Doctor's Hospital" were unsuccessful, perhaps because of the realism the viewers were exposed to such as the flaws of the doctors or the health care system. However, viewers seem to prefer reality tempered with fantasy. Patients in hospitals, such as those on dialysis, watch doctor shows on television because it helps them escape from the realities of hospital life (N.A.P.H.T., 1974). When a fictional physician treats illness, the audience wants to belive the patient will be cured. In "Medical Story," several episodes presented young, idealistic doctors losing hope while expressing concern for the imperfections of the health care system. One show had a young doctor question the ethics of giving painful experimental drugs to a terminally ill girl. In another episode, a young doctor challenged the ethics of ghost surgery; another episode presented a young obstetrician who was appalled by the hospital's policy of sterilizing indigent women.

"Doctor's Hospital," which had the first Jewish television doctor, also had a Puerto Rican physician and a woman physician as regular characters. In this series, accusations of incompetence frequently occur. In one episode, an intern accuses a veteran doctor of killing a patient due to poor surgical skills. Although lately there have been news stories of a doctor killing patients with curare and the suicide of drug-addicted gynecologist brothers, plots dealing with medical incompetence are incongruous with most people's view of doctors.

COMEDY SHOWS

Within a span of 24 years, there have been seven comedy medical programs. The first medical television comedy was the British series, "Doctor in the House" (1970-1973). This series presented the antics of seven medical students trying to maintain their sanity while pursuing the serious business of becoming a doctor.

In 1972, "Temperature's Rising" presented a loveable Black intern who frequently brought chaos to the bureaucratic structure of a hopital. Because of low ratings, changes were made to save the series. However, despite a title change to "The New Temperature's Rising Show," and the introduction of new characters, the series was cancelled in 1973.

The biggest "hit" comedy series is "M.A.S.H.," a black comedy set in Korea during the Korean War, has neither educational nor significant medical content. It is more about the uncertainties of war and medicine and the demanding role of surgeons. Surgeons joking during surgical procedures is common in reality (Goffman, 1961). Joking allows for "role distance" between a doctor and his patient and provides comic relief to a tension-filled situation. The popularity of "M.A.S.H." may be due, not only to humorous antics and verbal exchanges, but to the genuine concern the doctors have for saving their patient's lives and limbs.

"Doc" and "The Practice," two recent and unsuccessful comedy programs, each centered around an older doctor. Perhaps involving an older doctor in humorous situations is unacceptable to viewers who traditionally associate older physicians with maturity, experience, and a vast medical knowledge.

SUMMARY

The history of television's medical programming is erratic. If one format is successful, carbon copies of that format are likely to be produced. There now appears to be a trend toward racial minorities and women portraying both physicians and paraprofessionals. In past programs, women have generally portrayed either patients or minor characters such as nurses or receptionists, with only 7% of the physicians played by women. Only 20% of the television doctors are general practitioners while 23% are neurologists. The vast majority of the shows have been medical dramas (67%), followed by comedies (23%) and psychiatric dramas (10%).

In 1972 and 1973, as Figure 1 demonstrates, there were the largest number of medical shows on television with 10 each year. The number each year has since been declining.

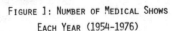

FIGURE 1: NUMBER OF MEDICAL SHOWS
EACH YEAR (1954-1976)

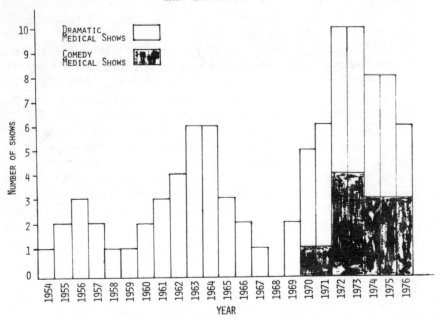

MARCUS WELBY, M.D.

"Marcus Welby, M.D." was first aired in September, 1969 and ran until 1976, making it the longest running medical show in the history of television. Dr. Welby, a veteran general practitioner is portrayed by Robert Young, best known for the lead role in "Father Knows Best," one of early television's most successful programs. Welby's young associate, Dr. Steve Kiley (James Brolin) had, because of financial problems, given up a residency in neurosurgery to work as a general practitioner with Dr. Welby. Dr. Welby, a widower, is a benevolent, father-like physician who rarely loses his temper except when it is for the patient's own good. Dr. Kiley is handsome, kind, concerned, and soft-spoken. The relationship between the two doctors is more equal than was the case in "Ben Casey" and "Dr. Kildare" where the older doctor patronized and often had to put the younger doctor in his place. Dr. Welby and Dr. Kiley seem to be close friends.

Working with the two doctors is Conseuela Lopez (Elena Verdugo), a bilingual nurse-receptionist. She is a mother figure with no family of her own, who seems to devote her life to Welby, Kiley, and their patients. All three get along extremely well.

Welby's practice is set up in his home in Santa Monica, California. Unlike the majority of medical shows in which most of the action takes place in the hospital, Welby and Kiley practice medicine wherever their patients are: on beaches, mountains, in patient's homes, as well as in their medical office and the hospital.

Social Characteristics of the Patients

Fifty "Marcus Welby, M.D." episodes were viewed for content analysis. In these 50 episodes, there are twice as many male patients as female patients (66% male versus 34% female). Thirty-six percent of the patients are children under 18 years old, and 44% are between 19 and 40. Only 18% of the episodes focus on patients between 41 and 60, and a mere 2% of the patients are 60 and over.

Thirty percent of the patients are married, 60% single, and 10% divorced, separated, or widowed.

Fully 94% of the patients are white and only 6% Black or Chicano. In one episode, a Black woman with sickle cell anemia, presented as an inherited and potentially fatal disease, wants to adopt a child. One episode presents a Black student protestor who is wrongfully hit by a police officer, and another revolves around a Chicano who develops gangrene because of incompetent medical treatment.

Over half (52%) of the patients are upper-middle or upper class, 40% middle class, and only 8% lower middle or lower class.

The occupational categories of the patients that are identifiable are as follows:

Occupation	Frequency
Student	14
Athelete	4
Businessman	4
Entertainer	3
Housewife	2
Nurse	1
Teacher	1
Photographer	1
Priest	1
Scientist	1

Diagnoses

Quick and fairly easy diagnoses are made in 62% of the programs. It is common to find Welby saying that he has a hunch as to the patient's ailment but more tests are needed. A young Black student in one episode has a sudden fit of rage. Welby's hunch is the obscure diagnosis of epilepsy brought on by a brain tumor, which is, in fact, supported by arteriograms.

Incorrect diagnoses are made in 12% of the cases. In two episodes, a visiting doctor makes the diagnosis. In another case, a correct diangosis would have been impossible because the ex-showgirl did not tell Dr. Welby about her silicone breast implant. Hiding such information from one's doctor occurs in 18% of the episodes and usually leads to dire consequences. The aforementioned showgirl undergoes a mastectomy, a young boy with dysautonomia develops pneumonia because he does not tell the doctor that he broke a bone while falling out of bed, and a jockey becomes comatose because he does not admit he has an amphetamine habit.

Even if the patient is not made to suffer because of his failure to confide in his doctor, the message of *potential* seriousness of concealing information from one's doctor is made clear.

Diseases and Treatment

William Nolen, a well known physician and popular author, in writing about doctor shows, notes that "in order to keep things dramatic, the writers often resort to rare diagnoses . . . three of the six general surgical problems that I saw were problems I have never encountered in 22 years of surgical practice" (Nolen, 1976). Over half (54%) of the Welby episodes dealt with rare diseases such as hypolipidoma, bends, Cushing syndrome, and dysautonomia. If a disease is rare, its treatment may be experimental. In 20% of the shows, the treatment provided is experimental or risky.

"Marcus Welby, M.D.," as an hour-long program, creates a need for more than the mere presentation of a disease and its treatment in order to sustain the interest of the audience. Therefore, most plots deal with such problems as family conflicts, emotional difficulties and experimental treatment. Patients often resist needed treatment and only a sudden acute

Table 2. DISEASES

Disease	Frequency
Cancer (i.e., liver, breast, uterine, cervical)	7
Heart disease	6
Diabetes	4
Addiction (drugs or alcohol)	3
Epilepsy	2
Leukemia	2
Venereal disease (Syphilis)	2
Autism	1
Bends	1
Bone infection	1
Burns	1
Cushing syndrome	1
Cystic fibrosis	1
Dysautonomia	1
Esophageal ulcer	1
Gas gangrene (aplastic anemia)	1
Hepatitis	1
Impotence	1
Juvenile rheumatoid arthritis	1
Learning disability	1
Meningitis	1
Myasthenia gravis	1
Plastic surgery	1
Psychosomatic asthma	1
Psychosomatic paralysis	1
Rabies	1
Sickle cell anemia	1
Stroke	1
Suicidal tendencies	1
Systemic lupis erythematosis	1
Tay Sachs disease	1

attack forces them to realize the seriousness of their condition and to follow the prescribed treatment. Treatment is resisted in 32% of the episodes. In one episode, a 30-year-old professional tennis player with myasthenia gravis refuses to give up tennis. In another, a poor Appalachian man refuses to take time off from work for some medical tests because he fears their outcome.

Sudden acute attacks occur in 56% of the episodes and either Welby or Kiley is present during the attack 34% of the time. Generally, the attack occurs when the physician is at the patient's home because he was just dropping by.

Surgical Procedures

Patients require surgery in 38% of the programs. Surgery provides the audience with drama and suspense. In medical practice itself, according to Parsons (1951:466), "there tends to be a bias in favor of operating . . . the surgeon is trained to operate. . . .For the patient and his family, in their state of anxiety and tension also, inactivity, just waiting to see how things develop is particularly hard to bear. A decision to operate will, in such a situation, almost certainly 'clear the air' and make everbody 'feel better.'"

In most cases where surgery is required, the surgery is unusually dangerous (68%). One patient, Welby's son-in-law, dies on the operating table, the only actual death in 50 episodes. It is emphasized, however, that the young man's heart was irreversibly damaged and that he would have died anyway.

Although only one death actually occurs, there are several episodes where imminent death is implied. In one episode, Kiley's young beautiful fiancee has a systemic lupis erythemalosis, an ultimately fatal disease. In another case, a 22-year-old ball player has terminal cancer of the brain.

Psychological and Social Aspects

Psychological or social drama is an essential ingredient in all of the episodes viewed. In all 50 shows, there was either a psychological problem or component, family conflict, or both. Family conflict was evident in 68% of the shows.

The Doctor-Patient Relationship

For the majority of people, their relationship with their physician is strictly professional. However, in 64% of these episodes, the doctor is a personal friend of the patient or his family, and in half of these shows, the doctor is shown socializing with the patient or family.

In discussing the social role of the physician, Parsons talks about the necessity of effective neutrality. But, he adds (1951:453), "the situation of medical practice is such as inevitably to 'involve' the physician in the psychologically significant 'private' affairs of his patients." In 74% of these shows, the doctor becomes involved in a patient's personal life.

Approximation to Reality

House calls are very much a thing of the past, and even when necessary, it is difficult to find a doctor who is willing to make them, or a patient who is willing to pay for them. Yet in 82% of the shows, at least one house call was made; both doctors would often come at the same time. The doctor sometimes went out of his way to make a house call on a patient who had not even called for the doctor. In one episode, a man gives up his business to run a survival camp in the country. He refuses to be operated on for a tumor and leaves the hospital. Dr. Kiley goes after him on his motorcycle and arrives at the camp just as he is having an attack. In another episode, after an actress has a stroke, her husband has a physical therapy room set up in their home. Dr. Kiley acts as her physical therapist and comes to her home several times a week. When her husband insists that she make a movie about stroke victims, both Welby and Kiley are there for the filming because they are afraid it might be too much for her; she does have another stroke.

MEDICAL COSTS

The financing of medical care is one of the major concerns and problems of the American people. Hospitalization, in particular, is unaffordable without medical insurance for most people. Yet the doctor's fee or medical costs were mentioned in only 10% of the shows. A boy in one episode, whose mother is poor and blind, wants to have plastic surgery on his ears and nose. Dr. Welby refers them to a doctor who will do the operation for free. In another episode, a boy from a poor mountaineer family is bitten by a rattlesnake and has to be admitted to the hospital. The mother is upset, and Dr. Kiley hands her the admitting forms and tells her not to worry about the cost, that they would work something out.

Private rooms are particularly expensive, and very few people can afford them, and hospital insurance usually covers only semi-private rooms. However, in over half the shows (54%), the patient was in a private room. When a patient shared a room, it usually was because of the story line.

OTHER PATIENTS

Doctors are notoriously busy, especially general practitioners. Once one gets an appointment, there is usually a wait in the waiting room before the doctor is seen. When the doctor visits the patient in the hospital, he usually cannot spend a lot of time with any one patient because of the many patients he must see. However, in only 14% of the shows were there any indications that the doctor had other patients in his office or in the hospital. The doctors' visits were never interrupted by other matters or phone calls not relevant to the case at hand. The receptionist was never harried, and always had time to chat with the doctor or patient.

MEDICAL INFORMATION

Medical shows provide entertainment and transmit medical information to the general population. Messages relayed through medical shows have such impact on the show's audiences that in 1955 a Physician's Advisory Committee on T.V., Radio, and Motion Pictures (PAC) was created to ensure the accuracy of the information given on medical programs. Since 1970, the PAC has consisted of four internists, a general practitioner, a surgeon, a psychiatrist, a dermatologist, a urologist, a radiologist, an ophthamologist, and a neurosurgeon. The committee member who is most qualified to judge a particular script, "will read the script, correct technical errors, point out medical booby traps, and return it to the producer. If there is some question about whether or not dramatic license should supersede technical accuracy, the producer will thrash it out with the appropriate PAC member" (Bell, 1970:84).

DISCUSSION

Based on our sample of 50 Marcus Welby episodes, one could conclude that the average American patient is a white, upper-middle class man who, when he gets sick, is cared for by a benevolent, paternalistic general practitioner who is a close friend of the family's, and who has endless time and patience to cure the physical and psychological ills of his patient-friend. Clearly, this is not the picture of the typical television viewer who is more likely to be female and lower middle to middle class (Bower, 1973).

False Expectations

Besides giving the viewer the impression that many rare diseases and complications are in fact common, these medical shows imply that most diseases are usually quickly and accurately diagnosed and cured by an operation or psychological insight. Death is rarely a reality. The uncertainties of medicine, so prevalent in the profession, are rarely found in these dramatic shows.

In real life, the average patient waits 27 minutes to see a general practitioner who spends approximately seven minutes with each patient and does not attend barbeques or bar mitzvahs with these same patients.

What effects, if any, may these false expectations have on the potential patient or on the medical profession?

Malpractice Suits. There has been a tremendous increase in malpractice insurance, making it a major concern of the medical profession. In discussing this increase in law suits, Dr. Roy G. Diessner (1975), president of the Minnesota State Medical Association wrote that:

> the television programs that cast the physician in the role of a superman performing miracles of diagnosis and cure do little to educate the patient and frequently aggravate the patient's unreasonable expectation for solutions to his own medical problems. I believe such programs are a disservice to medicine and are to be deplored.

The point is debatable since it is more likey for these false expectations to adversely affect the patient rather than the doctor. After all, a patient cannot sue a physician for not socializing with him, or for having other patients.

Conflict. Expectations can lead to difficulty in another way. Each member of a role-set, i.e., doctor, patient, nurse, etc., has different expectations of each of the other members. These differing role expectations or "clash of perspectives" are, according to Freidson (1961), the basis of conflict in the doctor-patient relationship. The physician may, for example, expect the patient to be the passive recipient of his medical advice and treatment, while the patient may wish to participate more actively in his or her treatment. The patient may demand to know the details about his or her disease, prescribed medication, and prognosis. This is, after all, information readily available to Dr. Welby's patients. If the patient sees the doctor as one who should know everything about his or her disease, and the doctor cannot supply all the answers, conflict is likely to result. Again, it seems unlikely that any of these conflicts would actually lead to a malpractice suit. A physician not being all-knowing or all-caring may be disturbing to a patient, but this is not sufficient grounds in themselves for a law suit. What may happen, as a result of these and other conflicts in the doctor-patient relationship, is that the patient may acquiesce, seek another physician, or demand to be treated as a person, not a disease.

Family Medicine. "Marcus Welby" may raise awareness and expectations in another area that may prove beneficial to both physicians and patients: the importance of the family in dealing with illness. The replacement of general practice by specialization has created a new generation of patients and doctors who have never had contact with a general or family practitioner. However, according to one medical sociologist, "There is renewed interest in the family as a significant element in the process of illness, so that in the initial approach to the patient, the family assumes renewed importance as part of the history and context in which illness has occurred" (Bloom, 1963:120).

This renewed interest in the family is reflected in "Marcus Welby" were the interrelationship between illness and the family is dramatically illustrated. As one internist wrote, "What is striking about the Welby show is the amount of psychiatric insight it presupposes on the part of its audience. Nowhere else in the world could the ordinary man's favorite program depend so heavily on ambivalencies of family life" (Halberstam, 1972). As Bloom (1963:135) put it, "the drama of family life is perhaps nowhere given fuller expression than in illness."

Perhaps the program does provide insight into aspects of the family and illness that would not ordinarily be accessible to the average viewer. In addition, what viewer would opt for a cold impersonal specialist who knows nothing about him personally, when he could have a warm, friendly general practitioner who knows the patient's family and cares? The medical profession is certainly not unaware of what Marcus Welby has done for the image of general practitioners.

Medical Information. Besides learning in a more general way about the significance of the family in the treatment of illness, other more specific aspects of the nexus between family and disease are illustrated by the depiction of genetic disorders, or diseases with genetic components such as sickle-cell anemia, Tay Sachs disease, and diabetes. Viewers with these diseases may not have received any information about the genetic consequences of these diseases. This may be particularly true of less educated viewers who are less likely to be medically sophisticated.

As was previously discussed, many episodes of "Marcus Welby" provide accurate, useful information about various diseases and medical problems. Numerous dramatic instances where lives have been saved bacause of medical information picked up from "Marcus Welby" and other medical programs have been reported in newspapers and popular magazines.

What the audience may learn from these shows may be considered helpful by them as potential patients, but may be considered dangerous by the medical profession. One doctor complained that two women with malignant growths, who had seen an episode of "The Bold Ones" about a doctor who performed unnecessary hysterectomies, cancelled their scheduled hysterectomies. The doctor was ultimately able to get one of the women to change her mind, but the other still refused the operation (Davidson, 1973).

It is perhaps understandable that an honest physician could be upset by this. However, the show did serve a useful function if it made people aware that there are indeed unscrupulous doctors, and that it may be a good idea to get a second opinion before agreeing to any operation.

These are just examples of the effect on a few viewers out of the millions who have seen and will see medical programs on television. The educational value of these programs has not yet been fully evaluated. Since most recent dramatic medical programs have physicians as program consultants, there seems to be little debate as to their authenticity and accuracy with reference to the diseases and technical material. It is, however, the lack of accuracy and realism in the more significant aspects of medical treatment, the doctor-patient relationship, that warrants our concern.

REFERENCES

BELL, J.N. (1970). "T.V.'s on-again romance with medicine." Today's Health, 48 (March):24-29, 83-84.

BLOOM, S.W. (1963). The doctor and his patient. New York: Russel Sage Foundation.

BOWER, R.T. (1973). Television and the public. New York: Holt, Rinehart and Winston.

DAVIDSON, M. (1973). "Viewer, heal thyself!" T.V. Guide, July 21-27.

DIESSNER, R.G. (1975). Unreasonable expectations." Minnesota Medicine, 58 (August):577.

FREIDSON, E. (1961). Partients' views of medical practice. New York: Russel Sage Foundation.

———(1970). Profession of medicine. New York: Dodd, Mead, and Company.

GOFFMAN, E. (1961). Encounters. Indianapolis: Bobbs-Merrill.

HALBERSTAM, M.J. (1972). "An M.D. reviews Dr. Welby of T.V." New York Times Magazine, January 16:12ff

National Association of Patients on Hemodialysis and Transplantation (1974). MAPHT News, 5:8.

NOLEN, W.A. (1976). "Examining the T.V. doctor shows." McCalls, January:54, 56, 58.

PARSONS, T. (1951). The social system. New York: Free Press.

SANDMAN, P.M. (1976). "Medicine and mass communication: An agenda for physicians." Annals of Internal Medicine, 85(3):378-383.

THE TREATMENT OF DEATH IN SYMPATHY CARDS

ABIGAIL STAHL WOODS
ROBERT G. DELISLE

In the television situation comedy, "Phyllis," Phyllis asked her boss, San Francisco Supervisor Valente, to attend her husband's "second" funeral. His response was "I hate funerals." She hastened to respond, "I don't want you to do anything which makes you feel uncomfortable." Caine (1974:61) might well have been part of Phyllis' conversation when she commented, "No one is comfortable in the face of death. In fact, it is this very discomfort, probably, which makes it so difficult to think of ways to help the one who suffered the greatest loss."

Generally, by nine or ten years of age, one "knows" that death is inevitable and irreversible for oneself and others (Nagy, 1948:3-27) and, if an American, has probably been exposed to death indirectly through television and film, if not directly through first-hand experience. Throughout life, then, most of us dislike being reminded of death and feel as uncomfortable as Valente and Caine describe, if not fearful and even angry about it. Many manage to deny death partially or altogether.

DENIAL OF DEATH

Virtually every adult text or tradebook on death deals with the denial of death. Most begin with this issue. Consider a sample:

Gordon: "Most of us are afraid to contemplate our own ending; and when anything reminds us that we too shall die, we flee and turn our thoughts to happier matters." (1972:13.)

Kavanaugh: "Words like 'dying', 'death', 'terminal', 'cancer', 'autopsy' and 'last rites' were not even whispered in my presence." (1974:5.)

Lifton and Olsen: "We don't talk about it; we try to conceal, deny, and bury it." (1975:5.)

Keleman: "We live in a time that denies death." (1974:3.)

Hendin: "Certainly death has become the taboo of our time. It is, in a very real sense, the last remaining one." (1974:10.)

Grollman: "Twentieth-century man is trying to remove death from life's reality." (1974:xiii.)

"Dying and denying are the basic counterparts in our contemporary society . . . Some people will refuse to think about death at all." (1974:xiv.)

Cutter: "Because of (this) almost universal denial, death always seems to come as a surprise." (1974:1.)

Kubler-Ross begins one book by writing (1975:x), "Death is a subject that is evaded, ignored, and denied in our youth-worshipping, progress-oriented society." In another, she describes denial and isolation as the first of five stages through which the dying and loved-ones of the dying progress in dealing with death (1969:38-49). Ernest Becker has written an entire book, a Pulitzer Prize winner, on denying death, which begins (1973:ix):

the idea of death, the fear of it, haunts the human animal like nothing else; it is a mainspring of human activity—activity designed largely to avoid the fatality of death, to overcome it by denying in some way that it is the final destiny for man.

ACCEPTANCE OF SYMPATHY CARDS

Sympathy cards are those commercially printed cards on the shelves of a card shop/display labeled "Sympathy Cards." One "knows" that they are intended to express sympathy to the living after the death of another. We will never know whether Supervisor Valente sent one to Phyllis; we do know that Lynn Caine received many. Anyone who has walked, albeit swiftly, through a card shop/display is aware that sympathy cards are as available as those dealing with birthday and graduation. Probably few adults have neither sent nor received one. The sending of sympathy cards, in fact, has become a common American post-death ritual.

Is it possible that the sympathy card ritual can exist side-by-side with denial of death? The two perceptions on which this question is based stimulated the undertaking of an investigation of sympathy cards: (1) the perception that Americans deny death, and (2) the perception that sympathy cards are an accepted, even common, American post-death ritual. The purpose of the investigation was to ascertain how sympathy cards deal with death.

METHOD

In an attempt to collect a representative sample of sympathy cards, a number of department stores in the metropolitan New York area were visited. Each store handled a variety of brands (Gibson, Hallmark, Norcross, and Paramount) and an attempt was made to balance the number of cards selected, an attempt which was soon frustrated because of availability. Seventy cards were selected: 30 from Norcross, 29 from Hallmark, 12 from Gibson, and 3 from Paramount.

Each card was analyzed for (1) the inclusion of the words "dead", "die," "death," (2) the use of substitute words for "dead," "die," "death," (3) reference to the deceased, (4) the theme of the inside message, (5) the intent of the message, (6) the use of qualifying words in juxtaposition with the word "sympathy," and (7) the cover art.

RESULTS

(1) Inclusion of the Words "Dead," "Die," "Death"

Each card was analyzed to determine whether the message included the words "death" (noun), "die" (verb), and "dead" (adjective or noun). It was found that none of these words appeared in the message of any of the cards examined. It was found, however, that certain substitute words did appear.

(2) Use of Substitute Words for "Dead," "Die," "Death"

Each card was analyzed to determine what substitute words appeared and the frequency of appearance. In descending order of appearance, the

following words appeared: "loss" (18), "sorrow" (15), "time of sorrow" (4), "this time" (2), and "left us" (2). Five additional substitute words appeared only one time each: "lose," "difficult hours," "gone," "such a time," and "hour of sadness." Out of the 10 substitute word possibilities, six are nouns or noun phrases which allude to the time or state of the card recipient ("sorrow," "time of sorrow," "this time," "difficult hours," "such a time," "hour of sadness"). The remaining four substitute word possibilities seem to focus more closely on some separation which the card recipient has experienced ("loss," "left us," "lose," "gone"). We stress "some separation" here because the words "dead," "die," and "death" are never actually used.
Examples:

> "The sympathy we're feeling for the loss that's come to you." (Paramount, 839.)
> "From someone who shares your sorrow." (Norcross, 923-4.)
> "May this time of sorrow that you are passing through . . ." (Hallmark, 291-6.)

(3) Reference to the Deceased

Each card was analyzed to determine what reference was made to the deceased. Fifty-three of the cards made no reference whatsoever to the deceased. Six of the cards referred to the deceased in terms of role (mother, father, etc.). Five of the cards referred to the deceased as "loved one," four as "dear one," one as "person," and one as "someone."
Examples:

> "Your loved one will be deeply missed." (Hallmark, 427-4.)
> "In the loss of your father there is little words can do . . ." (Hallmark, 425-4.)
> "We all share in the loss of someone who made the world a nicer place." (Norcross, 927-1.)

(4) The Theme of the Inside Message

While all the cards come under the general heading of "Sympathy Cards," each card was analyzed to determine what specific themes emerged in the message, excluding those words on the card cover. The following thematic clusters emerged: religious, literary, "non-message," sharing, memory, and sympathy. Messages with a religious theme referred to God, Bible, prayer, or religious environs. Messages with a literary theme quoted literary sources. Messages with a "non-message" theme conveyed an inability to express adequate sentiment. Messages

with a sharing theme mentioned the sharing of experience between the card sender and recipient. Messages with a memory theme made use of the word "sympathy" as an expression of the sender's feelings for the recipient. Four messages did not fall into any of the thematic clusters. The thematic clusters emerged in the following descending order of frequency: sympathy (25), sharing (11), memory (9), religious (9), "non-message" (9), and literary (3).
Examples:

Sympathy: "Thinking of you and extending deepest sympathy on your loss." (Paramount, 835.)

Sharing: "May there be comfort in knowing friends are there . . . Knowing that they care and share your sorrow." (Hallmark, 12-4.)

Memory: "The memory of your loved one will be an inspiration to many people—Such a wonderful person will never be forgotten." (Norcross, 8800.)

Religious: "May the gracious mercy that God has always shown be with you now so that you are not alone." (Hallmark, 294-7.)

"Non-message": ". . . too deep for words to express." (Gibson, 050-54.)

Literary messages included selections from Helen Steiner Rice (Gibson, 400-0017), Peter Marshall (Hallmark, 275-92), and Marjorie Frances Ames (Hallmark, 6-7.)

(5) The Intent of the Message

It became apparent that the message was expressed in themes through key words; thus, an analysis was made to determine which key words appeared and the frequency of appearance. Twenty-one different key words appeared and are listed in descending order of frequency: "sympathy" (67), "comfort" (15), "strength" (8), "consolation" (2), "sure" (2), "eased" (2), "courage" (2), "understand" (2), "faith" (2), "know" (2), "peace" (2), "knowing" (2), "heal" (1), "accept" (1), "sustained" (1), "surrounded" (1), "inspired" (1), "think" (1), "blessing" (1), "hope" (1), and "get through it" (1). The word "sympathy" conveys a generalized expression of the sender's feelings, whereas the other terms convey a more specific intent of an action or a state of being which the sender wishes for the recipient.

(6) The Use of Qualifying Words in Juxtaposition with the Word "Sympathy"

Sympathy is the largest thematic cluster (25) and the word most frequently repeated (67 times); thus, an analysis of how the word is used was undertaken. It was noted that the word "sympathy" was not always found to be unattended. A list was made to determine what qualifiers to the word "sympathy" were used and their frequency of appearance. While it appeared unqualified 35 times, it appeared qualified 32 times. In descending order of frequency the following qualifiers were used: "deepest" (16), "sincerest" (8), "deep" (4), "heartfelt" (3), and "loving" (1).

Examples:

> " . . . that deepest sympathy goes out to you." (Norcross, 8800.)
> "Extending deep and sincere sympathy to you." (Paramount, 833A.)

While the word "sympathy" appeared unqualified about half of the time, there were an abundance of superlative qualifying words. "Why?" one might ask. If one cannot be direct, does one compensate by being more strongly indirect? Another question: Are there really degrees of deepness in sympathy (deep, deeper/more deep, deepest)? Still another: Might there be a sympathy less than sincere, other than heartfelt, other than loving?

(7) Cover Art

Each card was analyzed to determine whether there was a clustering of cover art types and whether such art supported both the theme and intent of the message. The following clusters emerged: nature, person/animal, words alone, and decorative (cover art which did not clearly fit into the first three categories). In descending order of frequency there were 50 decorative covers, 11 nature covers, 6 words alone covers, and 3 person/animal covers. It would seem that there was no specific connection between cover art and message except in the case of religious cards. It would not seem that the other cover art specifically supported either the message theme or intent; covers and messages, in fact, seemed interchangeable.

CONCLUSIONS

Sympathy cards deal with death in a perplexing, if intriguing manner (particularly intriguing: blue "his" and pink "hers" sympathy cards):

- through cover art unrelated to death and, with the exception of those cards which fall into the religious thematic cluster, unrelated to the message within;

- through a message which falls into assorted thematic clusters (religious, literary, "non-message," sharing, memory, and sympathy), but which does not contain the words "death," "die," or "dead" in any form;
- through a message which contains substitute words for "death," "die," and "dead"—"loss" being the most frequent;
- through a message which either does not refer to the deceased at all or does so in terms of his/her role, or in terms like "loved one," "dear one," "person," or "someone."

Perhaps Lynn Caine (1974:61) was correct when she wrote that people "just want to get that letter (sympathy card) written, stamped and in the mailbox so they can stop thinking about it."

SOME FINAL NOTES

It is apparent that sympathy cards do exist side-by-side with denial of death in American society and paradoxically, but correctly, reflect this denial. As we become more able to deal with death, we may see that the glaring weakness of sympathy cards is similar to that of greeting cards in general: "that among their plethora of choices they do not give us the choices we might want, or need. That is the effect of the marketplace, lopping off the ends of the bell curve" (Rhodes, 1971:65).

It was one and one third centuries ago that greeting cards entered the marketplace. Henry Cole, an Englishman, found himself pressed for time before Christmas and asked an artist friend to design a printed card which he sent instead of his usual Christmas notes. Americans have since made greeting cards their own. It would seem, in fact, that no occasion has slipped past the visual acuity of the greeting card designers. The obvious occasions are prompted by religious and national holiday, birthday, wedding, graduation, anniversary, shower, promotion, goodbye, illness, bereavement; even the occasions of "thinking of you" and being a "secret pal." It would seem that every imaginable human feeling is an occasion worthy of a card. It would also seem that greeting cards have attempted to take on the role of expressing those feelings which tightened tongues cannot.

"How many times have you wanted to say 'Just because I love you doesn't mean you own me', or 'Let me get angry just once without apologizing for it'?" (Newsweek, 1970:88). This article continues with the notion that "Sensitivity cards are the latest panacea for the hung-up and the hopelessly tongue-tied. 'People have a need to reach out and say why they're reaching out,'" explains David Viscott, a Boston psychiatrist who devises messages for Sensitivity Cards. Apparently, Viscott feels that people have trouble expressing verbally such a need. To help them along, Sensitivity Cards discriminate subdivisions of sensitivity: "my hang-up" ("Sometimes I act the way I do because I think I have to"), "your hang-ups" ("I could give more if I knew you could accept it"), "mutual hang-ups" ("You don't listen to me and I suspect I don't listen to you"), and "no hang-ups" ("These are our beautiful years") (Newsweek, 1970:88). It was suggested in this article that the greeting cards which sell best offer more insight "into the country's commonly shared pent-up feelings." Consider the nationwide best sellers: "I saw something beautiful today and you weren't there to share it," and "I do love you even if I can't say it all the time," and "When I'm with you I feel complete." Or consider a particular city breakdown: New York's best seller, "Don't say you love me when you're only afraid of losing me"; and Los Angeles' best seller, "Thank you for touching my life"; and Houston's best seller, "This is no better—and it's much lonelier." The latter sentiment was designed for the occasion of divorce. (Newsweek, 1970:88).

It should be noted also that greeting cards are no longer a phenomenon created by and for white America (Newsweek, 1969:101). By 1969, four of the major greeting card companies had introduced a black line and new black companies have developed. It is, perhaps, hard to imagine life without greeting cards. They standardize and mechanize our relationships, give us time to breathe, save us time, as well as relieve our guilt and shyness (Rhodes, 1971:66).

Greeting cards have become a billion dollar-a-year industry (New York Times, 1974:50), 80% of which is controlled by the big five producers (Hallmark, American, Gibson, Rust Craft, and Norcross). Greeting cards account for half of the personal mail moved annually by the United States Postal Department (New York Times, 1975:13). They have, in fact, done for letterwriting what Colonel Sanders, Arthur Treacher, MacDonalds, and Burger King have done for eating. What they have not done is to help us deal with death directly; they have helped us deny death gently. The writers could find no contemporary cards in those sections of card shops/displays labeled "Sympathy Cards" (or elsewhere for that matter). One contemporary card, however, designed for a purpose other than death, was particularly a propos the sympathy card denial of death (Hallmark, 807-7):

Don't think of it as retiring . . .
Think of it as one big,
Gigantic coffee break!

REFERENCES

BECKER, E. (1973). The denial of death. New York: Free Press.

CAINE, L. (1974). Widow. New York: Bantam.

CUTTER, F. (1974). Coming to terms with death. Chicago: Nelson-Hall Company.

GORDON, D. (1972). Overcoming the fear of death. Baltimore: Penguin Books.

GROLLMAN, E. (1974). Concerning death: A practical guide for the living. Boston: Beacon Press.

HENDIN, D. (1974). Death as a fact of life. New York: Warner.

KAVANAUGH, R. (1974). Facing death. Baltimore: Penguin Books.

KELEMAN, S. (1974). Living your dying. New York: Random House.

KUBLER-ROSS, E. (1975). Death, the final stage of growth. Englewood Cliffs, N.J.: Prentice-Hall.

_____ (1969). On death and dying. New York: Macmillan.

LIFTON, R. and OLSEN, E. (1975). Living and dying. New York: Bantam. (1948).

NAGY, M. (1948). "The child's view of death." Journal of Genetic Psychology, 73:3-27.

New York Times (February 10, 1974) 50.

NEW YORK TIMES (December 21, 1975) 13.

Newsweek (May 5, 1969). Vol. 73:101.

NEWSWEEK (September 7, 1970). Vol.76:88.

RHODES, R. (1971). "Packages sentiment." Harpers, 243 (December):61-66.

CRIME AND LAW ENFORCEMENT IN THE MASS MEDIA

JOSEPH R. DOMINICK

AUTHOR'S NOTE: *The author would like to acknowledge the assistance of Linda Whitener in the preparation of this summary.*

INTRODUCTION

The main purpose of this overview is to examine and synthesize the research literature concerning crime and law enforcement as reported and portrayed in the mass media, particularly newspapers and television. In general, this summary attempts to address the following questions:

(1) How much of the media's attention is devoted to the portrayal and reporting of crime-related content?
(2) What are the defining characteristics of crime as reported in the press and television and as portrayed in TV entertainment programs?
(3) What are the main issues involved in the treatment of crime by the media?

This subject is important because media presentations of law-breaking, law enforcement and the legal process might be the major source of information for many Americans about these topics. As pointed out by former New York Deputy Police Commissioner Robert Daley (1972), "The average citizen meets a cop only when caught exceeding the speed limit . . . On such occasional glimpses of the law in action, plus TV shows, rest the entire knowledge of the average citizen." Further, Winick and Winick (1974), in discussing courtroom drama on television, suggested: "With courts so important in actual life, the manner in which and the frequency with which they are presented in the popular arts could be significant contributors to the way in which litigants and even court functionaries approach their tasks. For those not immediately involved with courts, the representation of the litigation situation may influence their expectations and impressions of a major American institution."

To sum up, it appears that for most people, direct exposure to crime and law enforcement procedures are not common. Perhaps Greenberg's (1969) discussion of the importance of studying violent media content is relevant here as well: "The vast majority of our exposure to violent acts has been indirect, as communicated through the mass media. What we have seen in the way of violent acts, what we know of violence and its general consequences has occurred primarily through an indirect, mediation process." The same statement could easily be made concerning information about crime and law enforcement.

Before beginning this summary, it is important to note the working assumptions and parameters used to define the topic area. Consequently, it seems appropriate to note what areas this review does *not* include. In the first place, there is a rather lengthy body of literature concerned primarily with the portrayal of violence and aggression on television. This review does not include this material, except to the extent that it deals specifically with crime and law enforcement. Readers who are interested in this topic should consult Greenberg's (1969) summary or the annual Violence Profiles issued by George Gerbner and his colleagues.[1]

Moreover, this summary does not touch upon the body of literature that concerns itself with the general questions of the effects of pretrial publicity on a fair trail or the related topic of TV cameras in the courtroom. Readers are referred to Kittross and Harwood (1970) and Gillmor (1966).

Throughout this entire review, the main research technique of interest will be content analysis. At its most basic level, content analysis is a method of studying and analyzing communications in a systematic, objective, and quantitative manner for the purpose of measuring certain message variables. As a research technique content analysis has certain strengths and liabilities and these should be pointed out before discussing the findings of this overview. On the one hand, content analysis provides for an objective and quantitative estimate of certain message attributes, hopefully free of the subjective bias of the reviewer. It also allows the analysis of relationships between content variables as well as being helpful in chronicling content changes over time. On the other hand, inferences about the effects of content on the audience are, strictly speaking, not possible when using only this methodology. More importantly, the findings of a particular content analysis are directly related to the definitions of the various content categories developed by the researcher. The validity of these definitions is an important consideration in the evaluation of any content analysis. In this regard, comparison across several studies done by different individuals is risky since the definitions used by the various investigators may not be identical. This is especially important for this summary because different definitions of "crime" and "law enforcement" were used by different authors.

CRIME IN THE NEWSPAPER

The reporting of crime news is an old tradition in American journalism, dating back to the era of the Penny Press in 1833. Benjamin Day's *New York Sun* was the first paper to employ a police reporter and the daily summary of local crime news became one of the most popular segments in the paper. Day's success quickly prompted imitators, among them James Gordon Bennett of the *New York Herald,* and crime reporting became a regular feature of newspaper journalism.

Crime news became more sensationalized during the 1920s when, perhaps as a response to competition from radio and motion pictures, tabloids, most notably the New York *Daily News,* featured simply written and often luridly illustrated crime stories. The *News* quickly became the daily newspaper with largest circulation in the U.S. Thus, from its early days, crime news has been a major staple in newspaper journalism and, evidently, a very popular feature.

Amount of Crime News

Several studies have attempted to catalogue the sheer volume of crime news as reported in various American newspapers. An early study (Deutschmann, 1959) measured the percentage of space devoted to crime news in a 30-day sample of seven daily New York papers and five daily Ohio papers. About 15% of available space was devoted to crime news in the New York papers compared with 10% in the Ohio press. The New York papers, however, varied considerably in the empahsis placed on crime coverage. A 1961 study of major Michigan dailies (Stempl,

1962) indicated that around 5% of their available content space was devoted to crime news.

In related studies, Otto (1962), using column inches as the unit of analysis, discovered that about 5% of the content of 10 major daily papers for a single day dealt with violent news (including a good deal of crime news). An analysis by Stott (1967) found that an average of approximately 12% of the news in four Ohio papers could be categorized as crime/accident news.

All of the above studies examined the reporting of individual crimes, and might be referred to as "event-oriented" studies. Less information is available concerning how newspapers cover the general *issue* of crime. One study, however, (Ryan and Owen, 1976) is relevant. In a content analysis of eight metropolitan newspapers, the authors found that news about the issue of crime was the most prominent of nine social issues studied, but in absolute terms, coverage was small, accounting for about 3% of the available news space.

In addition, it appears that newspaper attention is directed more toward coverage of violent crimes than toward other types. A survey (Cirino, 1974) of the front pages of the New York *Times* and the Los Angeles *Times* for three two-month periods in 1950, 1960, and 1969 disclosed that stories about individual violent crimes were featured twice as often as were stories about organized crime and three times more often than stories about "white collar" crime (price-fixing, food and drug violations, embezzlement, etc.).

Turning from newspapers to one possible source of their news, a study by Van Horn (1952) found that about 9% of the Wisconsin state Associated Press wire stories were concerned with crime and accidents. This figure corresponds to those determined by analyzing the actual coverage devoted to crime news.

Lastly, it should be pointed out that crime not only appears in the news columns of papers but also in the comic section. A study by Barcus (1961) revealed that the percentage of "crime and detective" Sunday comic strips rose from zero percent in 1900 to 16% in 1955-1959, with a high point of 23% in the 1945-1949 period.

In sum, to generalize from the studies reported above, it seems that a typical metropolitan paper probably devotes around 5-10% of its available space to crime news. Further, the type of crime most likely reported is individual crime accompanied by violence. Less than 5% of available space is devoted to covering the general issue of crime: its causes, remedies, etc.

Crime News: Differences Among Newspapers

One of the points made again and again by media researchers is that different newspapers devote different amounts of space to crime news. In the study mentioned earlier, Deutschmann found that crime news accounted for 7% of the space in the New York *Times* but 28% of the space in the *Daily News*.[2] The difference between these two papers in their emphasis on crime news has been a favorite topic of research and invariably the *Daily News* has been found to rely more heavily on crime news (Quinney, 1970; Otto, 1962; Bachmuth, 1960). A more recent investigation (Meyer, 1975) looked at a different aspect of the crime reporting in these two papers. The author investigated not quantitative differences in column inches devoted to crime stories, but instead differences in the way the same stories were reported. He concluded that while much of the two papers' coverage was similar, the *Times* reported more information about the official actions of the criminal justice system or, in other words, what legal processes take place after the crime is committed.

One possible reason for the difference in crime news emphasis by different papers might be competition. In a study on the effects of competition on the content of a single paper, Rarick and Hartman (1966) found that more competition was related to significantly more space being given to news that dealt with crime, disasters, and human interest.

Geographic differences in the amount of prominence given to crime news have also been examined. In a content analysis of crime coverage in Detroit and Atlanta papers, Cohen (1975) discovered that the Detroit papers had more than twice as much coverage as the Atlanta papers but that Detroit had more than four times as much crime, as calculated from police reports. Differences were also evident in the way crime news was reported in the two cities. Atlanta newspapers were more likely to give prominent coverage to crime related subjects.

Crime News and Amount of Actual Crime

Whether newspaper coverage of crime is related to the incidence of crime in reality has been the focus of at least two studies and both have found similar results. In an early study of Colorado newspapers, Davis (1951) found no relationship between the amount of crime news in newspapers and local crime rates.

In a more recent study, Jones (1976) found a similar pattern after analyzing St. Louis newspapers. Using a five-year timespan, the author compared the amount of coverage given certain crimes (using a specially constructed index) and the actual incidence of that crime as reported in the Uniform Crime Reports.[3] Jones' findings indicated that the press coverage of crimes gives a highly distorted version of the actual situation. Evidence that these findings are not confined to the U.S. is contained in a study by Roshier (1973) of newspaper crime coverage in the United Kingdom.

Issues

If we can abstract and infer from the above studies, it appears that most of them were prompted by the following questions: (1) Do newspapers place too much emphasis on crime news? (2) Does the reporting of crime news encourage other people to commit crimes? (3) Do newspapers report an "accurate" picture of crime and law breaking?

In attempting to answer the first question, the available evidence seems to suggest "yes and no" as a possible answer. If we contrast the amount of crime news against the total content of a newspaper, we find that only 5-15% of the typical paper is devoted to this coverage (with some papers, of course, exceeding this figure). This does not seem an excessive amount of attention, especially when the popularity of this content is taken into consideration. Swanson (1955) found that stories about major crime were read by 24% of the audience, compared to a readership rate of 20% for an average news item. Thus, in view of the popularity of crime news, it is perhaps somewhat surprising to find that newspapers do not carry more of it.

It is possible, however, that newspaper coverage overemphasizes certain kinds of crimes. The studies of Jones and Cirino indicate that individual violent crimes (especially murder) are covered to a far greater extent than property and white collar crime. Moreover, Ryan and Owen note that the amount of space devoted to examining the issue of crime constitutes only a small fraction of newspaper space.

Evidence surrounding the second question is scant and content analytic studies cannot suggest an answer. Audience research, however, does suggest some possibilities. One study (Payne and Payne, 1970) found that a certain category of crimes (what the authors labelled "instrumental" crimes—burglary, robbery, auto theft) decreased in Detroit during newspaper strikes. This could possibly indicate some support for the hypothesis that coverage of crime encourages imitation. A replication of this study, however, is four other cities also hit by newspaper strikes did not find similar results (Payne, 1974). Faced with this anomaly, the author concluded, "It seems probable that the relationship Payne and Payne found between newspaper publication and instrumental crime rates was simply a matter of chance. Such a relationship was in any case not strong enough to appear consistently in other cities . . . . There appears to be no general relationship between newspaper publication and crime rates." As a general summary, perhaps Haskins' (1969) conclusion following his review of the literature on this topic is still appropriate: "Therefore, one must conclude that there is no rigorous evidence one way or another as to whether violence in the print media has beneficial, harmful, or no effect."

As for the third question, studies summarized above suggest that the "mirror" theory of mass media (the media simply hold up a mirror to reality and reflect actual events and occurrences) is not entirely valid in so far as crime news is concerned. Davis and Jones point out no necessary relationship between the degree of press attention and actuality. Or as Funkhouser (1973) concluded after a content analysis of three major news magazines, "the amount of coverage of an issue did not necessarily bear any resemblance to the behavior of the facts of that issue."

CRIME AND BROADCAST NEWS

Far less information exists concerning the prevalence and dimensions of crime news in television. On the network level, a 1969 study of the NBC and CBS evening news (Cirino, 1972) found that NBC devoted a total of about 23 minutes to crime news over a two-month period. Roughly speaking, this would represent about 13% of the total available news time. CBS devoted slightly more than 31 minutes to crime news during this same period or about 18% of available newstime. Perhaps more importantly, Cirino noted that stories about individual crime were featured three times more often than stories about "establishment" or "organized" crime.

In a 1970 study, Lowry (1971) content analyzed the amount of "bad news" contained in network newscasts. He found that about 10% of all news items had to do with crime news. Looking at only those items defined as "bad" news, Lowry found that crime stories accounted for about 28% of all the items in this particular category. Crime stories tended to be short (most were under 30 seconds in length) and occurred toward the end of the newscast.

Local Stations

At the local level, one study (Dominick et al., 1975) suggested that the format of a local station's newscast is related to its coverage of crime and violence. In an analysis of the three networks' flagship stations in New York City, it was discovered that WABC, using the "happy talk" or "eyewitness" format spent significantly more time reporting violent stories (many of which concerned violent crime) than did its two competitors who employed other formats. In addition, with the "eyewitness" format, WABC placed its violent items more often in the first half of the newscast.

More recently, Powers (1977) has presented anecdotal evidence to suggest that the increasing use of "news consultants" or "news doctors" by local stations has lead to a greater emphasis on crime news, especially news of violent crimes.

Issues

In general, the main issues surrounding the reporting of crime news by television are less well articulated than their counterparts in the print media, partly because of the scarcity of research. Judging by the above studies, the main questions seem to be the following: (1) Does TV news over-emphasize or distort crime news? (2) Are local TV stations concentrating on sensational and violent crimes to boost their ratings? With regard to the former, we find that the percentage of time devoted to crime news by the networks is about the same as found in analysis of newspaper content. Similarly, there appears to be limited evidence tha TV also shows more of a preference for covering individual crime as opposed to other types. The limited data also suggest that a more detailed look is needed at the prominence given to crime coverage at the local level. No study seems to exist that correlates the amount of crime news coverage to success in the ratings.

CRIME AND LAW ENFORCEMENT IN BROADCAST ENTERTAINMENT

Historical Background

Shows featuring crime and law enforcement were not a major part of early radio dramatic programming. In fact, they never became as prominent a part of radio entertainment as they were later to become on TV.

Crime shows on radio. Radio dramatic programs carried by the networks featured law enforcement themes have shown wide variation over the years. For example, in 1932 only three hours were devoted to this type of programming. By 1940, this figure had risen to 5.75 hours. Eight years later, crime and detective programs were a substantial part of the national network's programming, comprising about 15 hours. In 1956, with TV attracting many audience members, about 6.25 hours consisted of this type of programming (Lichty and Topping, 1975). In terms of all evening programming, these figures represented about 4% of all program time in 1932; about 5% in 1940; 14% in 1948; and about 5% in 1956. Thus, while the absolute amount of time varied from season to season, it accounted for only a small proportion of all available evening program time. As we shall see, this is in marked contrast to the situation that was to occur later with prime time TV programs.

Crime in TV entertainment shows. Table 1 contains a listing of the percentage of prime time from 1953-1977 devoted to shows featuring as their main theme crime and law enforcement. As can be seen from the table, crime shows did not become a staple of prime time entertainment until the late 1950s when, prompted by the introduction of "adult Westerns" on ABC, and later by the success of a program called "The Untouchables," crime shows began to account for around one third of all prime time from 1959-1961. This trend levelled off during the 1960s but began to increase again during the early 1970s until it reached its peak in 1975 when almost 40% of the three networks' prime time schedules contained shows dealing with crime and law enforcement. More recently, the percentage has dropped slightly. Overall since 1970, shows dealing with crime have accounted for about 32% of prime time programming. Clearly, in recent years this programming has become a key element in mass entertainment.

The figures in Table 1 pertain to regularly scheduled network series. As Bailey (1970) has shown, the content of network special programming bears a rough correspondence to these figures, at least through 1968 (the last year for which data are available). The amount of special programming in which crime and law enforcement were major themes increased during the late 1950s until it peaked in 1960 with a total 10½ hours devoted to this topic. This figure was also on the rise during the late 1960s as well.

We might, at this point, speculate why this genre of programming has been so popular with networks. It would appear that the inherent conflict of good versus evil contained in this type of program is a common theme that is well understood and has great appeal to the mass audience which TV programs try to attract. In addition, crime shows are usually filled with action—chases, fights, gun battles—that are particularly attractive for a visual medium like TV. Finally, some writers have suggested that

Table 1. TIME DEVOTED TO SHOWS FEATURING CRIME AND LAW ENFORCEMENT IN PRIME TIME TELEVISION, 1953-1977[1]

Year	Number of Shows	% of Program Time	Total Program Time
1953	12	7	81.75 hours
1954	12	8	80.00
1955	10	7	71.00
1956	12	9	70.00
1957	19	17	69.50
1958	30	28	65.25
1959	37	33	69.50
1960	34	35	72.00
1960	34	35	72.00
1961	27	33	71.50
1962	14	17	71.50
1963	11	16	73.00
1964	11	16	73.00
1965	14	17	73.50
1966	18	20	73.00
1967	19	21	72.50
1968	19	23	72.50
1969	14	17	72.00
1970	17	23	73.00
1971	22	32	63.00
1972	19	29	63.50
1973	21	34	64.00
1974	20	36	64.00
1975	24	39	63.00
1976	20	32	63.00
1977	18	27	63.00

[1] Source: Data compiled by the author.

the "law and order" emphasis, popular during the late 1960s, manifested itself in popular entertainment in the increased number of police and detective programs that premiered during this period and shortly thereafter (Arons and Katsh, 1977).

Crime as Portrayed in TV Programs

The potential harmful effects of a steady diet of crime programs have prompted several content analyses of this genre since the early days of TV. In one of the first studies, Smythe (1954) found that 98% of all acts or threats of violence were found in entertainment programs. Somewhat surprisingly, only 28% of all the acts or threats were contained in crime dramas and 23% in Westerns. The remainder were found in general dramatic programs. About one sixth of all the violence identified in this analysis was committed in the interest of law and order. Cultural stereotypes were common as evidenced by the fact that 66% of all Italians shown on TV were portrayed as lawbreakers and 83% of the heroes were white Americans.

In a related study of TV in the early 1950s, Head (1954) analyzed more than 200 network programs. He found that crime and aggression were found more frequently in children's programs than in other types. In addition, he found that professional criminals were important elements in all these shows. Across all programs, homicide was 22 times as common as in real life. Further, Head noted that 17% of the jobs shown were connected with police work and that 17% of the characters were shown as criminals. Non-whites were infrequently portrayed in police work.

Ten years later, a study by the National Association for Better Radio and Television (1964) revealed that 192 hours of broadcast time in a single week were devoted to programs in which the commission of a crime was a major theme and more than 500 killings were televised. The number of hours of crime programming represented a 90% increase over 1952 and more than two thirds of the total crime programming was broadcast before 9 p.m.

Additional data on the frequency of crime in TV programs are contained in testimony presented to the U.S. Senate Subcommittee to Investigate Juvenile Delinquency during hearings conducted in 1955, 1961, and 1964. In 1955, subcommittee investigators studied a week's programming (from 4 to 10 p.m.) in nine separate cities plus a solid week of programs broadcast on four Washington, D.C. stations. Among other things, they found that 39 hours of programs on the D.C. stations featured crime and violence. This amounted to about 23% of all the program time analyzed. In the other nine cities, about 20% of all program time was devoted to crime and violence.

Further, testimony to this subcommittee revealed that the following incidents were broadcast before 9 p.m. during one week of programming available in the Los Angeles market in 1960: 144 murders, 52 justifiable killings, 13 kidnappings, 11 planned but unsuccessful murders, and four lynchings (U.S. Congress, 1955, 1965).

Since 1967, the most thorough analyses of television entertainment programs have been conducted by George Gerbner and his associates at the University of Pennsylvania. These studies contain valuable information about the portrayal of law enforcement over the years. In 1967, for example, criminals numbered 10% of all characters; they made up 20% of the killers and 24% of those killed. Forces of the law made up 13% of the killers but accounted for none of those killed. Criminals did not commit much of the overall violence coded by Gerbner and his colleagues, taking part in only two of every ten violent acts. Most criminals, however, were violent; 82% engaged in some violent act. Police and other law enforcement agents were almost as violent, with 70% of their number committing violence (Gerbner, 1970).

Further, when crime was featured, it almost always involved violent crime. Due process was indicated as a consequence of major acts of violence about 20% of the time. Violence was initiated by agents of the law about 40% of the time and they responded to violence in a violent manner on three of every ten occasions. Police restraint in the face of violence was rare, occurring only 10% of the time.

By 1969, however, a subtle change had taken place in the way in which crime and law enforcement were portrayed. As seen by the figures below, the process had become much less lethal. For example, in 1969, only 14% of the criminals were killers and only 5% were killed. For law enforcement officers, none were killers and none were killed. Police and criminals were equally violent that year, with about 73% of both groups involved in some type of violent activity. As was found in 1967, most violence was not related to crime and law enforcement. As a group, criminals accounted for only 8% of all violent roles while law enforcement agents accounted for 10%.

A 1972 study of crime that occurred in prime time network programs (Dominick, 1973) offers additional information about TV's treatment of law enforcement. Analyzing a week's worth of prime time programs, this study found that murder, assault, and armed robbery were the most frequently portrayed crimes. As was also noted by Gerbner, violent crime was the most prevalent type, accounting for about 60% of the 119 crimes coded for the week. When the frequency of TV crime was compared to the frequency of real-life law-breaking (as determined by the FBI's data), Blacks, young people, and lower class individuals were underrepresented in TV crime programs.

Lastly, a significant part of the legal process was not usually shown in TV drama. Specifically, only 5% of the criminals were shown during their trial or had post-apprehension legal processes (arraignments, pretrial hearings, jury selection) explicitly mentioned in connection with their case. In the TV world, the legal process usually ends with capture.

   This same tendency was found by Winick and Winick (1974), who concluded after analysis of 28 network courtroom drama series, that viewers were unlikely to see such events as arraignments, bonding, hearings, requests for bail reduction, plea bargaining, jury selections, jury deliberation, and cases that are disposed of without a trial.

   A different aspect of crime and law enforcement was the focus of a content analysis done by two law professors (Arons and Katsh, 1977). These investigators analyzed a random sample of crime dramas from the point of view of constitutional law. In 15 televised police dramas, they found 43 separate scenes in which serious questions could be raised about the propriety of police action. Included in the programs were 21 clear constitutional violations, 15 instances of police brutality and harrassment, and seven omissions of constitutional rights. The 21 clear constitutional violations occurred during scenes in which people were interrogated without being informed of their rights, in which evidence was taken without a warrant, or in which another form of illegal search was conducted.

   Related data are reported in an unpublished study by Tedesco (see Arons and Katsh, 1977) in which he found that the number of law enforcement characters on TV increased from 80 in 1969 to 168 in 1971. At the same time, the number of characters who were lawyers or other legal professional decreased from 25 to 18. He also found that in an average week's viewing during the 1969-1971 period the number of instances in which police failed to secure search warrants rose from 21 to 62. During the same period, the number of times per week that police failed to advise suspects of their right to counsel rose from 13 to 32. The author suggests that it is possible that these trends in TV content are correlated with the political values of the early years of the Nixon administration.[4]

   In addition to the above, there are several other studies, some reported in the popular press, that, although not following the classic content analysis methodology, may still tell us a great deal about the way law enforcement officers and those in the legal profession view TV crime drama. In short, they might be thought of as informal content analyses conducted by the very people who see themselves portrayed on screen. The first of these (Arcuri, 1977) consisted of a survey of 816 police officers concerning their attitudes about crime shows on TV. One of the major complaints these officers voiced had to do with the way all crimes were neatly solved by the program's conclusion. They also pointed out that TV shows portrayed all police departments with sophisticated equipment and that the role of the private detective was glamorized by TV and was totally unrealistic.

Similarly, Daley (1972), a former deputy police commissioner, suggested that unreal portrayals of police might be fabricating a myth that will hamper citizen-police relationships. In particular, he noted that certain police shows always show new equipment, neat offices and desks, radios that always work, and other paraphernalia that might suggest that police departments need little in the way of public tax funds for their operation.

Finally, Lewis (1974), a district attorney, argues that TV is brain-washing potential jury members by featuring programs that overemphasize the defense aspects of a case. Specifically, Lewis points out that, despite the many TV programs to the contrary, no defendant, in his experience, has ever admitted his or her guilt in court during a criminal trial. He also noted that many series erroneously imply that the legal process ends with capture and that an arrest "solves" a crime and closes a case.

Taken together, these last three "content analyses" seem to reinforce the conclusions reached by formal methods as well as sensitizing us to more subtle aspects that may have been overlooked by social scientists.

Summary

All in all, these studies suggest the following generalizations:

(1) Shows dealing with crime and law enforcement constitute a major element in prime time dramatic programming.
(2) The type of crime that is typically portrayed on TV is violent crime that is directed toward individuals.
(3) There is no correlation between crime as portrayed in TV programs and crime in the real world nor do TV criminals correspond to real-life criminals.
(4) TV police are far more efficient than are police in real life.
(5) Certain aspects of the legal process, consisting primarily of those events that occur after apprehension, are largely ignored in TV drama.
(6) Police work and criminal trials as seen on TV are not representative of the way they actually occur in real life.

Issues

Abstracting from the above studies, we find that much of the research impetus for this topic stems from concern about two major questions. (1) Does viewing of crime shows encourage the imitation of criminal activity? (2) Are crime shows cultivating misconceptions and biased views of this activity among audience members? We will consider each of these in turn. As before, we will have to turn to audience studies for possible answers since, by itself, content analysis is not sufficient to suggest a possible answer.

Evidence relating to the first of these questions is found in several places. There is certainly anecdotal evidence to support the proposition that certain disturbed individuals will directly imitate a crime they recently viewed on TV. Davison (1974) reported that a college athlete in Colorado was arrested after he had mailed letters threatening to kill the wife of a bank president unless he was paid $5,000. After his arrest, he stated he got his idea from a TV show. In addition, a juvenile court judge stated that two juveniles had committed a burglary by forcing a skylight, a technique they had copied from a TV program. Perhaps the most famous example occurred when Qantas Airways paid out over a half million dollars in a pressure bomb hoax in 1971 after a made for TV movie, "The Doomsday Flight," was shown on Australian TV. The film had used this device. When this same movie appeared on American TV in 1966, bomb threats against the airlines went up 80% in the following week. The broadcasting industry is aware of this situation. The code of the National Association of Broadcasters says, "The presentation of techniques of crime in such detail as to invite imitation shall be avoided." Many police shows, in fact, employ technical advisers, usually former police officers, to help them in this area (Monaco, 1977).

Additional evidence related to the imitation question is contained in research dealing with the larger question of whether televised violence prompts aggression in real life. Since violent crime is the most frequent type of crime portrayed, these data seem to have relevance. Since space precludes a comprehensive summary of this rather lengthy literature, we will consider only those studies that seem most pertinent.

A macro-analysis done by Clark and Blankenburg (1970) correlated measures of television violence with measures of environmental violence (the FBI's Uniform Crime Report) over a 17-year period (1953-1969). They found little correlation between incidents of violence shown on TV and real-life crime.

The over-all conclusions of studies using less global techniques (primarily experimental and survey techniques) have been somewhat inconsistent. Perhaps the best summary statement concerning this literature is given by Comstock (1975). As part of a research project that examined 2,300 different studies concerning television, Comstock was able to assemble over 30 articles which reviewed the literature pertaining to the issue of whether TV can be said to contribute to aggression or socially undesirable behavior. After doing what amounted to a "review of reviews," Comstock found differences among the appraisals offered by the reviews but went on to conclude, "A polling of the conclusions would lead one to accept the proposition that under at least some circumstances, viewing violence increases the likelihood of some form of subsequent aggressiveness." It would seem that this statement would apply to the viewing of violent crimes as well.

Considering the second question, we find again a certain amount of anecdotal evidence (some of which is mentioned above) that would suggest that certain police and lawyers feel that these shows are creating false expectations and misconceptions among the general public. Empirical evidence of this issue is available from at least two studies. As part of his Violence Profile, Gerbner (1977) has included a section containing data relevant to "cultivation analysis." Simply put, cultivation analysis investigates audience perceptions of social reality. It attempts to assess the degree to which television viewing is contributing to possibly distorted views of reality. The area of cultivation analysis most relevant to this study is the one involving perceptions of crime and law enforcement.

In this analysis, audience members are presented with questions that relate to reality and are given two choices for their answers. One of these choices corresponds more accurately to the "real world" while the other is more representative of the TV world. For example, two of the items that make up this index are "What per cent of all males who have jobs work in law enforcement and crime detection? One per cent? Five per cent?" In reality, the correct answer is 1%, according to the Census Bureau. On TV, however, about 12% of all male characters are in this line of work. Thus, 5% is labelled the "television answer" to this question. Similarly, "What per cent of all crimes are violent crimes, like murders, rape, robbery and aggravated assault? Fifteen per cent? Twenty five per cent?" The real world figure is about 10%; the TV figure is around 70%. Thus the second answer would be labelled the "TV answer." Gerbner and his colleagues have constructed an index using these questions and two others like them. They have administered this test to both children and adults. They have found significant positive correlations between amount of TV viewing and the scores on the index that reflect "television answers" to these questions about crime and law enforcement. The correlations, while small in the absolute sense (.16 in one sample of 573 adults; the same in a sample of 466 children), are robust and still reach statistical significance after the effects of key demographic variables are partialled out.

Additional information about the effects of viewing this type of program among children is provided by Dominick (1974). In a survey of 371 fifth graders in New York City, those children who were heavy viewers of crime shows were more likely to name a TV character associated with law enforcement as an identification choice. In addition, children who were high viewers also were more likely to think that most criminals usually get caught. Lastly, this study provides a clue as to the relative effectiveness of TV as an informal teaching device. The children were asked two series of three true-false questions to tap their knowledge of legal terms. One series had to do with knowledge of rights upon arrest, (a topic well-represented on TV shows) while the other concerned terms not usually treated on TV (functions of grand juries, definition of arraignment, Fifth Amendment Rights). The average score on the arrest rights scale was 2.5 out of a possible three; on the scale measuring knowledge about terms not commonly portrayed on TV, the average score was 0.5 out of three.

In sum, there is evidence to suggest that viewing of TV programs depicting crime and law enforcement is modestly but significantly related to somewhat distorted perceptions about these topics.

SPECIAL PROBLEMS

We turn now to a brief consideration of two issues that have recently assumed prominence among mass communication scholars and practitioners. The first can be traced back to the early days of American journalism; the second has become more salient with the advent of television.

Sensationalism

On August 10, 1977, David Berkowitz, the alleged "Son of Sam" killer, was arrested in New York City. On August 11, the New York *Post* had a large red headline, "Caught," and devoted a full 10 pages to the story. That day, all in all, the *Post* carried 16 stories on Son of Sam and 36 photographs. On the same day, the New York *Daily News* borrowed an idea from an earlier time and ran an extra edition in the early evening. This contained 12 Son of Sam articles, two columns and 17 photos. The New York *Times* was more reserved but still devoted two full pages to the story the day after Berkowitz's arrest.

The local television stations were also caught up in the rush. The New York CBS and ABC stations devoted two and a half hours each to the story while NBC spent two hours. Except for weather and sports, little else was mentioned in these newscasts. Further, the content of the coverage seemed not so much concerned with the content of the story as with the thrill of it. An ABC reporter, in a two-minute segment ostensibly covering Berkowitz's preliminary arraignment, referred to her own emotional reaction to the situation no less than 18 times (Tucker, 1977). Another reporter interviewed bar patrons that might have been Berkowitz's next target, while others perhaps exceeded journalistic propriety by asking survivors of the shootings questions such as "What would you do if you had Berkowitz in the room with you now?" Every station quickly rounded up psychiatrists who gave instant diagnoses of the suspect without ever having exchanged a single word with him.

The results of all this? Reportedly, newscast ratings were higher than usual. The *Post* sold over a million copies, 400,000 more than normal (the largest sale since Robert Kennedy was shot). The *News* sold 2.5 million; they normally sell about 1.9 million. Even the staid *Times* sold 50,000 copies more than usual.[5]

All too quickly, the atmosphere became circus-like. A lawyer reportedly offered to sell tapes of his conversation with Berkowitz to a local newspaper; a neighbor was asking $15,000 for an interview; an old girl friend sold Berkowitz's letters to the newspapers for $500. And the day after the arrest was reported, three newspaper photographers and a reporter were arrested for trespassing after they allegedly broke into Berkowitz's apartment and took pictures.

This brief case study raises some disturbing issues. Perhaps the New York media should not be criticized so much for overplaying the story as for the reasons why they did it. As Tucker noted, Son of Sam became "show biz." A column in the *New Yorker* (1977) warned, "By transforming a killer into a celebrity, the press . . . may have stirred others brooding madly over their grievances to act." Tucker perhaps summed it up best by writing, "Newsmen in a free society must balance the obligation to report facts against the necessity to excite an audience. When news organizations start opting for 'hype' in the guise of news, they risk the fate of the boy who cried wolf: when a real crisis comes, nobody will take them seriously."

Terrorism

In March of 1977, in Ohio, an ex-marine took two people captive. He finally agreed to trade one of them for a television set so that he could watch his own coverage. In February of the same year, an Indianapolis man abducted a mortgage company executive and held him captive for 62 hours. At one point in the ordeal, reportedly as a condition of surrender, the abductor demanded live coverage of a statement for the press. All three network affiliates immediately began to carry the event. For the next 25 minutes, the abductor, clutching the trigger of a sawed-off shotgun which was wired to the head of his captive, delivered a long, obscenity-filled diatribe that was carried in its entirety by two of the three local TV stations. This episode ended without surrender. Later, upon re-examining their actions, at least two of the three local TV news directors had second thoughts about their actions, realizing that a gunman had taken them hostage as well, and was essentially directing their 11 o'clock newscast with a shotgun. (Incidentally, the gunman was watching TV throughout most of the siege, closely following coverage of his own actions.)

Also in March, Hanafi Muslims took over three buildings in Washington, D.C. and held 134 persons hostage. Immediately, NBC assigned 18 minicam crews and 100 people to cover the story. An all-news radio station devoted 95% of all its coverage to the event during the 39-hour siege. Extremely conscious of the media aspects of the event,[6] the leader of the Muslims called up the anchorman of a D.C. station and read his list of demands over the six p.m. newscast. At another point, this same individual called a local radio station and demanded that the station immediately correct on erroneous story in which the group had been called "Black Muslims" or he was "going to kill somebody and throw him out the window."

In the same month, but this time in New York City, a gunman took over a church in Harlem and held two people captive. One of the first demands he made was to talk with John Johnson, a reporter for the local ABC station. He subsequently took the reporter hostage as well.

Taken together, these events highlight a growing problem concerning the proper way to cover terrorism, especially for the broadcast media.[7] As can be seen from the above, in many instances, the medium itself was manipulated by the individuals or the terrorist group involved.

A second issue, somewhat related to this, concerns the growing problem of police-media relationships during these events. Frank Bolz, in charge of New York City's Police Department Hostage Squad, highlighted some of these difficulties. Bolz described a situation in New Rochelle, New York, in which a radio reporter was broadcasting live the efforts of a police team trying to get into position by crawling across the rooftop of a building near the place where a gunman was holding hostages. Said Bolz, "If the perpetrator had been listening to the radio station he would have had a blow by blow description of what the police maneuvers were" (Friedman, 1977).

Further, one of the most troubling problems, according to Bolz, comes about when media reporters take it on themselves to telephone the abductors during the event. In the previously mentioned Washington, D.C. building takeover, a commentator from a talk show called up one of the Muslims during the siege and asked, "How can you believe the police?", seriously hampering negotiations.

A similar situation occurred in Calgary, Alberta, in March 1976, when two men were holding hostages. A deal was made in which the hostages were to be released in return for a certain number of doses of methadone. At this point, someone from the media called the gunmen and reportedly said, "Don't be stupid. If you give up all your hostages, you'll have nothing to deal with."

Many of the central issues surrounding this situation were highlighted in a panel discussion before the Radio Television News Directors Association (*Broadcasting*, 1977a). A Deputy Chief of the Washington Police Department urged that the public's right to know be counter-balanced by the rights of the police and hostages to reasonable safety. In part, he urged guidelines that would include prohibitions on tying up the phone lines in siege areas, interviewing suspects, and reporting police movements. A police psychologist suggested that the media refrain from naming names or describing the method of hostage taking. Another recommendation was the suspension of media competitiveness during the event. Said an attorney, "Some of the worst abuses would be avoided if everyone wasn't in a rush to scoop one another." This same problem was also noticed by policeman Bolz in simpler terms: "If one guy happens to make a phone call to the perpetrator and gets a scoop, all the others feel, 'We've been scooped by WWWW; we'd better get in there.'"

The other side of the coin was voiced by CBS' Walter Cronkite who said in a TV interview *(Broadcasting,* 1977b), "We cannot control the events that need to be reported. All we can do is be responsible in reporting the events that occur." Cronkite went on to say he was not sure journalists should be concerned with the consequences of what they do. "When we start worrying about the consequences, we're beginning to play another role other than that of reporters. We're beginning to play God. And I don't think I'm equipped to do that."

The entire problem has been made even more vexatious by technology. The emergence of ENG (electronic news gathering) equipment and minicams has made it far easier for TV news teams to cover events live. Some of the major problems have been pointed out by Saltzman (1975). In the first place, there is the danger of unexpectedly putting the inflammatory, slanderous, and obscene on the air (something that has already occurred during the Indianapolis kidnapping). Operating live requires split second decisions, with little time to contemplate the effects of the newsworthiness of what is being broadcast. Secondly, there is the danger of being used, or of creating a news story by covering it live. In addition to the examples mentioned above, in Los Angeles, a man holding hostages used the live coverage to try to negotiate his safe passage through police lines. Thirdly, there is the danger of giving viewers misinformation and rumor. In the pressures of a live broadcast, the difficulties of checking the accuracy of a report are immense. In the shoot-out between police and Symbionese Liberation Army, several rumors were broadcast, most notably that Patricia Hearst was involved. The risk of broadcasting wrong or inaccurate news is far greater during the coverage of live events.

In the wake of all this, a TV network, at least one wire service, and several newspapers have developed guidelines for the reporting of these events. CBS guidelines included (1) paraphrasing terrorist demands rather than broadcasting the voice or picture of the terrorist directly; (2) not covering actions live; (3) not monopolizing telephone lines to the terrorists; and (4) considering, but not taking as instruction, police suggestions about avoiding inflammatory phrases and reports (Levin, 1977). The guidelines set down by United Press International and several local papers seem consistent with those of CBS. In general, it appears fair to say that the upsurge of terrorism during 1977 has prompted much self-examination by the news media. How closely and how extensively the guidelines resulting from this examination are followed is another matter that can only be decided in time.

NOTES

1. These reports have been issued annually since 1967. Copies of the latest can be obtained from Dr. Gerbner at the University of Pennsylvania.

2. An old joke that circulates among journalists maintains that, if the *Daily News* prints a story about a crime, it's sensationalism. If the *Times* prints it, it's sociology.

3. The accuracy of these reports has been the subject of much debate.

4. Others would suggest an economic explanation. See Klein (1974).

5. These data and other observations on the New York media's Son of Sam coverage are contained in the September 1977 issue of *MORE*.

6. Reportedly, the leader of the Hanafi Muslims had considered taking over a TV station as well.

7. The June 1977 issue of *MORE* has a large section devoted to the problems of covering terrorists.

REFERENCES

ARCURI, A. (1977). "You can't take fingerprints off water: Police officers' views toward 'cop' television shows." Human Relations, 30(3):237-247.

ARONS, S., and KATSH, E. (1977). "How TV cops flout the law." Saturday Review (March 19):11-19.

BACHMUTH, R. (1960). "Juvenile delinquency in the daily press." Alpha Kappa Delta, 20(2):47-51.

BAILEY, R.L. (1970). "The content of network television prime-time special programming: 1948-68." Journal of Broadcasting, 14(3):325-336.

BARCUS, F. E. (1961). "A content analysis of trends in Sunday comics, 1900-59." Journalism Quarterly, 38(2):171-180.

Broadcasting (1977a). "Two sides of the coin on media and terrorists." April 4:78.

Broadcasting (1977b)."'Who's Who' looks into ethical questions of covering terrorists acts." March 21:28.

CIRINO, R. (1972). Don't blame the people. New York: Vintage Books.

_____ (1974). Power to persuade. New York: Bantam.

CLARK, D., and BLANKENBURG, W. (1970). "Trends in violent content in selected mass media." Pp. 189-243 in G. Comstock and E. Rubinstein (eds.), Television and social behavior: Media content and control. Washington, D.C.: U.S. Government Printing Office.

COHEN, S. (1975). "The evidence so far." Journal of Communication, 25(4):14-24.

DALEY, R.J. (1972). "Police report on the TV cop shows." New York Times Magazine, Nov. 19:39-40.

DAVIS, F. (1951). "Crime news in Colorado newspapers." American Journal of Sociology, 57 (June):325-330.

DAVISON, J. (1974). "The triggered, the obsessed and the schemers." TV Guide, Feb. 2:4-6.

DEUTSCHMANN, P. (1959). News page content of twelve metropolitan dailies. Cincinnati: Scripps-Howard Research Center.

DOMINICK, J. (1973). "Crime and law enforcement on prime time television." Public Opinion Quarterly, 37(2):241-250.

_____ (1974). "Children's viewing of crime shows and attitudes on law inforcement." Journalism Quarterly, 51(1):5-12.

_____ et at. (1975). "Television journalism vs. show business." Journalism Quarterly, 52(2):213-218.

FRIEDMAN, R. (1977). "Crisis cop raps media." MORE, June:18-21.

FUNKHOUSER, G.R. (1973). "Trends in media coverage of the issues of the 60's." Journalism Quarterly, 50(4):531-535.

GERBNER, G. (1970). "Violence in television drama: Trends and symbolic function." Pp. 28-187 in G. Comstock and Ed. Rubinstein, (eds.), Television and social behavior: Media content and control. Washington, D.C.: U.S. Government Printing Office.

_____ et al. (1977). "TV violence profile no. 8: The highlights." Journal of Communication, 27(2):171-180.

GILLMOR, D.M. (1966). Free press and fair trial. Washington, D.C.: Public Affairs Press.

GREENBERG, B. (1969). "The content and context of violence in the media." Pp. 423-449 in R. Baker and S. Ball (eds.), Violence and the media. Washington, D.C.: U.S. Government Printing Office.

HASKINS, J. (1969). "The effects of violence in the printed media." Pp. 493-502 in R. Baker and S. Ball (eds.), Violence and the media. Washington, D.C.: U.S. Government Printing Office.

HEAD, S. (1954). "Content analysis of television drama programs."

JONES, E.T. (1976). "The press as metropolitan monitor." Public Opinion Quarterly, 40(2):239-244.

KITTROSS, J., and HARWOOD, K. (1970). Free and fair. Philadelphia: Journal of Broadcasting Publications.

KLEIN, P. (1974). "Why TV is having a crime wave." TV Guide, January 12:28-31.

LEWIS, W.II. (1974). "Witness for the prosecution." TV Guide, Nov. 30:5-7.

LICHTY, L., and TOPPING, M (eds.) (1975). American broadcasting. New York: Hastings House.

LOWRY, D. (1971). "Gresham's law and network TV news selection." Journal of Broadcasting, 15(4): 397-408.

MEYER, J.C. (1975). "Newspaper reporting of crime and justice." Journalism Quarterly, 52(4):731-734.

MONACO, J (1977). "Why is Kojak so tough?" MORE, Feb.:42-44.

National Association for Better Radio and Television (1964). Crime on television: A survey report. Los Angeles: Author.

New Yorker (1977). "Notes and comment." August 15:21-22.

OTTO, H.A. (1962). "Sex and violence on the American newsstand." Journalism Quarterly, 40(1):19-26.

PAYNE, D. (1974). "Newspapers and crime: What happens during strike periods." Journalism Quarterly, 51(4):607-612.

PAYNE, D., and PAYNE, K. (1970). "Newspapers and crime in Detroit." Journalism Quarterly, 47(2):233-238.

POWERS, R. (1977). The newscasters. New York: St. Martins.

LEVIN, E. (1977). "What is news?" Pp. 28-33 in TV Guide, July 9.

QUINNEY, R. (1970). The social reality of crime. Boston: Little, Brown.

RARICK, G., and HARTMAN, B. (1966). "The effect of competition on one daily newspaper's content." Journalism Quarterly, 43(3):459-463.

ROSHIER, B. (1973). "The selection of crime news by the press." Pp. 28-39 in S. Cohen and J. Young (eds.), The manufacture of news. Beverly Hills: Sage.

RYAN, M., and OWEN, D. (1976). "A content analysis of metropolitian newspaper coverage of social issues." Journalism Quarterly, 53(4):634-640.

SALTZMAN, J. (1975). "The problems of covering news live." TV Guide, March 15:6-11.

SMYTHE, D. (1954). "Reality as presented by TV." Public Opinion Quarterly, 19(2):143-156.

STEMPL, G. (1962). "Content patterns of small metropolitan dailies." Journalism Quarterly, 39(1):88-90.

STOTT, M. (1967). "A content comparision of two evening network television programs with four morning Ohio daly newspapers." Unpublished M.A. thesis, Ohio State University.

SWANSON, C. (1955). "What they read in 130 daily newspapers." Journalism Quarterly, 32(4):411-421.

TUCKER, C. (1977). "The night TV cried wolf." Saturday Review, Oct. 1:56.

U.S. Congress, Senate, Committee on the Judiciary (1955). Television and juvenile delinquency. Washington, D.C.: U.S. Government Printing Office.

_____ (1965). Television and juvenile delinquency. Washington, D.C.: U.S. Government Printing Office.

VAN HORN, G.A. (1952). "A analysis of AP news on trunk and Wisconsin state wires." Journalism Quarterly, 29(4):426-432.

WINICK,C., and WINICK, M. (1974). "Courtroom drama on television." Journal of Communication, 24(4):67-73.

Deviant Media Behavior

Part 2

7

THE BARSEBACK "PANIC"
A Case of Media Deviance

**KARL ERIK ROSENGREN
PETER ARVIDSSON
DAHN STURESSON**

AUTHOR'S NOTE: *The research reported in this paper was supported by the Swedish Board of Psychological Defense. The authors gratefully acknowledge the valuable help, advice and criticism obtained from Dr. Kurt Törnqvist of that Board. The data also appear, in another context, in "The Bärseback panic: A radio program as a negative event." Acta Sociologica, 1975, 18(4): 303-321.*

INTRODUCTION

It is hardly any exaggeration to say that the news media live on, off, and for deviance. News reports to a large extent deal with concrete cases of deviance from generally shared norms and values. The overall picture of the world offered by the news media, therefore, may be said to be distorted, in spite of the fact that the individual reports more often than not seem to be quite correct or "true" (Marshall, 1977; Singletary and Lipsky, 1977).

Sometimes, however, the news media themselves deviate from what must be their own primary value: truth. In such cases, the public is very defenseless, because it lacks independent data from outside the media—"extra media data" (Rosengren, 1970, 1976, 1977; Katz, 1977:92)—with which to control the picture offered by the media. Such data are not easily available. This is a report about a case when it was possible to produce such extra media data, thereby demonstrating that the reports of the media were simply not true. It was also possible by means of the same extra media data to outline some causes and consequences of the media deviance, and to put that deviance within the framework of sociological theory. Finally, we looked at the behavior of the media when the results of the investigation were published.

THE BACKGROUND

According to press reports, Orson Welles' famous broadcast in 1938, *The War of the Worlds,* featuring an invasion from Mars, caused a "tidal wave of terror that swept the nation." The picture of widespread panic was elaborated by a classic investigation of the public reaction to the program, Cantril's *The Invasion from Mars* (1940, 1947). Cantril's main results, however, hardly bear out such an interpretation: 12% of the adult population listened to the program, 28% of the listeners believed the broadcast was a news bulletin, and 70% of those who misunderstood the program were frightened or disturbed. That is, some 2% of the adult population were excited by the program (Cantril, 1947:57-58).

No quantitative information about the amount of actual panic reactions is given, but anecdotal material from a purposive sample and from newspaper clippings conveys an impression of widespread panic reactions. This is also the way in which the program and the public reactions to it have lived on in memory and research.

There are, however, other conceptions about typical behavior under the influence of real or imagined disasters. Quarantelli (1960:58), for instance, denies the validity of what he calls the "panic image," characterized by "highly disorganized flight by hysterical individuals who have stampeded at the sight of actual or potential danger." Quarantelli's standpoint, based on years of disaster research, receives support from research on "hysterical contagion," e.g., Kerckoff et al, (1965) and Lemkau (1973).

There are, then, two diametrically different views about panic behavior in disaster. Grossly simplified: panic occurs, or it does not. The term "panic" may refer to an individual phenomenon (Guten and Allen 1972) or to a mass phenomenon. The latter is a special case of collective behavior, characterized by lacking social norms and relationships (ef. Brown, 1968:709; Weller and Quarantelli, 1973). Individual panic—impulsive, frantic, partly uncontrolled behavior—tends to occur when the individual

(a) perceives a strong threat toward his own existence;
(b) sees a possibility to escape; or
(c) believes that this possibility is soon to disappear.

If the three conditions are at hand for many individuals at the same time, many cases of individual panic may occur, sometimes so many that it may appear adequate to talk about mass panic.

A common way in which the escape possibility may disappear is that

(d)   this possibility does not appear sufficient for all those who want to use it.

If (d) is at hand, a special form of mass panic could occur, with ruthless and senseless fight for the scarce resource of escape. Brown (1968:743) calls this form of mass panic "escape panic," but a better term might be "escape panic struggle," to distinguish it from other forms of mass escape panics not characterized by intense struggle for the vanishing possibility of escape.

The somewhat unclear difference between Quarantelli and Cantril-Rosow-Schramm may now be expressed like this: in disasters (real or imagined), do cases of individual panic which are likely to occur grow into mass panics (or even into escape panic struggles), or do they tend to remain isolated cases, sooner or later to be taken care of by means of various informal mechanisms of social control?

Recently, an opportunity arose to test the two conflicting views about panic on a Swedish case of public behavior in a fictitious disaster. On November 13, 1973, the Swedish radio broadcast a fictitious news program about a future accident at Barsebäck, a nuclear power station then under construction in southern Sweden. The accident was said to take place in 1982. Through a fault in the cooling system, leakage was said to occur, and according to the fiction, radioactive stuff was carried southwards by the winds and also over the Sound toward (15 miles distant) Copenhagen in Denmark.

The producers of the program had regarded the fictitious bulletin—11 minutes in length—only as a means of catching the public's interest for a discussion about the future risks connected with nuclear energy. The program contained some realistic features: ambulance sirens, authentic program signals, and well-known radio voices. But before and after the program, it was explicitly said that the whole thing was fictional. Quite unexpectedly, it was mistaken for a real news bulletin by a substantial proportion of its public.

Within an hour, broadcast media reported widespread panic reactions in southern Sweden, and the next day, newspapers carried page-wide headlines on the panic. The program and the public's reactions gave rise to an extensive and lively debate in the mass media. Debates in the media, in political bodies and among the public were based mainly on the media image of widespread panic. This image was never seriously questioned, neither by the media, nor by anyone else.

At the request of the Swedish Board of Psychological Defense, an investigation was carried out, consisting of a survey among the population in the area, a qualitative content analysis of the mass media reports, and unstructured interviews with "victims" of the program, as well as with journalists, police and other key persons in the area (Rosengren et al., 1974 a, b: Göransson and Ruhnbro, 1973).

The results of this survey will be presented; then mass media reports of the public reactions will be analyzed. A comparison between the picture offered by the media and the results of the survey will be undertaken, and certain discrepancies will be found and discussed, inter alia in terms of the two conflicting research traditions outlined above. The outcome of the comparisons will be discussed against the background of a more general sociological frame of reference. Finally, some reactions from the media to the report of the investigation will be discussed briefly.

THE PUBLIC'S REACTION

The population of three municipalities in the area were selected for study: Löddeköpinge (the municipality in which the Barsebäck power station is situated), Lund, and Staffanstorp, a community with a population structure somewhat similar to that of Löddeköpinge (to a large extent white-collar commuters to the nearby cities of Malmö and Lund). Löddeköpinge has some 4,000 inhabitants, Lund and Staffanstorp some 59,000 and 13,000 respectively. From Barsebäck to Lund and Staffanstrop there are some 10 and 12 miles, respectively. Between Lund and Staffanstorp there about 6 miles. The Malmö-Lund area has some 400,000 inhabitants.

Two random samples of the population aged 15-79 were drawn from the population registers of each of the three municipalities. Each sample consisted of some 200 people; in all we approached some 1,200 individuals. Members of the first two samples were extensively interviewed regardless of whether they had listened to the program or not; in the second sample, only listeners were extensively interviewed. We used telephone interviews, complemented with questionnaires mailed to refusals and those we could not reach by telephone.

The period of data collection, then, started three and a half weeks, and ended 11 weeks, after the fictitious broadcast of the future atomic disaster. The bulk of the material—66% of the original sample—was

collected by December 21, when the telephone interviews were ter-
minated—five weeks after the event. The mail questionnaires contributed
another 23 percentage points, so that the total response rate was 89%.

Extensive comparisons between respondents and nonrespondents, as
well as between interviews and mail questionnaires, showed that the
material obtained was representative for the population of the three
municipalities, and that for all practical purposes, the answers obtained
by means of the two data-gathering techniques were comparable.

We had expected that the respondents would be somewhat reluctant to
admit that they had been taken in by the fictitious program, but our
definitive impression is that this was not the case at all. The widespread
publicity the incident had received probably had washed away any such
feelings. A more common reaction was anger directed toward the
producers and the medium.

The data are presented separately for each of the three municipalities,
and also for the municipalities combined. In the latter case the data are
weighted according to the differential sample proportions necessitated by
the differential sizes of the three municipalities.

Table 1. THE PUBLIC'S REACTIONS TO THE FICTITIOUS PROGRAM IN THREE MUNICIPALITIES IN SOUTHERN SWEDEN

Municipality	%	N	5	N	5	N	5	N
Loddekopinge	24	(335)	52	(86)	78	(45)	20	(35)
Lund	18	(363)	47	(66)	71	(31)	14	(22)
Staffanstorp	23	(371)	45	(85)	79	(38)	13	(30)
WEIGHTED TOTAL	19	(1089)	47	(237)	73	(114)	14	(87)

The bases of the percentages are given within brackets. These bases are obtained from the
column ot the left of the column in question. Thus, in Lund, 18% of 363 respondents had
listened to the program. This gives us 66 listeners in Lund, the base for column 2, in the case
of Lund. The percentages have been rounded off to the nearest integer. Two definitions of
"misunderstanding" have been used in the investigation, a narrow one and a broad one. The
former is used in this table (Table 2A and B).

The main results of the survey are summarily presented in Table 1. It
appears that in the area investigated, some 20% of the adult population
had listened to the program. About every second listener misunderstood
the program (every fifth till the end of the program). About 70% of those
who misunderstood were frightened or disturbed. Some 15% of the
frightened listeners also reacted behaviorally in one way or another. That

is, some 10% of the adult population in the area misunderstood the program, 7-8% were frightened, and about 1% reacted behaviorally to it.

In most cases the fear aroused by the misunderstanding was rather mild and of short duration. But in some cases it was said to have had effects lasting for hours (headaches etc.). The "behavioral reactions" to the program as a rule consisted of contacting family members, or others. Other reactions were to close windows, think over what to bring along in case of a possible evacuation, etc.

In spite of these results, the Swedish program must be considered a worthy rival to that of Orson Welles: 50% of the listeners misunderstood versus 28%; 7-8% of the population excited, versus 2% in the American case. Against the background of such data, it is all the more interesting to note that we did not find one single case of panic flight among our 1,089 respondents.

Three clusters of variables determine the amount of misunderstanding and connected reactions in a case like this: characteristics of the program, the situation at large, and the distribution of the population over certain key variables.

As to the situation at large, it is always possible to find more or less plausible a posteriori explanations. Cantril and his associates (1947: 153.) mentioned such factors as the economic and political strains of the late 1930s, presumably making large segments of the public prone to believe in an invasion from Mars. In our case we might point to an assumed widespread uneasiness about energy problems in general and nuclear problems in particular, increased by the October war in the Middle East and the oil crisis.

As to characteristics of the program, we did ask the subjects misunderstanding it what factors they thought had caused the misunderstanding. Realistic features such as ambulance sirens etc, were mentioned by 26% of those having misunderstood the program, 20% mentioned the fact that well-known radio voices were heard. Data such as these, however, tell us about *perceived* causative agents, not what factors in the program actually caused half of its public to misunderstand it.

When it comes to characteristics of the individual listener, we are on somewhat safer ground. A number of two- and three-dimensional cross-tabulations of individual characteristics against the dependent variable of misunderstanding the program or not were carried out. (In these tabulations we used two definitions of misunderstanding, a broad and a narrow one. The broad definition includes listeners who were doubtful for only a short moment; the narrow does not. As it turned out the two definitions gave much the same results. Tables 1 and 2A are both based on the narrow definition of understanding, while—for comparative purposes—Table 2B is based on the broad definition.)

Contrary to our expectations, the *social position* of the individual listener seems to have exerted only a slight influence on the way the program was perceived. Variables such as sex, education, social class etc. resulted in only small and inconsistent differences in the amount of misunderstanding. *Attitudes* toward mass media and nuclear energy had even less impact. *Knowledge* about the Swedish nuclear program had some effect, and especially so knowledge about whether the Barsebäck power station was in operation or not. Beside the latter, the most powerful single predictor variable of how the program was perceived was the *listening situation*. Those who tuned in the program after its beginning misunderstood it to a much higher degree than did those who listened right from the beginning.

Table 2. PERCENT MISUNDERSTANDING, LISTENING SITUATION, AND KNOWLEDGE ABOUT THE BARSEBACK POWER STATION.*

2A. Narrow Definition of Misunderstanding.

		Tuned in From the beginning		After beginning		TOTAL	
Knew Barseback	No	38%	(14)	82%	(58)	72%	(72)
not running yet	Yes	20%	(53)	39%	(105)	34%	(158)
TOTAL		26%	(67)	55%	(163)	48%	(230)

2B. Broad Definition of Misunderstanding

		Tuned in From the beginning		After beginning		TOTAL	
Knew Barseback	No	38%	(14)	97%	(58)	84%	(72)
not running yet	Yes	26%	(53)	72%	(105)	59%	(158)
TOTAL		30%	(67)	82%	(163)	68%	(230)

*Percentages weighted with respect to sampling proportion from the three communities. The bases of the percentages are within brackets. Broad definition of misunderstanding includes these doubtful for only a moment.

Tables 2A and 2B demonstrate the influence of the two most powerful independent variables. More than 80% of the less knowledgable listeners tuning in after the program had started misunderstood it, while it was misunderstood by only 20% of the knowledgable listeners who listened from the beginning.

Table 2A is based on the narrow definition of misunderstanding. Table 2B is an exact parallel of Table 2A, but based on the broad definition. The percentages of Table 2B are somewhat higher than those of 2A, just as they should be. It will be seen that the relationship between the three variables under study remains more or less intact.

In the lower right cells of the two fourfold tables, we find those individuals who tuned in after the program had started but who knew that the Barsebäck power station was not yet operative. A comparison between the two tables tells us that most of these respondents misunderstood the program according to the broad definition, but not according to the narrow one. That is, they were taken in for a short moment, but internal reference to their stock of knowledge told them that this could not be so.

Therefore, the proportion misunderstanding the program in this cell of the table sinks from 72% to 39% as we move from Table 2B to Table 2A. For those without this internal reservoir of knowledge, however, there seems to have been no correspondingly effective, external means of checking.

The data presented on the last few pages tell us that the listening situation did not function only as a filter for strong influences from social position, knowledge and attitudes. It also had an influence of its own, as can be seen from comparisons between columns, within rows of Tables 2A and 2B. The influence from social position, contrary to our expectations, turned out to be weak and inconsistent. Nor did attitudes toward mass media and nuclear energy have much of an influence. But knowledge was an important factor.

As far as they take us, Cantril's data offer much the same picture as ours. It is true that social position (especially economic status and education) seems to have exerted a somewhat stronger influence in the American case than in the Swedish one (Cantril, 1947:113). However, time of tuning in had a dominating influence in the interpretation of the Mars program, just as with the Barsebäck program (Cantril 1947:78).

Tables 2A and 2B provide us with some important information about the factors behind the differential interpretation of the program by different categories among its public. Now, let us turn to the consequences of the misunderstanding, behavioral and emotional. The number of behavioral reactions is so small in our material that it is not possible to look for causes of this type of reaction.

Only sex and place of living seem to have exerted some influence on the proportion of emotional reactions to the program, but even these results were rather inconclusive. It seems safe to conclude that emotional reactions to the misinterpreted program were socially determined to a much less extent than was the misunderstanding itself. Rather, the emotional reactions seem to have been basically human.

After all, if you have the impression that a serious nuclear disaster is developing in your close vicinity, it is only natural that you should be afraid. What needs explanation is that 30% reported misunderstanding the program without being afraid. Perhaps the misunderstanding was of such a short duration as to prevent any serious reflection on the possible consequences for the individual.

We interviewed in an unstructured way a relatively large number of key people in the area: policemen, shopkeepers, firemen, etc. Some of these told us about rumors of panic reactions, but no one had seen any panic with his own eyes, nor could anyone mention anybody who had seen any panic. We think that this result—in combination with our survey results—warrants the conclusion that what panic may have occurred as a result of the fictitious radio program must have been very unusual, if not virtually nonexistent.

However, when interviewing another key category—operators of telephone exchanges of police and mass media in the area—we did find evidence of some reactions. All in all, several hundred telephone calls must have gone to the police and the mass media in the area.

The callers either sought information or advice or—more often—wanted to vent anger at the program having deceived them or some member of their family. Still other calls came from people living in other parts of the country, wishing further details of the "event," since they had relatives living in the area.

THE MEDIA REPORTS

The mass media covered the Barsebäck incident extensively. We undertook a qualitative content analysis of the national newspapers published in the three large cities of Sweden (Stockholm, Gothenburg and Malmö), and also of two local and regional papers published in the nearby cities of Landskrona and Helsingborg.

Most of the journalists' instantaneous beliefs and opinions about what had happened were based on telephone calls from the public directed toward the mass media and the police. Key roles in this connection were played by the local radio station at Malmö and the police stations at Malmö and nearby Lund.

The journalists at the radio station were alerted by a sub-editor at a regional newspaper, who in turn had been called up by a friend living at Barsebäck who had seriously misinterpreted the program. For a moment the sub-editor, too, had believed a disaster had occurred. Very soon the radio people got their own calls from the public, relayed to them by bewildered exchange operators. Within an hour they would have their regional afternoon news bulletin on the air. Time did not permit any control at Barsebäck, but the agitated telephone callers were real enough, and some telephone controls were undertaken with, for instance, the police of Malmö and Lund.

At the Lund police station, a weeping woman was the first to call. She and her father took their turns at the telephone, and both of them were convinced something terrible had happened. Other calls of much the same nature followed. The policemen at the phone had received no prior information and did not know what to tell the callers. However, they soon got better information and could deny that there had been any catastrophe. Then the reporters from, radio, newspapers and television started calling. Under the circumstances, the policemen could only confirm that they, too, had received many calls. They also relayed the content of some of the more bizarre calls they had received. So did the Malmö police.

By now, time was running out for the journalist responsible for the report from the Malmö radio. He knew he would be the first to report on the event. He may have been doubtful for a time. Panic or no panic? But after the calls to the police, he hardly had any choice. Panic was the main theme of his message; panic in a whole country, perhaps two.

After an hour of hectic journalistic work, the situation had been defined. The panic picture was on its way, and it would prove to be a viable one. It was now 6:20 p.m. Within little more than an hour the broadcast media had five national and regional news programs scheduled on radio and television. In every one, a prominent place was given to the Barsebäck panic, as it was now called. Next to nothing was detracted from the original regional news bulletin. In some cases, further vivid and bizarre details were added. During the same hour, the national news agency distributed their reports, based mainly on the regional bulletin. Not until 10 p.m.—five hours after the fictitious disaster program had been broadcast—did the first eyewitness reports from Barsebäck get through. No panic had been found in Barsebäck, but for the surrounding communities the panic picture was reinforced by repeating the old tales from the first regional news bulletin.

All in all, the reports of the mass media may be summarized thus:

(1) Many people were scared by the fictitious program.
(2) For a considerable period of time, an unspecified but presumably large number of telephone exchanges of police and fire stations, as well as those of hospitals and the mass media were jammed by telephone calls from a large number of agitated people.
(3) Panic reactions of various kinds occurrred to a large extent and at several places in the area.

This was the socially accepted picture of reality upon which editoralists, radio critics, experts, authorities and opinion leaders at large now had to comment. It was never seriously questioned. On the contrary, it was explicitly taken for granted and embroidered upon.

Given this conception of what had happened, the comments of the mass media must be considered fairly moderate. The program was condemned without exception. Explanations of the reported panic phenomenon were sought in lack of information, the situation at large, lack of psychological balance, etc. Reduced confidence in the radio, and consequent damages to the Swedish psychological defense, were mentioned as possible consequences of the incident.

The matter was also discussed in Parliament, and the Minister for Culture and Education was questioned by two MPs from different opposition parties whether he was planning any measures to prevent the same thing from happening once more? The Radio Council ruled that it did not approve of the form of the program, but refuted the objections made against its balance and objectivity.

Two things are common to all or most of the rather diverse comments being made to the incident. First, the panic picture was never seriously questioned; rather, it formed a starting-point readily taken for granted by the commentators. Second, most of the comments were made to a purpose by more or less obvious spokesmen for various interest groups— politicians, administrators, businessmen, technicians, researchers, proponents and opponents of nuclear energy.

COMPARISON BETWEEN MEDIA PICTURE AND SURVEY DATA

The media reports and results of the survey, as well as related, more qualitative data, have been presented in the two previous sections. In Table 3 the two sets of data are confronted with each other.

Table 3 brings to the fore some general differences between data from survey research and mass media reports. The former are precise and quantitative, the latter vague and qualitative or quasi-quantative, and sometimes downright contradictory.

Table 3.
SURVEY DATA VERSUS MEDIA PICTURE

	Survey Data	Media Picture
Misunderstood the program	10% of population in the area.	Many.
Behavioral reactions	1% of population. in most cases contact with family, neighbors, etc. No escape panic.	Widespread escape panics.
Authorities, organizations etc.	Short excitement, two telephone exchanges fammed for a short time.	Great and lasting bewilder-ment, many important telephone exchanges jammed for consider-able time.

On the basis of Table 3 and other, more detailed comparisons made possible by the two independent sets of intra- and extra-media data (Rosengren 1970, 1977), we conclude that the mass media

(1) Exaggerated the extension of strong reactions of fear and anger;
(2) Exaggerated the extent of telephone calls to various public organs, as well as the number of telephone exchanges jammed, and the length of the jamming; and
(3) Very much exaggerated or even invented the public flight reactions.

The outcome of the comparison provides additional evidence when we want to choose between the two conflicting conceptions of panic behavior in actual or imagined disaster-situations represented by Quarantelli and by Cantril-Rosow-Schramm earlier in this paper. Here is another case where, according to stereotyped opinion, mass panic should occur. And occur it did—but only in the media reports. In reality, the behavioral reactions were rather mild, and they only comprised a small fraction of the population in the area (about 1%). The outcome, then, is in agreement with Quarantelli's perspective, but the media reports are rather similar to the conceptions vaguely embraced by Cantril, Rosow, and Schramm.

We take this result to indicate that in the actual or imagined disasters, there is one type of behavior that tends to occur in reality, and another that may be characterized as a stereotype, embraced by various segments of our culture—researchers and journalists alike. This stereotype probably is an important factor behind the exaggerated reports of the press often found in cases like the one under study (Quarantelli, 1960:70).

The argument may be expressed in terms of the "hierarchy of assistance seeking" established by Rosow (as quoted by Quarantelli, 1960:74). There are five levels in this hierarchy:

(1) family and intimates,
(2) place of work, church, familiar shops, etc.,
(3) aquaintances,
(4) radio stations, police, newspapers, etc., and
(5) disaster organizations.

The dividing line between on one hand levels (1)-(3), and on the other levels (4)-(5) is an important one from theoretical as well as practical points of view. When a certain number of disaster reactions have reached this sphere, authorities cannot but act in one way or another, regardless of the actual nature of the disaster. Of crucial importance in this connection are two circumstances, which in the case under study do not seem to have been quite clear to the agencies involved:

(1) A tiny fraction of a large population—even less than a tenth of a percent—may amount to quite impressive absolute numbers, especially when put in relation to the relatively limited input channels of, say, police and mass media.
(2) The individuals approaching police and mass media in a case of actual or imagined disaster are those for whom the earlier levels of the assistance seeking hierarchy have either failed, not been used, or not been available. These individuals, then, tend to be much more excited than the average member of the population (who has either had no need for any assistance hierarchy at all, or has received adequate response at lower levels of that hierarchy).

In combination, the two circumstances tend to result in a concentration of atypical and relatively infrequent reactions in sometimes fairly large absolute numbers at an important level of the assistance hierarchy: the level where privacy ends and the public sphere of society begins. What may be a small proportion of atypical cases tends to appear to the journalists as a large number of genuine reactions.

Under heavy time pressure, the journalists have to define loosely structured situations and present them in a meaningful way to the public. To solve their difficult task, they cooperate, of course, drawing on the technical and human resources at their disposition by their news organization. But under certain conditions this very process of cooperation may function much as a rumor generator.

The processes reviewed so far are those causing the journalists to misperceive the situation against their will, as it were. To these factors must be added strong elements in the journalists' professional training, inducing them to seek, report and stress deviance, the unique and sensational aspects of social life. It is only too evident that these elements of the journalistic professionalization offer a fertile seedbed in cases like the one under study. In their search for the deviant case, the journalists themselves are always tempted to deviate.

We find in our material instances where there is small doubt that the distinction between on one hand isolated cases of intense reactions, and, on the other, mass panic has been consciously blurred. Even cases where the line between the fiction of the program and the presumed reality of the actual news reports have been deliberately neglected, do occur.

But there are other elements in the professional training of the journalists, inducing them, on the contrary, to tell the truth, to control statements of sources, etc. Why did these forces not operate? They did operate sometimes, but circumstances were not favorable to them. The time for control was rather short for the team behind the very first report of the incident, the one broadcast over the regional radio. Here, time did hardly permit on the spot controls. Furthermore, it so happened that the police, too, had been a victim of the mechanisms just described. Temporarily, at least, they seem to have misperceived the situation as much as the journalists, taking the atypical calls for indicators of widespread panic.

Next we shall turn the focus from the specific mechanisms of the cases at hand to regard instead the incident against the background of a somewhat broader frame of reference.

THEORETICAL INTERPRETATION OF THE RESULTS

In this section, the Barsebäck incident will be regarded in the light of theories and concepts developed by Merton (1957), Boorstin (1961) and van Gennep (1960). Drawing upon and combining these theoretical arguments, we hope to arrive at a deeper understanding of the event.

Merton's notion of "trained incapacity" (Merton, 1957:197) may be applied also to the profession of journalism. Tuchman (1973) among others has shown that the news media may be regarded to advantage as bureaucracies established to process in a routine manner events which are—in detail, at least—unpredictable. The news media have been successful in this; so successful, indeed, that they have often been criticized for being oriented too exclusively toward events. The capacity to handle events seems to have brought about a trained incapacity to handle structures and slow processes of a macro character. We think that one way of circumventing this difficulty may be to apply a combination of van Gennep's (1960) and Boorstin's (1961) key concepts.

In his fascinating study of the rites of passage, van Gennep (1909) discusses season ceremonies used to mark, for instance, the transition from summer to autumn. Common to season ceremonies and passage rites proper is the function of turning a sometimes almost imperceptible process into a socially manageable event.

Boorstin (1961:11) has defined a pseudo-event as an event staged in order to be reported in the news media. Some pseudo-events could be regarded to advantage as functional equivalents, in a society of electronic media, to the primordial rites of passage found in technologically less advanced societies (as well as in our own). The function common to "legitimate pseudo-events" and to rites of passage is their capacity to turn processes into events. Since pseudo-events have come to connote something rather shoddy, another term should be found to denote such legitimate pseudo-events. Funkhouser (1973:73) suggests "event summary" for a different, but related phenomenon; we feel that the term "summary event" covers the phenomenon.

In some cases, "summary events" are already consciously and successfully used to overcome the trained incapacity of journalists ot report on structures and slow processes. In other cases, the proper social invention is still waiting for its ingenious inventor to step forward.

Trying to find out which summary events have already been invented, it appears that very often they are events staged to summarize positive or functional processes or structures. As a matter of fact, there seems to be a whole host of institutionalized summary events, the function of which are to focus the attention of the environment, including that of the mass media, on slow positive processes, good and lasting structures, happy states of affairs: inaugurations, anniversaries, jubilees, expositions, etc. Summary events connected with negative, slow processes of bad states of affairs seem to be somewhat less frequent, and also less socially accepted. They have not always been institutionalized. At the same time there seems to be a growing need for such "negative summary events."

We have also seen attempts to create new institutionalized summary events: sit-ins, teach-ins, etc. Just as when in the past, the now institionalized types of negative summary events were turning up for the first time (workers' demonstrations, etc.), these new forms of collective behavior have a tendency to be somewhat unstable; sometimes they run out of control, turning into violent conflicts, brutal police attacks, etc. They are seen as collective deviant behavior and often treated as such by society. All the same, such institutionalized negative summary events are much to be preferred to the nightmarish scenes of panics, riots, excesses, and abuses which might follow if the institutionalized warning signals were not there to be heeded by those in responsible positions (Dreistadt, 1072).

We think that the Barsebäck incident may be seen in the light of the above arguments. The originators of the fictional news program were, in fact, intuitively groping for a negative summary event, highlighting the possibly increasing risks for nuclear fall-out, accidents, and disasters of one type or another. Their intentions were the very best, but their solution could have been more prudent. The fictitious disaster fit in only too well with an established pattern of news reporting. (Disasters tend to be first reported in radio.) The program was misunderstood by some of its listeners, and a tiny proportion of the population reacted by calling up the police and the mass media. In the hands of the journalists with their trained incapacity to perceive the world in terms other than those of sudden and unpredictable events, this was enough to create a sensation: the "panic" of Barsebäck.

Paradoxically, the originators of the program succeeded by failing. There was, at last, a certain revitalization of the debate on nuclear energy. It was a healthy debate, perhaps, but its foundations were somewhat shaky: a fictitious disaster, a fabricated panic. Again, Thomas and Thomas (1928:572) were right. The disaster and the panic were defined as real, and consequently they had real effects.

The lessons to be learnt from the Barsebäck incident are several and diverse. They range from (1) broad generalizations, to (2) doubts on a classic, to (3) specific recommendations. Here are some:

(1)   There seems to exist a widespread but not very accurate stereotype about mass panic in situations of real or imagined disasters.

(2)   This stereotype may have influenced the shape of a classic investigation in the area, Cantril's *The Invasion from Mars*, and also the way this classic has been interpreted and reshaped in scientific and popular tradition.

(3a) Because the stereotype seems to be embraced by many journalists also, mass media reports about panic reactions should be received with scepticism.

(3b) Fictional news programs about disasters should be avoided. Quantitative data show that they are easily misunderstood.

The most important lessons, however, are more general. The search for institutionalized, socially accepted negative summary events should be intensified. Society must be careful not to mistake new types of negative summary events for "ordinary" deviant behavior. Also, the media must be able to see through the paraphernalia of new summary events to the real message.

EPILOGUE

When the report of the investigation was published by the Swedish Board of Psychological Defense, next to nothing happened. The newspapers dutifully published the press release—but in their back sections. The local radio station arranged a debate, and some columnists cracked a joke or two about sociologists unable to see what so many journalists had been able to see. The rest was silence. The fact that the whole Swedish news system had been proved misleading in an important test case was not publicly recognized.

Then the angry authors wrote an article in the leading Swedish quality newspaper, calling the journalists by various names. This time TV reacted, and in two one-hour programs on prime time the débâcle of the news media was made fairly clear to the public.

Half a year after the publication of the report, the *Journalisten,* the journal of the Swedish Journalists' Union, asked the radio and TV news editor responsible for the first broadcast reports about the alleged panic, as well as eight editors of leading newspapers—all having given a misleading picture of the "panic"—whether they had discussed the matter with their staff or taken any steps to prevent similar mistakes in the future? Only TV had done something about it, establishing an internal handbook for controls to be undertaken in similar exigencies. Seven editors denied that their newspapers had made any mistakes, although they admitted that other newspapers might have failed. One editor did not know—he was in America at the time.

It would seem, then, that media deviance is as hard to admit as other deviance, or harder. It is interesting to note, however, that the only news desk to do anything at all to prevent similar mistakes in the future was a

TV desk. Swedish broadcast journalists tend to be younger and better educated than their counterparts in the press. This fact did not help the broadcast journalists when it came to the question of panic reporting itself, but it may have exerted a contributing influence in making them more open to criticism and suggestions from the outside.

REFERENCES

BOORSTIN, D.J. (1961). The image. London: Weidenfeld and Nicholson.
BROWN, R. (1968). Social psychology. New York: Free Press.
CANTRIL, H. (1947, 1940). The invation from Mars. Princeton: Princeton University Press.
DREISTADT, R. (1972). "A unifying theory of dreams, a new theory of nightmares, and the relationship of nightmares to psychopathology, literature, and collective social panic behavior." Psychology, 9 (4):19-30.
FUNKHOUSER, G.R. (1973). "The issues of the sixties: An exploratory study in the dynamics of public opinion." Public Opinion Quarterly, 37 (1):62-91.
GENNEP, A.V. (1960). The rites of passage. London: Routledge & Kegan Paul.
GORRANSSON, L., and RUHNBRO, C. (1973). Karnkraften. Ett informations-problem. Belyst med ett aktuelt exempel: Barseback olyckan. University of Lund (mimeo).
GUTEN, S., and ALLEN, V.L. (1972). "Likelihood of escape, likelihood of danger, and panic behavior." Journal of Social Psychology, 87 (2):29-36.
KATZ, E. (1977). Social research on broadcasting: Proposals for further development. London: BBC.
KERCKHOFF, A.C., BACK, K.W., and MILLER, N. (1965). "Sociometric patterns in hysterical contagion." Sociometry, 28 (1):2-15.
LEMKAU, P.V. (1973). "On the epidemiology of hysteria." Psychiatric Forum, 3(2):2-14.
MARSHALL, H. (1977). "Newspaper accuracy in Tucson." Journalism Quarterly, 54(2):165-168.
MERTON, R.K. (1957). Social theory and social structure. Glencoe: Free Press.
QUARANTELLI, E.L. (1960). "Images of withdrawal behavior in disasters: Some basic misconceptions." Social Problems, 8(1):68-79.
ROSENGRAN, K.E. (1970). "International news: Intra and extra media data." Acta Sociologica, 13 (2):96-109.
        et al. (1974b). Katasrofen i Barseback. En fingerad nyhetssandning och dess foljder. Appendices. Psykologiskt Forsvar No. 66. Stockholm: Beredskepsnamnden for psykologiskt forsvar.
        et al. (1974a). Katasrofen i Barseback. En fingerad nyhetssandnung och dess foljder. Stockholm: Allmanna Forlaget.
        (1976). "International news: Four types of tables." Journal of Communication, 27 (1):67-75.
        (1977). "Bias in news: Methods and concepts." Paper presented to the Mass Communication Division, ICA Convention, Berlin, May 29-June 4.
ROSOW, I. (1973). "The social context of the aging self." The Gerontologist, 1 (1):82-87.

SCHRAMM, W. (1973). Men, messages, and media: A look at human communication. New York: Harper & Row.

SHIBUTANI, T. (1968). "Rumor," In D.L. Sills (ed.), International encyclopedia of the social sciences. New York: MacMillan.

SINGLETARY, M.W., and LIPSKY, R. (1977). "Accuracy in local TV news." Journalism Quarterly, 54 (1):362-364.

THOMAS, W.I., and THOMAS, D.S. (1928). The child in America. New York: Alfred A. Knopf.

TUCHMAN, G. (1973). "Making news by doing work: Routinizing the unexpected." American Journal of Sociology, 79 (1):110-131.

WELLER, J.M., and QUARANTELLI, E.L. (1973). "Neglected characteristics of collective behavior." American Journal of Sociology, 79 (3):665-685.

Comparative
Studies

Part 3

Part 2

THE CASE OF RAPE
Legal Restrictions on Media Coverage of Deviance in England and America

GILBERT GEIS

AUTHOR'S NOTE: *I want thank the National Center for the Prevention and Control of Rape, National Institute of Mental Health, for a grant (MH 28868) which made possible the research upon which this chapter is based, and the Institute of Criminology, Cambridge University, for providing working facilities.*

Legal restrictions on the press are much more prevalent in England than in the United States. This situation correlates (though by no means necessarily in a causal manner) with greater English concern with personal privacy, and with a rather low crime rate though one, particularly in regard to property offenses, that is beginning to rise considerably (Wilson, 1976). Conformity is accorded high social value in Britain, and class distinctions are pronounced (Runciman, 1966; Westergaard, 1976). In addition, as John Fowles (1977) has noted, the prototypical English person tends to hide emotions and to wear a public mask, a manner that can exasperate more ebullient outsiders. An American, noting the complacence with which the British generally accept inconveniences that his countrymen would not tolerate, was moved to observe caustically that "the English think incompetence is the same thing as sincerity" (Kilborn, 1977).

In the United States, the crime rate is high, privacy is relatively unprotected (most certainly for "public" figures), and there are great variations in life styles. The

American mass media, largely unencumbered by legal reins, are avid in their pursuit and dissemination of both the relevant and the prurient. The following vignette of the spiel of a guide conducting a tour of a newspaper office indicates the variant professional and popular faces of American mass media (Kanin and Kanin, 1958:2-3):

> And now we're coming to the city room. . . . Here you see a part of the twenty-five hundred highly trained specialists employed by the Evening Chronicle—editors, reporters, photographers who work tirelessly to make it possible for you to sit in your armchair and witness history in the making. Men and women who uphold the highest tradition of American journalism, who are dedicated only to the task of making you the best-informed newspaper reader on earth.
>
> At that instance, a copy boy came through with an armful of our latest edition right off the presses, and the headline screamed, HATCHET MURDERER SLAIN IN LOVE NEST.

Judges in Japan

In Japan, criminal court judges are agreeable to holding press conferences both before and during the course of a trial over which they are presiding. "At one of these conferences," Belli and Jones (1960:125) observe, "there may be as many as fifty reporters firing questions, television, radio, moving pictures and flash cameras." The carnival atmosphere of sessions such as these is aptly conveyed by way of Albert Einstein's (MacDonald, 1961:186) remark that the ideal news photographer should come from a very large family where the battle for nourishment and attention precludes any possibility of learning taste, sensitivity, or manners.

Japan, compared to the United States, has an extraordinarily low crime rate (Bayley, 1976); indeed, crime control is so effective that a postwar drug use epidemic was quickly excised (Geis, 1978a; Brill and Hirose, 1969), a goal that continues to evade other democracies. In Japan, the relatively unfettered approach to publicity regarding criminal deviance, juxtaposed to low Japanese crime rates, warns us to be wary of simple conclusions about the relationship between media practices and behavioral causes or consequences. But we can conclude that in at least one other country what American jurisprudents would regard as prejudicial and inflammatory publicity does not produce outraged indignation, whatever other impacts it may have.

The Soviet Approach

In the Soviet Union, contrary to Japan, an ethic of considerable sensitivity to the personal integrity and the right to privacy of persons is articulated as underlying media avoidance of stories about deviants and criminal offenders. The confidence of Russian people in the fairness of their criminal processes has never been systematically studied, though there are indications that they are not viewed in any better light, if as well, as similar proceedings in the United States (Feifer, 1964). The Soviet view is that, if a crime is highlighted, it is apt to become an "opiate" (or, perhaps, a cocaine-like stimulant) for the masses, deflecting attention from more important social, political, and economic matters. A Moscow Police Commissar (Arensky, 1956:11) with high self-righteousness, extols his country's media policy in the following terms: "We Russians are not accustomed to filling our newspapers with stories of personal tragedy or of the unhappy accidents that befall various individuals, nor are we interested in publicizing the passions of unfortunate men and women who are led to commit crime either because of their feelings or ambitions."

In Moscow, there is little hesitation about walking alone at night or letting small children play out of sight in parks. Evidence suggests (Shipler, 1978:1) that "some of the fearlessness stems from ignorance . . . because violence is rarely publicized . . . just as some of the fear in New York may be exaggerated by detailed reporting by radio, television, and the press." Key questions arise: What, if any, are the consequences of the Russian, the Japanese and other media policies in terms of crime rates, public attitudes, justice, social health and malaise, and similar outcomes? How, if at all, might such consequences be determined? We will return to these issues subsequently.

RAPE AND THE MASS MEDIA

General Considerations

The criminal offense of rape offers a particularly fruitful subject for examination in regard to legal restrictions on the mass media. Rape has received intense scrutiny in recent years, with leaders of the feminist movement denoting it as the "quintessential" (Brownmiller, 1975:49; Griffin, 1971:35) representation of male exploitation of women. The offense carries for the victim a heavy load of personal jeopardy, both physical and emotional (Russell, 1975). The violence in rape can be enormously fear-inspiring: victims interviewed by Burgess and Holstrom (1974) said that their major concern during the rape was not sexual, but was focused on the terrifying anticipation that they might be killed or maimed.

The sexual component in rape makes it a particularly sensitive event in a culture such as that of the United States with its puritan heritage. Wits may say that old folk today yearn for earlier times when the air was clean and sex dirty, but a more accurate statement would show continuing deep inhibitions and repressive and condemning attitudes toward sexual deviance within American society. Female virginity may no longer be the saleable commodity it once was (Thomas, 1959), but unrestrained sexual activity or untoward sexual experience, even as the innocent victim of male aggression, still implies soiling and damage. Perhaps the most prominent difficulty of women who have been raped is their inability to shed the idea that they themselves somehow were responsible for what happened to them: they blame the clothes they wore, their inattention to clues in the depredator's behavior, their failure to defend themselves more effectively.

For the offender also rape can carry considerable derogatory weight. In prisons persons sentenced for rape are regarded as low status inmates, subject to the scorn of those who have been incarcerated for more "manly" kinds of crimes, such as armed robbery, or more skillful exploits, such as perpetration of con games.

Feminist writers say that male anger at rapists derives from the outraged belief that rape represents an intrusion into their territory, and an impairment of goods and chattels that "belong" to them. An equally if not more persuasive explanation is that rape draws condemnation from males because it victimizes relatively helpless persons and invades areas of personal privacy in an ugly and despicable fashion. Successful seduction may rate high among achievements that men applaud in other men; but sex through employment of force is considered outside permissible limits. As sexual etiquette changes so that mutual attraction rather than (or in addition to) seduction becomes the password for sexual intercourse, rape moves even farther beyond the pale, being defined as a testament to failure in a situation in which most are believed readily able to succeed.

As a consequence, men who have much to lose in terms of rape accusations against them (public figures, in particular) sometimes believe themselves notably vulnerable to simulated charges of rape, and in a nervous way they seem to feel at the mercy of women they might offend in "innocent" ways. The mass media represent the vehicle by which masculine fears and fantasies of ruined reputation can be translated into reality. Important men can come to view the media as constituting a force that, if unchecked, might collude with women to "get" them. Because men control the power, both in the media world and in the legal realm, it is instructive to see what they have done and tried to do to forestall such possible threats.

The absence of a constitutional measure such as the First Amendment has allowed the British Parliament to impose restrictions more freely upon the press than is true in the United States. However, this provides only a partial explanation of the striking differences between the two countries. Another part may lie in nothing more profound than historical chance, so that an almost happenstance original event forms a precedent that inexorably leads to subsequent developments. The media clause of the First Amendment to the American Constitution is, after all, only a barebones provision: "Congress shall make no law . . . abridging the freedom . . . of the press." These skeletal words might readily have been interpreted to exclude from their reach the several states as well as the executive and judicial branches of the federal government. *Near v. Minnesota* (1913), the landmark Supreme Court ruling that enunciated the principle that no prior restraint could be imposed on publications, served to cement today's standards for freedom of the American press, and provided for the general (though not total) suzerainty of the first amendment press guarantees in their inevitable conflicts (see e.g., Simons and Califano, 1976) with other constitutional and statutory provisions—almost as if, by being first, the amendment was presumed to be ascendant over its followers.

In England, an early authoritarian monarchy seems to have left behind remnants of a spirit that supports the view that confidentiality of government processes and regard for personal privacy are of much greater significance than press liberty. Britain's Official Secrets Act is one of the the most restrictive provisions found in any democracy, and it stands in sharp contrast to the growing emphasis on freedom of information in the United States (Montgomery et al., 1978). As Sir William Haley (1974:11) has noted: " 'The right to know'—a phrase coined in America— is not yet an accepted British concept."It has truly been said (Graham, 1974) that had a scandal such as Watergate taken place in England (a situation, it needs emphasizing, that commentators uniformly regard as less likely to have occurred there than here), British newspapers early on would have been effectively restrained from unearthing and publicizing the kinds of materials that were to bring down the Nixon administration.

The element of personal restraint that characterizes British society might well, as noted earlier, provide a major clue to the country's more extensive restrictions on the press, though, at their worst, British newspapers, epitomized by *News of the World,* can be as or much more vulgar than American counterparts. While England has a good deal less crime than America, British interest in the gorier manifestations of the phenomenon, measured by things such as the Notable British Trials series and a coterie of best-selling mystery story writers, seems no less intense than that of Americans.

The English Judicial Proceedings Act of 1926 decreed that evidence in matrimonial cases, such as divorces, could no longer be reported, but only the names of the parties, the issues between them, and the summing up or judgement (Ginsberg, 1959:291). At about the same time, the British inaugurated an informal (but rigidly followed) court-media agreement to camouflage the identity of blackmail complainants (Hepworth, 1975). Newsworthy episodes of both types of actions—blackmail and sensational divorce cases—are much more likely (compared to street crimes) to involve prominent and "respectable" persons in potentially embarrassing situations. In a parallel way, the movement in the United States for legal recognition of a right to privacy (Warren and Brandeis, 1890) was motivated most fundamentally by a desire to shield the peccadilloes of the social leaders from more common ears and eyes in order to, according to one commentator, "elevate the moral standards of the masses" (Franklin, 1963:112).

Similarly, it was the trial of a person of some prominence that preceded the adoption in Britain of the law mandating that details of preliminary hearings were not to be published in the media. In 1957, Dr. John Bodkin Adams was acquitted on the charge of murdering one of his patients. At Adams' preliminary examination the prosecution had introduced widely reported evidence of circumstances in which two other patients had died. This material was not used at the trial (Bedford, 1961). Subsequently, an investigatory committee (Great Britain, 1958) recommended, and Parliament enacted, a law forbidding the reporting of the proceedings of preliminary examinations, though the hearings would remain open to the public (Geis, 1961).

Almost two decades later, when feminist pressures led to parliamentary review of the laws and procedures for dealing with the crime of rape, these British precedents would help greatly to bring about the extension of anonymity to rape trial personae. Degrees of secrecy prevailed in divorces, in blackmail cases, in juvenile delinquency proceedings, and in preliminary hearings, it was stressed, and no seeming meretricious consequences had ensued from such truncating of press and public information. Opponents said, of course, that if you also allowed the defendant and/or the complainant in rape cases to be shielded from media identification, there was no telling where it all might stop.

In the United States today, "gag" orders on the press are becoming more commonplace in regard to reporting of criminal episodes and criminal trials, though the appellate courts tend to view such orders with a jaundiced eye. On the contrary, in Britain, as Walter Gellhorn (1960) has observed, newspaper editors will be heavily fined and imprisoned for publishing stories about evidence that later may be introduced into a trial. A British judge, Sir Patrick Hastings (1954:75), sets forth the principles that prevail in the relationship between the media and the reporting of crime in his country:

> One of the most salutary principles of English justice bears the somewhat curious appelation of the rule against "contempt of court." Under that rule no one is permitted to interfere in the slightest with the administration of justice either civil or criminal. In some countries it is the practice to make a feature in the Press of forthcoming trials; opinions are expressed, and possibilities explored; the probable result is frequently anticipated; no doubt the Editor would justify his action as exemplifying the freedom of the press. In England an editor similarly engaged, would find himself within two or three days before the Royal Courts of Justice, and the only freedom he would enjoy would be during the comparatively short period before his removal to Brixton Prison.

A demand in rape cases is for protection from adverse publicity that is said to attach and to linger in a particularly destructive way around the persons of the participants. Unlike blackmail cases, in which many, if not most, of the complainants have engaged in deviant and perhaps criminal behavior, the parties to the rape episode may be totally innocent of wrongdoing, with the complainant a victim of a brutal sexual attack, or the defendant the object of a false accusation or a mistaken identification. Parallel circumstances might prevail in other forms of crime, of course, but rape has been singled out for judicial and legislative attention in regard to media coverage because of its presumably particularly scandalous character.

The "innocence" issue that differentiates rape from blackmail also distinguishes it from juvenile delinquency adjudications where both in the United States and Britain anonymity is typically provided for the charged youngster (Geis, 1958, 1962, 1965; Note, 1977). An assumption is made in delinquency cases that public identification may lead to further unfortunate labeling (Lemert, 1951), thereby hindering the ability of the delinquent to secure legitimate employment and to achieve community acceptance. It is presumed that such rebuffs ultimately are likely to push the offender toward further law violations. No persuasive empirical evidence supports this commonsense view, and it is not altogether unlikely that labeling also may have inhibitory consequences on wrong-doing and, though this seems less probable, may promote a determination to confound public opinion through the performance of praiseworthy acts. Most likely, diverse outcomes probably result from labeling in different proportion in any cohort of adjudicated delinquents.

For the rape victim, the assumption is that public broadcasting of her identity places her in further jeopardy, embarrasses her in later social interactions, inhibits her willingness initially to report the offense, and otherwise serves to harm her above and beyond the injury already criminally inflicted by her assaailant. These commonsense ideas, it needs noting, are no better supported by empirical data than those referring to the possible sequelae of identification of juvenile delinquents.

The foregoing, then, are some issues underlying public discussion and legislative and judicial action on media practices in regard to rape. The precise form that such actions have taken in the United States and in England will be indicated in the following sections of the chapter.

The United States

In the United States, the issue of rape gradually gained precedence on the feminist agenda for reform of the criminal justice.system. An early feminist foray into the issue of prostitution proved something of a standoff: feminists divided over whether the prostitute represented the truly liberated female, trading independently in the capitalist market-place, or whether she was symbolic of exploitative sexual relationships between all men and women. The crime of rape, however, clearly divided by sex into victim and victimizer categories: it was a prime subject for united feminist attention. Besides, gross and remediable inequities existed in the criminal justice system handling of rape offenses. The symbolic strength of rape reform is indicated by the rapid diffusion of the movement from the United States to societies where the problem—that is, the rate of rape—is only a small fraction of what it is in America, such as the Netherlands (Doomen, 1976), Norway (Lykkjen, 1976), and France (Fargier, 1976). The sexist nature of the preexisting criminal justice processes may be appreciated through the roster of recent juridical changes. Corroboration rules, the cautionary instruction (Geis, 1978b), and cross-examination inquiries into the complainant's sexual background all have fallen by the wayside. The exemption of husbands from charges of rape by their wives is being excised from the law (Geis, 1978), and forceful sexual acts other than vaginal penetration are being incorporated into rape statutes (Cobb and Schauer, 1974).

That the matter of the relationship between rape and the media did *not* become a problem in the United States, though it did in England, is noteworthy. Several explanations suggest themselves. First, many of the militant feminists in America writing about rape themselves were or had been practicing journalists, such as Susan Brownmiller, Susan Griffin, Nancy Gager, and Cathleen Schurr. As such, they were deeply indoctrinated into the American newsroom belief that news is what happens now (and not what is told retrospectively at the end of a criminal trial), and that the "who" of a news story is an essential element whose amputation would be lethal to the corpus. To challenge press sovereignty would be to commit heresy.

In addition, there is a well-established practice in the United States of media discretion in the publishing of the names of rape victims. Though Vicki McNickle Rose (1977:85) maintains that "[a]lthough victims' names can . . . be withheld voluntarily by the media, this possibility is unlikely," there is no doubt that many, perhaps most, American papers do not identify rape victims in crime stories. We also know that rape victims themselves, studied in depth and quoted at length in a very considerable literature, do not bring up media identification as an issue of concern. Sutherland and Scherl (1972) note that counseling should prepare victims for possible publicity, but victims testify to fear of the rapist, immobilization, hostility to the courts, self-guilt, and a plethora of other rape-associated conditions without including media attention among their problems (e.g., Burgess and Holstrom, 1974; Russell, 1975).

Lastly, though again satisfactory information is sparse, it seems apparent that the feminists, pressing for reform of rape laws, could not strategically afford to alienate the mass media in the United States by focusing upon an issue, such as law-imposed victim anonymity, that comes close to being blasphemy against a sacred media cause. Without media support, rape reforms (and feminist causes in general) would be much more lonesome and less rewarding social and personal enterprises than they have proven to be. In England, as we shall see, the press itself was not inhospitable to restrictions on identification of participants in rape trials; by espousing such a cause the feminists did not risk losing a powerful ally.

Although the feminist surge into the area of the crime of rape has not concerned itself in the United States with media identification of victims, there has been legislative and court activity on the subject over the years. It began with enactments by three states, South Carolina (1909), Georgia (1911), and Florida (1911), that prohibited publication of the names of rape victims. The Florida statute, similar to the other two, reads as follows (Fla. Stat. Annot. s. 974.03):

No person shall print, publish, or broadcast, or cause to be printed, published or broadcast, in any instrument of mass communication the name, address, or other identifying fact or information of the victim of any sexual offense.... An offense under this section shall constitute a misdemeanor of the second degree.

That all three states were southern may well testify to concern with identification of white victims of black rapists: miscegenous rape always has played a powerful role in defining the ingredients and parameters of the law of rape.

Wisconsin followed with a 1925 statute of the same nature as that of the southern triad, and it became the only one of the four enactments to be subjected to constitutional attack. The Chief Justice of the Wisconsin Supreme Court thought that the law was within the limits of legislative power, and pointed out that the first amendment does not protect all speech. He also found the following redeeming virtues in the law (State v. Evjue 1948:312):

[It protects] the victim from embarrassment and offensive publicity which no doubt have a strong tendency to affect her future standing in society. In addition to that it is a well-known fact that many crimes of the character described go unpunished because the victim of the assault is unwilling to face the publicity which would follow prosecution.

The Wisconsin ruling noted further that "there is a minimum of social value in the publication of the identity of a female in connection with such an outrage" and that disclosure of the information would only feed into a "morbid desire" to connect the criminal events with a specific person.

The Cox case (1975), however, ended the practice of forbidding media identification of rape victims when they are named in public records. A 15-year-old girl had become drunk at a party, was raped by six young men, and died thereafter. The boys were first charged with murder, but that allegation was dropped, largely because the death was regarded as inadvertent. Had the murder charge stood, no restrictions would have been placed on media identification of the victim though, had they been tried as juveniles, the offenders would not have been publicly identified. Eight months following the incident, during the trial of the defendants, a radio newscaster broadcast the victim's name. Her father recovered damages on the ground that, in violation of specific statutory injunction, the broadcasting corporation had invaded his privacy and caused him emotional distress. The award was upheld in the Georgia Supreme Court (Cox, 1973:134), where it was said:

> A majority of this court does not consider this statute to be in conflict with the First Amendment. We think the General Assembly of Georgia had a perfect right to declare that the victim of such a crime should not be publicly identified by the news media.

The U.S. Supreme Court thought otherwise, however. The Cox (1975) case represented for the Court its first encounter with the tension between the first amendment and a privacy action based on public disclosure of wholly accurate information (Note, 1975). The Court did not attend to the possible effect on the amount of rape which might be reported if anonymity prevailed, nor did it deal, even in passing, with the trauma of the raped girl's father. It merely indicated in its 8-1 ruling that "in this instance and in others reliance must rest upon the judgment of those who decided what to publish or broadcast" (Cox, 1975:496).

It is apparent that the Supreme Court wanted to define public records, such as court indictments, as open to all, and available for media dissemination. There is a strong hint between the lines of the Cox decision that the Court felt revelation of the rape victim's name in this instance was a mistaken judgment, but one that was not apt to be repeated often. In addition, as a commentator has observed (Note, 1975), the Court left the door wide open (though no jurisdiction has yet chosen to pass through it) for a state to enact a statute which would shield the identity of a rape victim by not having her name appear on any public record. Precedent exists for such a move. In the Blumenthal (1960) case, the Eighth Circuit court ruled that a defendant in a Mann Act case was not deprived of constitutional guarantees where the indictment failed to name the "victim," as long as he himself was given that information. It remains arguable what might ensue were the defendant to transmit the identification to the media thereafter and they were to publish the name. Or suppose that the newspaper by its own investigation discovered the identity of a complainant not named on any formal judicial record? (McKeever, 1976). Nor did the Court spell out possible boundaries on legislative attempts to provide crime victims with anonymity. Must some reasonable justification exist for singling out a particular category of complainants? The Cox case commented only on a narrow issue, excluding from the protectable areas of privacy material to be found in judicial records open to inspection by the public (Virgil, 1975). What lies beyond these limits remains uncharted.

Another case, one in which the accused had an office as a practicing physician located within sight of my home, provides material for further review of some of the intricate issues posed by media coverage of deviance and crime. The complainant was a 22-year-old patient of the 54-year-old doctor. She sought treatment for a back injury, and later maintained in court that the doctor had injected her with valium, and that while she was disoriented and semi-conscious he had raped her and forced her to participate in acts of "sexual perversion." She said that she was confused and powerless to prevent what he did: "I felt like a vegetable." The doctor insisted that the woman had consented. "She went out of her way to entice me. I'm not proud of what I did, but I did nothing she didn't agree to." The woman was identified in the suburban newspapers as Miss G., while both the doctor's full name and office address were indicated each day during the two weeks of the trial. The conflicting stories of the parties were moved no nearer to resolution by the playing of a tape that the doctor had made (why?, spectators wondered) in the midst of an act of intercourse. The dialogue on the tape indicates how precarious judgment can be in rape trials (Welborn, 1976):

> The doctor says: "What really turns you on most of all?"
> The woman replied: "Most of all?"
> The question is repeated. The woman giggles: "I don't know. Different things. I don't know. I can't think right now."
> Later, the doctor asks: "Do you like that?"
> "I don't know," she responds. "Is it good for my back?"
> The doctor then answers: "Anything that relaxes you is good for your back."

It took the jury of eight women and four men two days to decide on a verdict of not guilty. The jury foreman said that the tape had played some part in the decision, but that jurors had been influenced mostly by the fact that the woman had returned for treatment two days after the doctor admittedly had tried to seduce her during an earlier appointment.

It was at the time of the verdict that the *Los Angeles Times,* the area's largest newspaper, ran its first story about the case. That story identified by name both the complainant and the doctor, though the suburban newspapers continued to use only the doctor's name in their final writeup.

I was away from the area for almost a year following the conclusion of the rape trial. When I returned home, the doctor's nameplate was gone from the medical building. I was told by a receptionist and another doctor in the suite that the accused practitioner had felt compelled to move to a low-status job in an emergency room elsewhere in the county. They suggested that he would not welcome any questions from me about the rape case. "He's still very angry," they said.

Great Britain

The diffusion of public concern with denominated social problems is a subject that had not received much scholarly attention. Becker (1963) designated as "moral entrepreneuers" those who attempt to impose their judgmental standards of behavior on others. The concept describes a process whereby members of a power group single out for interdiction acts usually committed by persons less powerful than themselves. There is a corollary process, one in which organized outsiders designate issues that they regard as needing emendation. They operate as "issue energizers," telling others those things about which their consciences should ache, and where their attention should be directed. At the moment, for instance, poverty has retreated into a penumbral state, while withdrawal of American investments in South Africa has assumed preeminent importance for "issue energizers."

Rape reform has been the consequence of such a movement. It was a denominated problem in the United States (and, most assuredly, a very real problem as well, but so are numerous other matters which are overlooked). The tendrils of the reform movement then spread outward from America to arouse concern in areas, such as Britain, which, at least by American standards, do not have a notable rape problem. Barbara Toner (1977), an Australian journalist resident in London, became England's Susan Brownmiller, and rape crisis centers soon appeared in the larger British cities.

Fuel for the reform movement was supplied by the Law Lords decision in the Director of Public Prosecutions v. Morgan (1975), a ruling that declared that a subjective test was to be the standard for determination of guilt in a rape prosecution; that is, if the accused himself believed that the victim had consented, and he could get a jury to accept the truth of his belief, it would not matter whether or not the victim had indeed consented or whether or not a reasonable person would have concluded that she was consenting. This decision, highly unpopular in pro-feminist circles, was followed by some ill-tempered judicial dicta in the Stapleton case. Justice Milford Stevenson, in summing, said: "It was, as rape goes, a pretty anemic affair. The man has made a fool of himself, but the girl was almost equally stupid. This practice of hitch-hiking must be stopped." The rapist was given a two-year suspended sentence (Toner, 1977:9-37).

By the end of the reform process, Britain's new Sexual Offenses (Amendment) Act of 1976 had achieved for the first time in the country's history a statutory (as opposed to a commonlaw) definition of rape, one that softened the Morgan ruling slightly by indicating that recklessness in determining consent would support a rape conviction. The new law also limited cross-examination inquiries into the complainant's sexual background. By far and away, however, the most extraordinary aspect of the British legislation was the restriction placed by Parliament against the identification of *either* the complainant *or* the defendant in a rape prosecution. How this came about is what will occupy us for the remainder of this section.

First, informative data was available to British authorities about the extent of press identification of rape victims. Keith Soothill and Anthea Jack (1975) had surveyed the practices of six newspapers for the years 1951, 1961, and 1971. They found that in each of the years about one person in four involved in court proceedings for rape cases could expect some publicity in the national press. *The News of the World* proved to be the major chronicler of rape. It had, Soothill and Jack (1975:702) observed, "developed . . . a distinctively titillating style of reporting sex crimes." Each year, some cases—those with a murder, sexual activities, and a celebrity were most favored—would become "a national soap opera." Soothill and Jack also pointed out that acquittals had risen from 19.3% of all rape charges in 1951 to 28.5% in 1971. This means, they noted, "that an increasing number of *men* who are subsequently acquitted by the courts are in danger of having their names emblazoned across the newpapers, while the case is in progress" (1975:702).

The Heilbron Commission, appointed to recommend rape law revisions in the wake of agitation following Morgan, considered anonymity one of its key agenda items. It first called for statements from parties with views on the issue. The statements have not been published, but the Home Office provided me the list of those who had submitted their views and gave permission to contact them for copies of their submissions. Most responded graciously, though the reply from the Metropolitan Police testifies to the point that the idea of freedom of information has not made deep inroads into the thinking of the British bureaucracy. The operative sentence of the Metropolitan Police letter says: "After careful consideration we have decided that little purpose would be served by supplying you with this information."

The distribution of responses to the Heilbron question regarding the issue of anonymity for the victim in a rape trial took an interesting form, one very different, I suspect, than it would be if equivalent organizations were canvassed in the United States. The four women's groups, not surprisingly, all urged anonymity for the victim, with the Rape Counselling and Research Group going a step further by suggesting that the anonymity shield not be breached on acquittal of the defendant, because acquittal often means merely that the charge could not be proven, not that the man did not commit the rape. Two of the women's groups, in addition to pressing for anonymity of victims, went beyond the question posed by advocating that defendants also be protected from identification. The Women's National Commission, an advisory group to the government, said: "We would not suggest that injustice is confined to one sex and it is clear that a man may be wrongly accused of an offence and, in consequence of publicity suffer—albeit not physically—no less than the woman."

The three media groups that addressed the idea were divided. The British Broadcasting Company favored no identification. "It is our view that the public interest would not suffer if, in the very small number of such cases which we report, this particular piece of information were not available." The Press Council thought the decision ought to be left with the judge, while the Guild of British Newspaper Editors, responding through a joint committee established with the Council of the Law Society, recommended anonymity, with the judge allowed to determine at the conclusion of the trial whether to reveal the complainant's name.

It was the legal community, rather than the press groups, which was adamant in its opposition to blanket victim anonymity. A survey of judges, reported by their association's executive secretary, found 104 of them favoring victim anonymity at their discretion, nine favoring anonymity for both defendant and complainant, five flatly opposing any anonymity, and only one favoring it as an absolute condition for the victim only. Justice, whose membership is made up of affiliates of the British section of the International Commission of Jurists, thought that victim anonymity offered "a deceptively simple facade" of reform, whereas it most fundamentally represented a retrogression, "a further erosion of open public justice." Finally, the Criminal Bar Association came out strongly against anonymity. In the most thorough submission on the subject, it considered pro and con arguments in detail. Leaving discretion with the judge, it thought, could be tolerated only if there was "a clear understanding that anonymity was to be the exception and not the rule." It concluded that "rape victim anonymity is contrary to the basic principle of open justice, is of doubtful practical need, is unfair to innocent defendants, would be difficult to apply fairly and is likely to produce more personal and practical harm than its absence."

The Heilbron Committee (Great Britain, 1975:para. 143) devoted seven of the 41 pages of its report to anonymity. It believed that "one of the greatest causes of distress to complainants in rape cases is the publicity which they sometimes suffer when their names and personal details of their life are revealed in the Press." The recommendation was for a statutory ban on the publication of the name or identifying particulars about the complainant, but with a discretionary power in the judge to eliminate the restriction if convinced that the interests of justice would be served by doing so. The idea that the defendant should be anonymous was rejected on the ground that the defendant's equality should not be with the victim, but with other accused persons, and that, besides, "acquittal will give him public vindication" (1975:para. 178).

Parliamentary action came soon thereafter through a Private Member's bill introduced with government approval by a Labor M.P. who sought to implement most—but not all—of the Heilbron recommendations on rape reform. In particular, the Parliamentary bill omitted the proposal that rape juries be constituted of at least four men and four women, a suggestion singularly odd in view of the uncertain empirical evidence on male and female juror's performance on rape juries, combined with the folklore belief that women tend to be tougher than men on their complaining sisters (Lynch, 1975:100; Pekkanen, 1977:177).

On the bill's second reading, members of the minority Conservative party proposed anonymity for the defendant (Great Britain, 1976a). The rationale for concern for the male accused of rape, the debates clearly reveal, was not based in compassion for the plight of falsely accused criminal defendants, but rather founded primarily in self- and class-interest, raised by the prospect of a rape accusation against a well-placed member of society. One debater made the concern very explicit (1976a: col. 838):

> When a defendant claims, as part of his defence, that there is a conspiracy against him with the object of destroying his character because of *his position in society or politics,* would it not be fair to give him the kind of defence that the Bill would provide for women? [Emphasis added.]

The case of a candidate for Parliament whose career had been ruined because of a rape accusation came in for comment. The man, it was claimed, was "completely innocent" but he was ever after "jocularly known throughout Labour Party circles as the Brighton rapist" (Great Britain, 1976a:col. 95). A defendant in a rape case, it was pointed out (1976a:col. 96), "may well be shunned in the clubs to which he is accustomed to go." Undergirding the move toward defendant anonymity was the male-expressed thesis that women can be vicious, vindictive, and vengeful.

The provision for defendant anonymity was passed in Standing Committee by a vote of nine to two. The government acquiesced, and a few weeks later the new clause was accepted by the full House of Commons. The House of Lords, "an anthropological zoo" one M.P. called it during debates on the rape bill, went along sputteringly, with members deploring the anonymity provision for defendants, but acceding because they did not want to wreck the reform effort totally, as they would have to do in order to eliminate the objectionable clause. With the Queen's pro forma approval, the measure entered law as one of the most unusual provisions in Anglo-Saxon jurisprudence—a derelict on the waters of the law—or, perhaps, (though much less likely) a precursor of an extraordinary shift in the relationship between the media and all criminal defendants. The measure provided for anonymity of defendants and complainants in rape cases. The victim could be identified at either the trail or the appellate stage if the judge were convinced that such a step might impel persons to come forward who could serve as witnesses or that without such identification the defense would be substantially prejudiced. The defendant, if convicted, could be identified at the end of the trial. The naming of complainant, if the defendant was acquitted, was to be at the judge's discretion.

It is worth noting that, though both the Morgan case and the deliberations of the Heilbron Committee received extensive coverage in the American press, there was no mention by the American media (at least that I have located) of the enactment in Britain of the law granting anonymity to defendants and complainants in rape trials.

FURTHER CONSIDERATIONS

How do we appraise so distinctively different legal approaches to the matter of media coverage of rape cases as those in England and the United States? The first task seems to be to set forth matters that appear to be of importance; the next to attempt to determine the possible impact of the differing media approaches. First, though, it is worth noting that the issue itself may not have great significance, that is, that the power of the press in general may be vastly overrated, so that it matters little what policy is adopted. T.S. Matthews (1959:163), a former news magazine editor, has noted:

> A piece of clap-trap is that the Press has enormous power. This delusion is
> . . . taken for granted by the public-at-large, who are apt to be impressed by
> anything that is said three times; it is continually adverted by the Press
> itself, and it is cherished by Press Lords, some of whom, at least, should
> know better.

If what is done does make a difference, however, a key question concerns the relationship between media policy and the amount of rape; another, the impact of the policies on real and alleged victims and on real and alleged rapists, both in terms of their present involvement and their later situation. There are also matters of general wellbeing, involving balances between an informed public and a compassionate public policy. We will briefly consider a few of these and other issues in this section. A fundamental background observation, though, must be that no approach, that of Britain, America, or any other jurisdiction, will produce unilateral results. There will be some gains and some losses, and advantages to some persons and disadvantages to others attached to any chosen option. Even if we could delineate all likely outcomes of any policy, there remains the insoluble issue of equivalency: is the conviction of one innocent person worth or not worth the acquittal of seven, nine, or 59 guilty rapists?

Labeling and the Media

The result of the process of labeling or, as Lemert (1951) calls it, "secondary deviance," can be activated through the agency of the media. A person is accused, his ill-fame is broadcast, and his person and act deplored. He finds it difficult not to introject the definition of self propounded by powerful agencies and to avoid the stigma now attached to him by persons who learn of his behavior. In rape, a similar process often leads to derogation of the victim, a process that proves hurtful in personal relationships, destructive of privacy, and otherwise deeply meretricious. It is arguable whether notoriety as a rape victim might for some persons in some instances carry positive consequences. If nothing else, it could transform a secret and secretive event into a matter of public concern.

Those who learn of the event may be more considerate and more understanding of what otherwise might be regarded as peculiar behavior on the part of the victim. Failure to identify the victim in the media also conveys the sense that what happened to her is a shameful matter, something that ought to be kept hidden away. Thus, ironically, the drive for anonymity, by statute in Britain and by practice in the United States, may result in precisely the opposite consequences, at least in the long run, than those alleged in its favor, by further imparting to the act of rape a particularly dirty, ugly, shameful nuance, rather than serving to portray it and its victims as no more than part of the regular criminal scene.

That views such as the foregoing may be shared by at least some rape victims can be seen from the comments of Sadie Kendall whose rape led to the California Supreme Court decision in the case of People v. Rincon-Pineda, a decision which limited the range of cross-examination of rape victims and repudiated the ancient cautionary instruction that had the juries instructed that rape is an easy charge to make and a difficult one against which to defend. In a 1978 interview with myself and my wife, Ms. Kendall, whose name had been kept out of the papers, noted:

> The thing I object to is that there seems to be this attitude that rape is something embarrassing and sinful, and that your name should be protected. Now I was claiming privacy about all areas of my life except the rape. That is public. I in fact did not object if they wanted to use my name in the newpapers. But it was assumed—"Don't worry, dear, we won't use your name" [imitating an oversolicitous official]. That seems to me to be very much a symptom of the way society views rape.

Social Atmosphere

Too few commentators on legal arrangements take into account their eddying effects; that is, the lesson that is conveyed by the selected formula. It has been said (Gorer, 1955), for instance, that almost unfailing courtesy of the British police, itself perhaps a consequence of the fact that they do not carry weapons, conveys to the public, which in turn reproduces it, an attitude of politeness and respect. Conversely, it is sometimes argued that use of capital punishment transmits to the society the lesson that killing is a legitimate retaliatory response. Rebecca West (1955:107) in a vignette from the Nuremberg war criminal trials captures the feelings that may distinguish civilized from uncivilized media approaches:

It seemed that when people had never seen a man, or had seen him only once or twice, they did not find anything offensive about the idea of photographing him while he was being sentenced to death, but that if people had seen him often the idea became unattractive. The correspondents who had attended court day in, day out, knew how the defendants hated the periods of each session when it was part of the routine for the cameras to be put on . . . it might be right to hang such men. But it could not be right to photograph them when they were being told they were going to be hanged. For when society had to hurt a man it must hurt him as little as possible and must preserve what it can of his pride, lest there should spread in that society those feelings which make men do the things for which they get hanged.

How, in such terms, do the variant approaches of the United States and Britain to media identification of persons accused and accusing of rape function? The view noted above is but one segment of a highly complex equation. The issue is an empirical one, though hardly susceptible at the moment, if it ever will be, to a sure conclusion. To take but one matter: some "guilty" but acquitted rapists who escape identification in Britain may regard this as a testament to the foolhardiness of the system and an invitation to further depredation. Others may take it as a god-sent reprieve, and from there on behave more acceptably.

Crime Control

Undoubtedly, a major impetus to the anonymity provisions is concern for eliciting a larger number of rape complaints. Dukes and Mattley (1977) suggest that other factors, particularly victim fear combined with a feeling that the police will provide a haven, are those most apt to lead to the reporting of rape. Identification in the media may have only a marginal impact on reporting. It has been alleged that some major factor—10 seems particularly popular—of rapes remain unreported to the police. The assumption is that women do not report these episodes because, in part, they are afraid of being identified and further humiliated. The reason for encouraging complaints is straightforward. The more complaints the greater likelihood of apprehending and convicting offenders because corroborative evidence and further clues to the identity of the offender will become available. This is particularly important because studies indicate (Heppner and Heppner, 1977) that in more than 50% of the cases a rapist will rape again and will show increasing violence in doing so. The relationship, on the other hand, between anonymity and spurious complaints remains for the moment unknown, though commentators uniformly suggest that the number of such ill-founded reports had in the past been considerably overestimated.

It can also be said that the anonymity provisions in Britain will tend to reduce newspaper concern with rape, and in this manner, perhaps, deescalate an emotional buildup that has in the past led to considerable reform. The amount of rape in a social system probably varies in terms of social definitions of proper male behavior in particular circumstances, as that behavior is defined by groups and by individuals within such groups. Publicity can be counter-productive in regard to broadcasting the fearsome attributes of a rape event and can encourage a person determined to gain a reputation for aggression and "masculine" virility. Rewrite men, as Duffy and Lane (1959:123) observe, have been known to transform "morons into 'Reckless Mobsters,' cowardly gunmen into 'Fearless Lawbreakers' and bombers into 'Don Quixotes.'" Similarly, Sampson (1974) testifies that the ITT white-collar crime scandals, for instance, "established the company's corporate identity" and that reservations for Sheraton hotels set a new record after the fraud revelations. Matters such as these require close empirical monitoring for rape, with exquisite research designs, before we will gain any insight into the manner in which the identification process operates.

CONCLUSION

The ramifications of media policy in regard to rape in Britain and the United States can be traced in further outline, but the foregoing should suffice to indicate the great complexity of the issues and the importance of trying to determine the variant consequences of so different a set of guidelines as the two countries have adopted.

My personal policy preference, with all its trade-offs, is for the American approach, though I would be inclined to identify the rape victim more freely than is presently done. I believe that anonymity plays directly into the sniggering innuendos that surround rape and make it a special kind of criminal offense today. Anonymity is founded on the view that there is something degrading about being raped, something very different from being the victim of robbery or burglary. The anonymity provision suggests that the public will in some subtle or not so subtle manner conclude that the victim in a way contributed to her own fate, that therefore it will think less of her, and that her reputation will be compromised. These suppositions obviously have a substantial basis in fact, but it is (as I see it) superficial treatment to resort to anonymity to camouflage the more fundamental issue. The fight will be better fought by

firm and repeated insistence that it is no different to be raped than to be
victimized by other criminal offenses, that the offender is totally to blame.
The incentive for such a basic campaign could be seriously undermined
by the anonymity provisions that push rape into shadowy status.

Anonymity for the person accused of rape, however important it might
prove in particular cases (for instance, the episode detailed earlier in this
chapter involving an accused physician), stems not from a fellow-feeling
of compassion for all offenders, but rather from an interest in providing
special protection to the better-positioned. There is no logic to shielding
the accused rapist and leaving open to public identification the accused
burglar or robber. I am not insensitive to the harm done by publicity.
George Whitmore's plaintive note—he had been accused of a rape-
murder—tells it all (Shapiro, 1970:107): "Please forgive me not saying
much. I've been in the papers so bad that I don't feel like a human any
more. Did you read the papers?"

It will not do, in light of statements by victims of the media such as
Whitmore, to fail to mention the sensationalism that often dictates the
manner in which the media cover crime news, particularly news containing sexual and/or violent elements. Their pious pronouncements aside,
the media are primarily business enterprises, and they cater to and create
a market not notable for its dignity or even-handedness. An Australian
writer attending a rape trial was startled at the discrepancy between what
of importance she thought was happening and what she read the following
day in the newspapers. That the victim had been menstruating at the time
of the charged assault and that her tampon had been pushed deep into the
vaginal channel was taken by the viewer as not unpersuasive evidence to
the point that she had not consented. The media made no mention of this
fact and sent forth a story that, as the spectator saw it, was much more
favorable to the defendant than the court proceedings justified (Scholz,
1977:132-133).

The nature of media reportage concentrating on ephemeral and
sensational ("newsworthy") events, in contrast to more subtle and
significant trends, introduces considerable distortion into the understanding of audiences and readers who depend upon it for their comprehension of what of importance is occurring in the world (Janouch,
1953:75, quoting Franz Kafka; Cater, 1959; Bell, 1965:193). Nonetheless, I would generally agree with Sorensen (1975:146): "We would be a
more vulnerable nation by far if the public . . . accepted any limitation on
journalism's probing eye, whatever its motes and beams." My opposition
to anonymity for either rape defendants or rape complainants rests on the

ground (perhaps, but hopefully not, based on wishful thinking) that accurate information is essential for decent existence, and that the best redress of injustice will take place only when we are fully informed about those processes and persons involved in and victims of injustice.

REFERENCES

ARENSKY, G. (1956). "Moscow at midnight." Pp. 9-24 in K. Singer (ed.), My greatest crime story. New York: Hill and Wang.

BAYLEY, D. (1976). Forces of order: Police behavior in Japan and the United States. Berkeley: University of California Press.

BECKER, H.S. (1963). Outsiders: Studies in the sociology of deviance. New York: Free Press.

BEDFORD, S. (1961). The faces of justice. New York: Simon & Schuster.

BELL, D. (1965). The end of ideology. New York: Free Press.

BELLI, M.M., and JONES, D.R. (1960). Belli looks at life and law in Japan. Indianapolis: Bobbs-Merrill.

Blumenthal v. United States (1960). 284 F.2d 46 (8th Circuit).

BRILL, H., and HIROSE, T. (1969). "The rise and fall of a methamphetamine epidemic: Japan, 1945-55." Seminars in Psychiatry, 1:179-194.

BROWNMILLER, S. (1975). Against our will: Men, women and rape. New York: Simon and Schuster.

BURGESS, A.W., and HOLSTROM, L.L. (1974). Rape: Victims of crisis. Bowie, Md.: Brady.

CATER, D. (1959). The fourth branch of government. Boston: Houghton Mifflin.

COBB, K.,and SCHAUER, N.R. (1974). "Michigan's criminal sexual assault law." University of Michigan Journal of Law Reform, 8:217-236.

Cox Broadcasting Corporation v. Cohn (1973). 200 S.E.2d. 127 (Georgia).

_____ (1975). 420 U.S. 469.

Director of Public Prosections v. Morgan (1975). 2 All-England Reports 347.

DOOMEN, J. (1976). Verkrachting. Baarn, The Netherlands: Anthos.

DUFFY, G. and LANE, B.W. (1959). Warden's wife. New York: Appleton-Century-Crofts.

DUKES, R.L., and MATTLEY, C.L. (1977). "Predicting rape victim reportage." Sociology and Social Research, 62:63-84.

FARGIER, M. (1976). Le viol. Paris: Bernard Grasset.

FEIFER, G. (1964). Justice in Moscow. New York: Simon and Schuster.

FOWLES, J. (1977). N.Y. Times Book Review, Nov. 13.

FRANKLIN, M. (1963). "A constitutional problem in privacy protection: Legal inhibitions on reporting of fact." Stanford Law Review, 16:107-148.

GEIS, G. (1958). "Publicity and juvenile court proceedings." Rocky Mountain Law Review, 30:101-126.

_____ (1961). "Preliminary hearings and the press." U.C.L.A. Law Review, 8:397-414.

_____ (1962). "Publication of the names of juvenile felons." Montana Law Review, 23:141-147.

_____ (1965). "Identifying delinquents in the press." Federal Probation, 29:44-49.

_____ (1978a). "Illicit use of central nervous system stimulants in Sweden." Journal of Drug Issues, 8:189-197.

_____ (1978b). "Lord Hale, witches, and rape." British Journal of Law and Society, 5:26-44.

_____ (1978c). "Rape-in-marriage: Law and law reform in Britain, the United States, and Sweden." Adelaide Law Review, 6:284-303.

GELLHORN, W. (1960). American rights. New York: Macmillan.

GINSBERG, M. (1959). Law and opinion in England in the 20th century. Berkeley: University of California Press.

GORER, G. (1955). "Modification of national character: The role of the police in England." Journal of Social Issues, 11:24-32.

GRAHAM, K. (1974). "The freedom of the American press." Pp. 75-91 in Freedom of the press. London: Hart-Davis, MacGibbon.

Great Britain (1958). Department committee on proceedings before examining magistrates. Command 479. London:HMSO.

_____ (1975). Report of the advisory group on the law of rape. Command 6352. London:HMSO.

_____ (1976a). House of Commons, Parliamentary Debates 905:Feb. 13.

_____ (1976b). House of Commons, Parliamentary Debates. Official report of standing committee F [Sexual Offences (Amendment) Act] March 24-April 7.

GRIFFIN, S. (1971). "Rape: The all-American crime." Ramparts, 10:26-36.

HALEY, W. (1974). "Introduction." Pp. 9-18 in Freedom of the press. London: Hart-Davis-MacGibbon.

HASTINGS, P. (1954). Autobiography. New York: Roy.

HEPPNER, L.P., and HEPPNER, M. (1977). "Rape: Counseling the traumatized victim." Personnel and Guidance Journal, 56:77-80.

HEPWORTH, M. (1975). Blackmail: Publicity and secrecy in everyday life. London: Routledge & Kegan Paul.

JANOUCH, G. (1953). Conversations with Kafka. New York: Praeger.

KANIN, F., and KANIN, M. (1958). Teacher's pet. New York: Bantam.

KILBORN, P. (1977). "Explaining the British dilemma." New York Times, Jan. 30.

LEMERT, E.M. (1951). Social pathology: A systematic approach to the theory of sociopathic behavior. New York: McGraw-Hill.

LYKKJEN, A.M. (1976). Voldtekt: Ei bok om kvinneundertrykking. Oslo: Pax Forlag.

LYNCH, W.W. (1975). Rape: One victim's story. New York: Berkeley Medallion.

MacDONALD, J.D. (1961). One Monday we killed them all. New York: Fawcett.

McKEEVER, J. (1976). "Publication of true information on the public record." Duquesne Law Review, 14:507-520.

MATTHEWS, T.S. (1959). The sugar pill: An essay on newspapers. New York: Simon and Schuster.

MONTGOMERY, D.G., PETERS, A.H., and WEINBERG, C.B. (1978). "The Freedom of Information Act: Strategic opportunities and threats." Sloan Management Review, 19:1-14.

Near v. Minnesota (1913). 283 U.S. 697.

Note (1975)."A state may not impose civil liability for the accurate publication of a rape victim;s name obtained from publicly available judicial records maintained in connection with a public prosecution." Georgia Law Review, 9:963-979.

Note (1977). "The press and juvenile delinquency hearings: A contextual analysis of the unrefined first amendment rights of access." University of Pittsburgh Law Review, 39:121-139.

PEKKANEN, J. (1977). Victims: An account of a rape. New York: Popular Library.

People v. Rincon-Pineda (1975). 123 Cal. Rptr. 119, 538 P.2d 247.

ROSE, V.M. (1977). "Rape as a social problem: A byproduct of the feminist movement." Social Problems, 25:75-89.

RUNCIMAN, W.G. (1966). Relative deprivation and social justice. London: Routledge & Kegan Paul.

RUSSELL, D.E.H. (1975). The politics of rape: The victim's perspective. New York: Stein and Day.

SAMPSON, A. (1974). Whitmore. New York: Pyramid.

SCHOLZ, B. (1977). "Profile of a gang rape." Pp. 116-135 in P.R. Wilson (ed.), Delinquency in Australia: A critical appraisal. St. Lucia: University of Queensland Press.

SHAPIRO, F. (1970). Whitmore. New York: Pyramid.

SHIPLER, D.K. (1978). "Rising youth crime in Soviet troubles regime and public." New York Times, March 5.

SHOBLAD, R.H. (1972). Doing my own time. Garden City, N.Y.: Doubleday.

SIMONS, H., and CALIFANO, JR., J.A. (1976). The media and the law. New York: Praeger.

SOOTHILL, K., and JACK, A. (1975). "How rape is reported." New Society, 32:702-703.

SORENSEN, T. (1975). Watchmen in the night: Presidential accountability after Watergate. Cambridge: MIT Press.

State v. Evjue (1948). 33 N.W. 2d 305 (Wisconsin).

SUTHERLAND, S., and SCHERL, D.J. (1972). "Crisis intervention with rape victims." Social Work, 17:37-42.

THOMAS, K. (1959). "The double standard." Journal of History of Ideas, 20:195-216.

TONER, B. (1977). The facts of rape. London: Hutchinson.

Virgil v. Time, Inc. (1975). 527 F.2d 1122 (9th Circuit).

WARREN, S.D., and BRANDEIS, L.D. (1890). "The right to privacy." Harvard Law Review, 4:193-220.

WELBORN, L. (1976). "Jurors listen to intimate tape in Santa Ana rape trial." Santa Ana Register, Dec. 17.

WEST, R. (1955). A train of power. New York: Viking.

WESTERGAARD, J. (1976). Class in a capitalistic society. New York: Basic Books.

WILSON, J.Q. (1976). "Crime and punishment in England." Public Interest, 43:3-25.

9

HOW MUCH HEAT? HOW MUCH LIGHT Coverage of New York City's Blackout and Looting in the Print Media

ANDREW KARMEN

It was a sultry evening in July 1977 when the thunderstorm struck and the lights went out in New York City. The failure of electrical power triggered an upheavel in the balance of social, economic, and political power. What followed was a "night of terror" for some, but "Christmas in July" for others. By the time darkness gave way to daylight and police control was reimposed, merchandise was missing from 2,000 stores in black and hispanic ghettos, and over 3,000 "looters" were jammed into the sweltering city jails.

As the communications capital of the world revived, the mass media became preoccupied with the social problems and lessons revealed by the blackout. The reactions of commentators in the print media to the looting is the subject of this study because they shed light on how deviance is presented in the mass media.

METHODS AND DATA

A composite picture of editorial comment about the looting during the blackout will be pieced together through a content analysis of the 45[1] articles that appeared in nationally distributed magazines, newspapers, and columns.

A review of how social scientists analyzed urban uprisings in the recent past will add an historical dimension to this study. Data on the looters and opinion polls on public reaction to the looting will be used to evaluate the content of the 45 articles.

In order to investigate any relationships between ideology and reporting, several sub-sets of publications with acknowledged political or racial outlooks will receive special attention. Conservative and neo-conservative perspectives will be gleaned from the *National Review* (two articles: editorial staff, 1977; Edelson, 1977) and *Commentary* magazine (Decter, 1977). The liberal viewpoint will be from the *Nation* (editorial staff, 1977), the *New Republic* (editorial staff, 1977), and the *Progressive* (Dreyfus, 1977). Independent (of any political party) radical analyses will be taken from the gradualist socialist bi-weekly newspaper *In These Times* (Koning, 1977), and the revolutionary socialist weekly newspaper the *Guardian* (editorial staff, 1977). Three publications with a black perspective are *Ebony* (editorial staff, 1977), *Jet* (editorial staff, 1977), and the weekly *New York Amsterdam News* (editorial staff, 1977). In these articles, how much heat was generated, and how much light?

PROFILES OF THE PARTICIPANTS

According to popular stereotypes, a typical 1960s rioter was part of the "criminal riff-raff" that haunts ghetto streets—a "dangerous class" of "delinquents, drop-outs, hustlers, troublemakers, hoodlums, and idlers." Most social scientists who studied police records discovered that arrestees were generally a representative cross-section of lower-income, young, inner-city men (Oberschall, 1968:269; Lang and Lang, 1968:259; Kerner Commission, 1968:127; Janowitz, 1969:406; Skolnick, 1969:146).

Who Were the Blackout Defendants?

The Criminal Justice Agency (CJA) of New York City (1977:1-25) received information from bail recommendation interviews on over 3,000 defendants charged with either burglary, possession of burglar's tools, possession of stolen property, petit or grand larceny, criminal trespass, criminal mischief, arson, robbery, riot, obstructing governmental administration, resisting arrest, disorderly conduct, or possession of a weapon. In its preliminary report, the CJA provided information about a control group of "typical arrestees" from the same parts of the city who passed through the judicial system the previous month. The CJA profile can be compared to the profile of a typical rioter from the 1960s and to the profile of the typical arrestee in 1977.

The CJA data about the blackout defendants confirmed that 96% were black or Spanish surnamed, 93% were male, and 75% were under 30. The report recognized four categories: employed; unemployed; welfare recipient; student. Forty-five percent of the blackout defendants had jobs. Although this is less than the proportion of gainfully employed persons arrested during riots in the 1960s, as reported by the Kerner Commission and Fogelson and Hill, economic conditions were more depressed in the New York City ghettos in 1977 then they were from 1964 to 1968. The proportion of typical arrestees from the same boroughs of the city who had jobs when they were apprehended was 30%. Thus, the blackout defendants were more likely to have jobs than typical arrestees, but less likely to be employed than the rioters of the 1960s.

Compared to the control group, the blackout defendants had smaller proportions of unemployed people and recipients of public assistance. Furthermore, the Brooklyn District Attorney's Office analyzed the same bail recommendation forms in greater detail for a sub-sample of the defendants, and found that a large percentage of the unemployed were enrolled in anti-poverty programs and job training courses, leaving only 11% as jobless and "idle" (New York Times 1977:34). His office also calculated the average take-home pay of the blackout defendants with jobs to be about $3.40 an hour, adding up to approximately $135 a week or a little over $7,000 a year. The CJA breakdown by income classes revealed that nearly a third of the employed defendants cleared more than $7,500 a year after taxes. Hence, to categorize the defendants as "poor" is accurate, but to characterize all of them as part of an "underclass" is to overstate the case, since most of the 45% who were employed were the "working poor," or the "underemployed."

Sixty-four percent of the blackout defendants had been arrested previously, and 43% had prior convictions. But Fogelson and Hill found that between 40 and 92% of rioters in various cities in the 1960s had police (contact) records, and that somewhere between 50 and 90% of young men in ghetto neighborhoods had police records. Sixty-nine percent of the control group of typical arrestees had been apprehended before by the police. Hence, the proportion of young men with police records was similar for all three groups—the 1960s rioters, the blackout defendants, and the typical arrestees—and probably was not over-represented considering the pool of people from which they were drawn.

The Looters In Print

Reviews, comment, and editorial opinion were subjected to content analysis to determine if any discrepancy existed between the looters' print media image and the blackout defendants' profile. How frequently certain characteristics were mentioned in the press were compared to how they were actually distributed among the defendants. (See Table 1.)

Table 1. PROFILE OF THE PARTICIPANTS

Author	Criminals	Unemployed	Welfare	Underclass	Employed
Axthelm					
Baker	x	x	x	x	
Boeth, et al.					
Breslin					
Buchanan	x		x		
Business Week					
Christian Science Monitor		x			
Clines	x				
Coombs	x	x	x	x	
Decter	x	x			
Dreyfus	x	x	x	x	
Ebony	x	x			
Edelson		x		x	
Guardian		x			x
Gutman					
Hamill		x	x		
Jet	x	x			
Jones		x			
Kempton	x			x	
Koning	x	x	x	x	
Kraft			x		
Lerner	x	x	x	x	
Lewis		x			
Lewellyn, Walinsky	x	x	x		
Lipsyte		x		x	
McCall		x			
McGrory		x			
Merrick	x	x	x		
Nation		x		x	
National Review	x			x	
New Republic		x	x	x	

Table 1. PROFILE OF THE PARTICIPANTS

Author	Criminals'	Unemployed	Welfare	Underclass	Employed
NY Amsterdam News	x	x			
NY Times		x		x	
New Yorker		x		x	
Plate	x			x	
Ravitch	x				
Riley	x	x	x		
Safire	x				
Time	x	x	x	x	
Van Horne	x	x		x	
Village Voice					
Wall Street Journal		x			
Weusi		x			
Wicker					
Will	x	x	x		
45	22	30	14	16	1

In nearly a third of the articles (14 out of 45 cases or 31%),commentators claimed that "welfare recipients" took part in the looting. Although this was indisputably true, only 10% of the defendants were on public assistance. Thus, welfare recipients were singled out for unwarranted attention in the press. Similarly, the looters were described as "unemployed" in two thirds (30 of 45, or 67%) of the cases. This categorization also appeared too often in the media, since only 30% were out of work, able bodied, and not responsible for raising children. An even more misleading aspect of the media coverage was its lack of recognition that people with jobs also looted. Although 45% of the defendants were employed, in only one case (2%) was it specifically stated that some of the participants were workers.

In nearly half of the articles (22 of 45, or 48%), the looters were labelled "criminals" or denounced in similar terms like: "thieving mob" (Safire); "hard core thug types" (Clines); "hoodlums' (Ravitch); "vandals" (Van Horne); "outlaws" (Riley); "lawless and defiant" (Llewellyn and Walinsky); and "calculating, cold, professional thieves" (Kempton). Since 64% of the blackout defendants had records of prior arrests and 43% had been convicted previously, the frequency of occurrence of "criminality" as a descriptive characteristic was not out of line with the reality.

In over a third of the articles (16 of 45, or 35%), the participants were called members of an "underclass," or were allegedly drawn from the ranks of: "scum of the city" (Lipsyte); "ruffians; pariah class; litter of the streets; rag, tag and bobtail" (Kempton); "debris" (Koning); "miserably poor" *(Nation);* "parasites" *(National Review);* "those on welfare and food stamps for doing nothing" (Llewellyn and Walinsky); "idle, menacing, strutting, violence prone" (Decter); "street blacks" (Coombs); "idle poor and unemployables" *(New York Times);* and "riff-raff" (Van Horne). Indeed, it appears that these condemnatory terms, and the more sociological category "underclass" refer to essentially the same people who used to be tagged "criminal riff-raff." If the number of articles branding the participants as criminal types is added to the number decrying their extreme marginality (some authors used descriptions from both sets of unfavorable allegations), commentators in 28 cases (62%) used terminology that social scientists in the 1960s tended to avoid as prejudicial and inaccurate because it accentuated the negative and assumed the worst.

Ideological differences between liberals and conservatives affected the tone of the descriptions of the participants more than the specific characteristics. Both liberals and conservatives referred to an unemployed underclass, although their alleged assistance from the welfare system was mentioned by the liberal *New Republic* and the *Progressive,* while their alleged participation in crime was scored in the conservative *Commentary* and the *National Review.* Black-oriented publications did not use the term underclass at all, but consistently identified a criminal element among the participants. The gradualist socialist publication presented the looters in the same light as the liberal and conservative commentators, but the revolutionary socialist newspaper avoided the use of any negative or condemnatory terms.

PORTRAIT OF THE VICTIMS

A History of Tensions

The residents of ghettos have long harbored two sets of grievances: their relationships as customers and their roles as hired help. After the first Harlem uprising, Basso (1935:210) identified local merchants' discriminatory employment practices as the major source of the community's antagonism. Black civil rights groups during the Depression had been frustrated in attempts to get neighborhood people jobs in local stores.

In the wake of the second Harlem rebellion, Lee and Humphrey (1943:98-99) contended that sheer desperation with their outcast status motivated considerable numbers of ghetto dwellers to loot the available symbols of "white exploitation"—chiefly pawn shops and groceries.

Shortly before the third Harlem insurrection in 1964, Caplovitz (1967:45-53) discovered that the poor may pay more for less because they face a dilemma–either to endure consumer exploitation at the hands of ghetto merchants who extend them credit, or to suffer deprivation. Carmichael and Hamilton (1967:20) charged that the ghetto was "sapped senseless" by commercial exploitation. Stores which extended "easy credit" relied on pressure tactics as often as legal actions (to repossess goods and garnish wages) to collect outstanding debts from hard-pressed customers on installment plans. Jacobs (1965:3-27) noted that merchants specializing in "lay away" deals for over-priced goods were actually selling credit itself, and sought to maintain their customers in constant debt.

The owners of ghetto enterprises looted during the 1964 Harlem rebellion reportedly were bewildered and incensed because they perceived themselves as serving a depressed community that badly needed retail outlets. The reality, Clark (1964:28) argued, was that local residents were not grateful but resentful because the store owners were viewed as outsiders and colonizers who kept a hated structure of oppression intact.

The Kerner Commission (1968:274-277) investigated the exploitation of disadvantaged consumers and noted that much of the violence during uprisings was directed at stores that were widely believed to charge exorbitant prices for inferior goods.

Consumer exploitation was rooted in the powerlessness and lack of educational and financial resources of the urban poor, according to Tabb (1970:37-40). He doubted that replacing white entrepreneurs with black ones would alleviate customers' problems, given the realities of marginal businesses.

Allen (1970:134, 153) noted that white-owned stores were the main targets of looters and arsonists because they were the most visible symbols of exploitation. But he predicted that "black capitalism" would not guarantee benefits to the entire community, because "blacks were capable of exploiting one another just as easily as whites."

Hayden (1967:29-33) interpreted the Newark looting as "people expropriating property to which they felt entitled," rationalized or justified with "this is owed me." He reported that there was little hostility and quarreling over who got what because there was, for a change, enough for all.

The Harris Poll (1967) confirmed that a tremendous gulf separated white and black perceptions. Confronted with the statement, "White shopkeepers in Negro neighborhoods have gouged Negro customers," only 14% of the whites but 58% of the blacks concurred. Campbell and Schuman (1968:13) interviewed inner city blacks for the Kerner Commisson in 15 locales that had experienced uprisings and found that 56% felt they had been overcharged in neighborhood stores, and 42% asserted they had been sold spoiled or shoddy merchandise.

Berk (1968:125-131) questioned merchants in 15 cities for the Kerner Commission and found a substantial number who would admit that they felt embattled and surrounded by untrustworthy, even hostile customers, employees, and neighbors. Berk concluded that from 25 to 50% of the enterprises conducted their businesses in ways that demanded improvement if they were to escape the wrath of a hostile community during future uprisings.

The strained relations between the store owners and their ghetto employees can be partly understood in light of the "wage-theft system" (Liebow, 1967:37-40). Owners of small businesses frequently expect that employees will steal some of their merchandise, so they offer lowered wages to offset their anticipated losses. By underpaying their hired help, proprietors set up a classic situation of entrapment. Employees who do not steal back the unpaid value of their labor are economically penalized, while those that do attempt to catch up may suffer pangs of guilt and are fired and perhaps even arrested when they are caught.

Customer Relations In the Seventies

The massive indictment of ghetto retailing that appeared in the social science literature of the 1960s should sufficiently explain the sources of tension between storekeepers and their employees and customers at that time. Is there any reason to believe that customer relations in the neighborhoods that were looted during the blackout have improved over the past decade?

Some of the more flagrant abuses that flourished in the past have been toned down. Legal prohibitions against bait and switch advertising and unspecified interest charges have been enacted. If the law now restrains merchants, then perhaps consumer exploitation has lessened and relations are improved. But other basic sources of conflict have probably intensified. Certainly, prices have risen sharply over the last decade, and many low income workers and public assistance recipients have not been able to keep up with inflation. Interest rates for credit have jumped. The quality of merchandise has deteriorated.

A woman who complained that the rich and powerful are rarely punished for their illegal escapades told a *New York Times* reporter,

"Some of the stores deserved to be ripped off because they cheat us all the time, charging high prices for junk" (Sheppard, 1977:40). A Harlem reverend said he could understand the "hatred and resentment of those who did the looting . . . it was a chance for the poor people to strike back effectively at their oppressors" *(New York Amsterdam News,* 1974:A4). Harlem's State Senator McCall remarked that "they broke into the stores because they don't feel any allegiance to them. They know the owners don't live here and the prices are much higher than downtown" (Kelley, 1977:3). The director of Spanish Harlem's Chamber of Commerce told the *New York Times* that "if they (merchants) had shown some interest in the community, they might not have been looted" (Asbury, 1977:26). Businesses that were spared had ties to the community and had demonstrated sensitivity to its needs (Hunter-Gault, 1977:A4).

Shortly after the blackout, pollsters asked a nationwide sample whether the looters' seized the opportunity to "get even" with ghetto merchants. This rationale was accepted by a quarter of the whites and a third of the blacks *(New York Times*/CBS News Poll, 1977:5-7).

The Merchants In Print

The portrayal of the victimized merchants was subjected to content analysis. Three categories were set up. If nothing negative appeared about the marketing practices of the merchants and something positive was written about their businesses, the characterization was termed "innocent." Descriptions of the looting which specifically claimed that the targets were picked at random or that the destruction was indiscriminate were also considered as assertions that the merchants were innocent victims. If the commentators charged that the merchants precipitated the attacks by their unpopular practices, then the description was classified as "responsible" (merchants had at least in part caused their stores to be singled out). If some stores "got what they deserved" and others were hit unjustly, then the category of "both" was scored. Some articles did not describe the victims at all (16 of 45 cases). (See Table 2.)

More than half of the commentators (25 of 45, or 55%) described the victims in favorable terms that made it seem they were totally innocent and not at all responsible. The merchants suffered "heartbreaking losses" (Wicker); they "lost their life's work and savings" *(New York Times);* his store was "his entire life" (Breslin); they had "worked and saved all their lives" *(Time);* "he was incapable of cheating anyone" (Kempton); and they were "decent people" (Van Horne). Surely, a substantial number of the businesses were corporations and chain stores,

Table 2. PORTRAIT OF THE VICTIMS

Author	Innocent	Both	Responsible
Axthelm			
Baker	x		
Boeth, et al.		x	
Breslin	x		
Buchanan	x		
Business Week	x		
Christian Science Monitor	x		
Clines	x		
Coombs	x		
Decter	x		
Dreyfus			
Ebony			x
Edelson			
Guardian			
Gutman			
Hamill	x		
Jet			
Jones	x		
Kempton	x		
Koning			
Kraft			
Lerner			
Lewis			
Llewellyn, Walinsky	x		
Lypsyte		x	
McCall	x		
McGrory	x		
Merrick	x		
Nation	x		
National Review			
New Republic	x		
NY Amsterdam News	x		
NY Times	x		
New Yorker			
Plate			
Ravitch			
Riley	x		
Safire	x		
Time	x		
Van Horne	x		
Village Voice		x	
Wall Street Journal			
Weusi			x
Wicker	x		
Will	x		
45	25	3	2

but their ownership was consistently depicted as proprietorships. They were "hard working" (Hamill), "courageous" when they defended their property (Buchanan); "envied because they were successful" (Coombs); "leading productive lives" (Will); "middle class suppliers" *(Nation);* "victims of unfairness" (Baker); "striving and loved" *(New York Amsterdam News);* "believers in the American dream of capitalist free enterprise" (Riley); "providers of jobs to those willing to work" (Clines); and "deserving of more community and customer support" *(Christian Science Monitor).* Llewellyn and Walinsky (1977) contended that black and hispanic entrepreneurs faced unusually high overhead costs. *Business Week* (1977) lamented the merchants' losses and noted that some who were insured would not get fully reimbursed.

The merchants and their enterprises were criticized for their questionable business practices in only four of the articles. Hence, the merchant's side of the story received the lion's share of attention in the print media. Of the 45 articles, 55% exonerated them from any charges of provocation, 4% suggested they were responsible for their plight, 7% deemed them partly responsible but partly innocent, and 35% did not describe them in either favorable or unfavorable terms. The deviant and inflammatory practices of an estimated 25 to 50% of the stores were not overlooked by 24% of the whites and 34% of the blacks in the Times/CBS Poll, but were cited by only 11% of the commentators.

WHY IT HAPPENED

Messages Received In the Sixties

By the end of the sixties, urban uprisings had become a regular summertime occurrence, and their meaning was most frequently taken as a call for change, at least among social scientists.

The Kerner Commission (1968:1) stated, "This is our basic conclusion: Our nation is moving toward two societies, one black, one white— separate and unequal." Clearly, the consensus among the Commission members was that uprisings were mostly protests rather than outbreaks of wanton criminality.

Skolnick (1969:339-340) reported to the National Commission on the Causes and Prevention of Violence that few serious official riot commissions attempted to explain ghetto "disorders" purely as the work of criminal elements or "riff-raff" types. He proposed that looting be viewed as a form of collective protest that was largely instrumental in its selective targeting of stores with a reputation for discrimination and exploitation.

Similarly, Gans (1969:46) denied that ghetto rebellions were examples of impulsive mob behavior. Gans saw looting as a community event that united ghetto dwellers in the realization that for once they could have some control over their own fate, if only for a little while.

To Rustin (1966:29-35), the rational aspect to looting was highlighted by the tendency to spare white-owned businesses with a reputation for fair deals and nondiscriminatory practices. To Rainwater (1967:25), the instrumental character of looting was in its primitive but direct attempt to be a mechanism of income redistribution. Geschwender (1968:304) went further and interpreted rebellions that led to the destruction of black-owned businesses that had the same strained community relations as white-owned ones as attacks on a system of exploitation by emergent social movements, rather than mere hostile outbursts by enraged people against specific antagonists.

Quarantelli and Dynes (1970:171-177) proposed that looting during civil disorders be considered normative behavior for some strata of American society. Large numbers of people representing a cross-section of the ghetto community selectively and spontaneously worked together in pairs, family units and teams amidst a "carnival atmosphere" and received strong open local support during uprisings.

Outside of sociological circles, outbreaks of looting are usually cited as evidence of the existence of "human depravity" when social controls are lifted (Quarantelli and Dynes, 1968:9; Dynes and Quarantelli, 1968: 169-173). The "evil of looting" is attributed to "man" himself and not social conditions and environmental forces. The authorities then devise mechanisms to establish or reassert formal, repressive, effective police controls over those who would use civil strife as a cover for their criminal inclinations and animalistic proclivities.

Public Reaction In 1977

Because the looting followed a blackout caused by a thunderstorm, the popular 1960s explanation that uprisings were provoked by "subversives" did not surface in 1977. But some widely acknowledged symbols of protest were also absent. Most of the energy of ghetto residents was directed at emptying out stores rather than at fighting the police, and "soul brothers" were apparently not passed over during the blackout. So explanations centering on "third world liberation," had less support in the data surrounding the 1977 event than they had in the 1960s.

The majority of looters were swept up in mass arrests and crammed into inadequate detention facilities from several days up to a full week before being sent to court for arraignment (Levine, 1977:28). Few public officials and media personalities criticized this disregard for the constitutional rights of accused persons who had not been convicted of any crime.

The *New York Times*/CBS News (1977) public opinion poll taken immediately after the blackout confirmed that the majority of respondents, black and white, tended to view the looting as lawlessness rather than as protest. The most direct interpretation that looters seized the opportunity to get even with local merchants was soundly rejected, as was the argument that the "poor and needy" stole out of desperation. Most people also rejected the situational explanation that violence tends to happen on hot summer nights.

How Commentators Interpreted the Looting

The reasons cited by the commentators can be compared against the external criteria of the profiles of public opinion about the looting documented by the *New York Times*/CBS News Poll. (See Table 3.)

Table 3. REASONS FOR THE LOOTING

Author	Poverty desperation	Unemployment frustration	Discrimination	Criminal inclinations	Hot night
Axthelm				x	
Baker	x	x		x	
Boeth et al.	x	x	x		
Breslin	x	x		x	
Buchanan				x	
Business Week					
Christian Science Monitor	x	x	x		
Clines		x		x	x
Coombs		x		x	
Decter				x	
Dreyfus	x	x	x	x	
Ebony	x	x	x		
Edelson				x	
Guardian	x	x	x		
Gutman	x		x		
Hamill	x	x		x	
Jet	x	x		x	x
Jones				x	
Kempton				x	
Koning	x	x	x	x	
Kraft	x	x			
Lerner	x	x		x	
Lewis	x	x	x		
Llewellyn, Walinsky		x		x	
Lipsyte				x	
McCall		x			

Table 3. REASONS FOR THE LOOTING (Cont'd)

Author	Poverty desperation	Unemploy- ment frustration	Discrim- ination	Criminal inclinations	Hot night
McGrory				x	
Merrick	x	x	x	x	
Nation	x	x			
National Review				x	
New Republic	x	x		x	
NY Amsterdam News		x		x	
NY Times	x	x	x		
New Yorker	x	x	x	x	
Plate		x		x	
Ravitch				x	
Riley	x			x	
Safire				x	
Time	x	x		x	
Van Horne	x		x	x	
Village Voice	x	x		x	
Wall Street Journal					
Weusi	x	x	x		
Wicker	x	x	x		
Will				x	
45	25	28	13	31	2

One reason partly accepted by the public but totally rejected by the commentators was the situational factor that "violence tends to break out on hot nights." Thirty-five percent of the whites, 14% of the blacks, and 4% of the commentators accepted this as plausible.

Poverty and the desperation it engenders, and unemployment and the frustration it produces were two reasons cited more frequently in the print media than in the public opinion poll. Only 15% of the whites and 24% of the blacks thought the looters broke into stores because they were "poor and needy," but 55% of the commentators cited the desperation of the poverty-stricken. Forty-seven percent of the whites and 51% of the blacks thought the looters were frustrated because they were out of work, while 62% of the commentators pinpointed unemployment as a root cause. But the most popular motivation cited by whites, blacks, and commentators alike was "criminal inclinations."

In order to weigh the competing claims sometimes offered by the same commentator about why the looting occurred, the themes of the interpretations were classified as "mostly protest," "mostly lawlessness," and "mixture of both." (See Table 4.)

Table 4. MEANING OF THE EVENT

Author	Mostly protest	Both	Mostly lawlessness
Axthelm			x
Baker		x	
Boeth et al.	x		
Breslin		x	
Buchanan			x
Business Week			
Christian Science Monitor	x		
Clines		x	
Coombs		x	
Decter			x
Dreyfus		x	
Ebony	x		
Edelson			x
Guardian	x		
Gutman	x		
Hamill		x	
Jet		x	
Jones			x
Kempton			x
Koning		x	
Kraft	x		
Lerner		x	
Lewis	x		
Llewllyn, Walinsky		x	
Lipsyte			x
McCall	x		
McGrory			x
Merrick		x	
Nation	x		
National Review			x
New Republic		x	
NY Amsterdam News		x	
NY Times	x		
New Yorker		x	
Plate		x	
Ravitch			x
Riley		x	
Safire			x
Time		x	
Van Horne		x	
Village Voice		x	
Wall Street Journal			
Weusi	x		
Wicker	x		
Will			x
45	12	19	12

Articles arguing that the looting was in reality a protest by people facing great hardships were in the minority. Only 12 of 45, or 26% of the commentators interpreted a message of general discontent from the specific attacks delivered to ghetto merchants, and blamed economic forces and social conditions. The largest group of articles, 19 of 45, or 42%, fell into the contradictory category of a mixture of both lawlessness and protest.

As many articles considered the looting as "mostly lawlessness" as did "mostly protest." Twelve of the 45, or 26%, contained statements that reduced the actions in the streets to purely criminal offenses with no redeeming social or political implications. A number of commentators specifically denied the protest interpretations of their opponents.

In all three of the articles considered to be representative of the conservative viewpoint, the importance of social conditions like widespread poverty and desperation, and pervasive unemployment and frustration was denied. Instead, emphasis was placed on the socialization process and the morality (or alleged lack of it) of deviant individuals. Hence, conservatives interpreted the looting as plain lawlessness. All the liberal and the black-oriented publications stressed combinations of social system failures and personal shortcomings as reasons for the looting, and interpreted the events as mostly protest or both protest and lawlessness. Because so many commentators straddled this line and avoided a definite stance, it appears the polarization of opinions evident in the 1960s has blurred and the center of gravity has shifted rightward. Many who decry social injustices today feel compelled to denounce "inexcusable opportunism" with equal fervor. Although the locus of the looting was in ghetto neighborhoods, and 96% of the participants were black or hispanic, only the two radical publications, one black-oriented magazine, and one liberal author within the sub-sets pointed to the persistence of racial discrimination as an underlying grievance fueling the uprising.

The whole event was quickly dubbed "the night of the animals," a phrase attributed to an anonymous policeman. In the *Amsterdam News,* a black shopkeeper called his attackers "animals," a black politician denounced arsonists who burned his headquarters as "jackals," and the headline story claimed the black community was split over whether the looters were "animals or victims" *(Amsterdam News,* 1977:A1, A4). A headline in the reputedly liberal *Globe* in racially tense Boston trumpeted an hispanic shopkeeper's words: "Like mad dogs and animals going wild" (Rosenthal, 1977:1).

These and other instances of "animal" and animal-like descriptions of the looters and their behavior tended to emanate from those sectors that previously were cited as the most hostile to the plight of ghetto residents, the police and local merchants. What is striking is that the "offhand" or "uninhibited" remarks of unsympathetic actors caught up in conflict situations actually seemed to be echoed, if not magnified and concentrated, in a number of the articles, especially ones that interpreted the looting as "mostly lawlessness" or "both."

The looters were branded as "animals"–in the nonracial sense–they have no human guilt pangs" (Safire); "animals and scum—perhaps they are" (Baker); "a new creature, like the Loch Ness monster" (Edelson); "a multiheaded beast" (Hamill); "piranhas" (Will); "young sharks" (Jones); "urban insects" that scurry around, live in hordes and infest sections (Decter); "an unstoppable swarm" (Boeth et al.); "swarming," "scavenging," and travelling in "packs" *(Time);* "prowling" *(New Republic);* moving "roachlike" (Clines) and "swarming like driver ants" (Edelson). Perhaps the most blatantly offensive was "welfare mommas lumbering about like overfed heifers" (Buchanan). A total of 15 articles, or 33% printed animal or animal-like descriptions without negative comment or quotation marks as a sign of disavowal.

The use of the animal metaphor was condemned in only three (7%) of the articles. Gutman (1977) devoted his entire piece to dissecting how animal analogies have been used historically to try to separate the behavior of the rebellious (striking, rioting, looting) from the social, economic and political conditions that shaped their discontent.

DEVIANCE, SOCIAL SCIENCE, AND THE PRINT MEDIA

The content analysis has demonstrated that most commentators made little or no attempt to understand this outbreak of deviant behavior from the standpoint of the participants. Instead, many chose to closely identify with the victims, and to portray their plight in sympathetic, personalized, and anecdotal terms. The gulf of race and/or class that separated the authors from the participants was rarely bridged. The outwardly expressed motives of the looters, if acknowledged, were dismissed as rationalizations, while the widely known deviant and provocative business practices of a portion of the ghetto merchants were usually overlooked. The result frequently was a reductionist tirade against "mob behavior" misrepresented by psychologistic or biologistic (animalistic) metaphors.

The readily accessible findings of prior social science research on similar uprisings were largely ignored. Those few commentators who attempted to explain or comprehend the events from a sociological perspective within an historical context were castigated as "apologizing for" or "excusing" the illegality that occurred in the ghetto streets that night.

The consensus of social scientists in the 1960s who studied urban uprisings generally leaned in a liberal direction: a cross-section of young ghetto men retaliated against local merchants who antagonized them in their roles as consumers and workers during a spontaneous rebellion against the hardships of poverty, unemployment, and discrimination. In 1977 the closest approximation of this formerly liberal view was found in the editorial of the revolutionary socialist newspaper the *Guardian*. Liberal commentators tended to emphasize the emergence and development of an "underclass driven to desperation and criminality by idleness, public assistance and social decay." Conservative authors demonstrated a preoccupation with a "criminal riff-raff underclass, pampered by permissiveness" that plundered innocent and helpless small business men during an "orgy of lawless, animalistic outbursts." These two points of view have a great deal in common. Both denigrate the backgrounds and accomplishments of the participants; exonerate their immediate, petty antagonists, the victimized merchants; divert attention to the alleged faults and flaws within the moral codes, personalities, families, or peer groups of those who behaved in a deviant manner; and totally overlook the social, political and economic forces that the deviants claim exploit, alienate and oppress them as workers and low-income consumers.

NOTES

1. This is not a sample but the entire universe, although a few articles meeting these criteria may have been overlooked. If the same author(s) wrote a series of articles, they are considered as installments of a single piece.

REFERENCES

ALLEN, R. (1970). Black awakening in capitalist America. Garden City, N.Y.: Anchor.
ASBURY, E. (1977). "Looted business owners seek federal assistance." New York Times, July 19:26.
AXRHEIM, P. (1977). "A walk on the wild side." Newsweek, July 25:31.
BAKER, R. (1977). "The unfairness of it all." New York Times, July 19:35.
BASSO, H. (1935). "The riot of 1935." New Republic, April 3:209-210.

BERK, R. (1968). "Doing business in the ghetto: Retail merchants." Supplemental studies for the National Advisory Commission on Civil Disorders, 125-132. Washington, D.C.: U.S. Government Printing Office.

BOESEL, D., BERK, R., GROVES, G., EIDSON, T.,and ROSSI, P. (1968). "White institutions and black rage." In P. Rossi (ed.), Ghetto Revolts, New York: Transaction.

BOETH, R., GEIMAN, E., BOYD, F., ABRAMSON, P., and WILLIAMS, D. (1977). "The plunderers." Newsweek, July 25:23-27.

BRESLIN, J. (1977a). "Black deeds done in the heart of darkness." New York Daily News (syndicated column), July 15:5.

———— (1977b). "Open wounds fester in heat, dirt and smell." New York Daily News (syndicated column), July 17:5.

BUCHANAN, P. (1977a). "The looting: A night of people failure." New York Daily News (syndicated column), July 18:55

———— (1977b). "Hungry Folks Rob Food, Andy, Right." New York Daily News (syndicated column), July 21:58.

Business Week (1977). "The steep price tag on the blackout." August 1:20-21.

CAMPBELL, A., and SCHUMAN, H., (1968). "Racial attitudes in fiften American cities." Supplemental studies for the National Advisory Commission on Civil Dosorders. Washington, D.C.: U.S. Government Printing Office.

CAPLOVITZ, D. (1967). The poor pay more: Consumer practices of low income families. New York: Free Press.

CARMICHAEL, S., and HAMILTON, C. (1967). Black power. New York: Vintage.

CARMODY, D. (1977). "Pathos, heroics, humor on a night to remember." New York Times, July 15:14.

Christian Science Monitor (1977). "Lessons from the looting." July 18:28.

CLARKE, K. (1965). Dark ghetto. New York: Harper and Row.

CLINES, F. (1977a). "Down these mean streets." New York Times, July 15:16.

———— (1977b). "The night of the looters." New York Times, September 3:40.

COOMBS, O. (1977). "The tragedy of Le Mans: The new civil war begins." New York Magazine, August 8:43-45.

DECTER, M. (1977). "Looting and liberal racism." Commentary, September:48-54.

DREYFUS, J. (1977). "Black progress: Myth and ghetto reality." Progressive, November:21-25.

DYNES, R., and QUARANTELLI, E. (1968). "What looting in civil disturbances really means." Trans-Action, May:9-14.

Ebony (1977). "The tip of the iceberg." September:132.

EDELSON, M. (1977). "Bastille day '77'." National Review, August 5:870.

FOGELSON, R., and HILL, R. (1968). "Who riots? A study of participation in the 1967 riots." Supplemental study for the National Advisory Commission on Civil Disorders. Washington, D.C.: U.S. Government Printing Office.

GANS, H. (1969). "The ghetto rebellions and urban class conflict." In R. Connery (ed.), Urban riots. New York: Vintage.

GESCHWENDER, J. (1968). "Civil rights protest and riots: A disappering distinction." Social Science Quarterly, 49:474-484.

Guardian (1977). "What the blackout illuminated." July 27:10.

GUTMAN, H. (1977). "As for the '02 Kosher-food rioters." New York Times, July 21:38.

HAMILL, P. (1977a). "Blackout looting." New York Daily News (syndicated column), July 15:3.
_____ (1977b). "Five solid ways Jimmy Carter can help our city." New York Daily News (syndicated column), July 18:4.
Harris Public Opinion Poll (1967). Attitudes about the riots.
HAYDEN, T. (1967). Rebellion in Newark. New York: Vintage.
HUNTER-GAULT, C. (1977) "Where looting's part of life." New York Times, July 15:4.
JACOBS, P. (1965). "Keeping the poor poor." New Politics, 5:1-27.
JANOWITZ, M. (1969). "Patterns of collective racial violence." In H. Graham and T. Gurr (eds.), Violence in America. New York: Signet.
Jet Magazine (1977). "What caused the looting when the lights went out?" August 4:12.
JONES, G. (1977). "New York's looters: Budding anarchy?" US News and World Report, August 1:14.
JONES, M. (1969). "Deception in the marketplace of the poor: The role of the Federal Trade Commission." In F. Sturdivant (ed.), The ghetto as marketplace. New York: Free Press.
KELLEY, K. (1977). "N.Y.C. blackout spotlights poverty." Guardian, July 27:1.
KEMPTON, M. (1977a). "The pride of the 44th." New York Post (syndicated column), July 15:53.
_____ (1977b). "Law and disorder." New York Post (syndicated column), July 16:17.
Kerner Commission (1968). Report of the National Advisory Commission on Civil Disorders. Washington, D.C.: U.S. Government Printing Office.
KONING, H. (1977). "New York's dissident looters: Human rights means different things to them." In These Times, August 24-30:17.
KRAFT, J. (1977). "Lessons of New York." New York Post (syndicated column), July 18:30.
LANG, K., and LANG, G. (1968). "Racial disturbances as collective protest." In L. Massoti and D. Bowen (eds.), Riots and rebellion: Civil violence and the urban community. Beverly Hills, Cal.: Sage.
LEE, A., and HUMPHREY, N. (1943). Race riot. Detroit: Dryden.
LERNER, M. (1977). "Feeling the pain at the birth of a new underclass." New York Post (syndicated column), July 27:33.
LEVINE, A. (1977). "The law went dark, too." New York Times, August 20:28.
LEWIS, A. (1977). "The mind of the north." New York Times, August 15:27.
LIEBOW, E. (1967). Tally's corner. Boston: Little, Brown.
LIPSYTE, R. (1977). "The strange logic of looting." New York Post (syndicated column), July 15:13.
LLEWELLYN, B., and WALINSKY, A. (1977). "Blackout lessons." New York Times, July 31:sec. 4, p. 17.
LYNN, F. (1977). "Survey shows New Yorkers link lootings to thievery, not protest." New York Times, August 27:1.
McCALL, H. (1977). "Reply to an editorial in the New York Amsterdam News." New York Times, August 5:21.
McGRORY, M. (1977). "A true disaster." New York Post (syndicated column), July 18:31.
MERRICK, F. (1977). "Night of terror." Time, July 25:12-22.
Nation (1977). "People in the dark." August 6:100.
National Review (1977). "Rip-off time." August 5:869.

New Republic (1977). "The mugging of New York." July 30:5-7.

New York Amsterdam News (1977a). "Editorial on the blackout." July 23:1.

_____ (1977b). "Black opinion mixed on looting; Merchants, politicians outraged." July 23:1, 4.

New York City Criminal Justice Agency (1977). "A demographic profile of defendants arrested in New York City's blackout: A preliminary report." New York City.

New York Times (editorials) (1977a). "Wednesday the thirteenth." July 15:22.

_____ (1977b). "A blind night: Let the nation heed the "animals." July 17: sec. 4, p. 20.

_____ (1977c). "What New York can do for Mr. Carter." July 19:34.

_____ (1977d). "My grandfather and the looters." July 23:18.

_____ (1977e). "The geography of civility." July 28:18.

_____ (1977f). "50% of 176 cited in looting held full-time jobs." August 15:34.

_____ (1977g). "Legal Aid Society may turn out to be unlikely victim of blackout." July 25:42.

New York Times/CBS News (1977). "Poll, July 1977." New York City.

New Yorker Magazine (1977). "The talk of the town: Notes and comment." August 8:15-17.

OBERSCHALL, A. (1967). "The Los Angeles riot of August 1965." Social Problems, Winter:322-341.

PLATE, T. (1977). "Why the cops didn't shoot." New York Magazine, August 1:29-32.

QUARANTELLI, E., and DYNES, R. (1968). "Looting in civil disorders: An index of social change." American Behavioral Scientist, 11:7-10.

_____ (1970). "Property norms and looting: Their patterns in community crises." Phylon, 31:168-182.

QUINDLEN, A. (1977). "The city on a morning without any electricity: Odd mixture of unrealism and business as usual." New York Times, July 15:15.

RAINWATER, L. (1967). "Open letter on white justice and the riots." Trans-Action, September:25.

RAVITCH, D. (1977). "Not always a matter of justice." New York Times, July 27:19.

RILEY, C. (1977). "Time is no longer running out; It's gone." New York Times, July 17: sec. 4, p. 12.

ROSENTHAL, R. (1977). "Like man dogs and animals going wild." Boston Globe, July 15:1.

RUSTIN, B. (1966). "The Watts manifesto and the McCone report." Commentary, 41:29-35.

SAFIRE, W. (1977). "Christmas in July." New York Times, July 18:27.

SHEPPARD, N., Jr. (1977). "Youths offer loot and excuses." New York Times, July 17: sec. 1, p. 40.

SKOLNICK, J. (1969). The politics of protest. New York: Ballentine.

TABB, W. (1970). The political economy of the black ghetto. New York: Norton.

Time (1977). "The American underclass: Destitute and desperate in the land of plenty." August 29:14-27.

VAN HORNE, H. (1977a). "Dark portent for the future." New York Post (syndicated column), July 15:43.

_____ (1977b) "Hinterland's view of looters." New York Post (syndicated column), July 18:28.

_____ (1977c). "Looting provides city's bigots with an excuse to hate." New York Post (syndicated column), July 25:28.

Village Voice (1977). "Here comes the neighborhood." July 25:1-14.

Wall Street Journal (1977). "Power and finance in New York City." July 19:12.
WEUSI, K. (1977). "A Brooklyn community leader takes a different look at the looters."
    New York Amsterdam News, July 23:2.
WICKER, T. (1977a). "A prophecy fulfilled." New York Times, July 17: sec. 4, p. 21.
_____ (1977b). "Yazoo city and the Bronx." New York Times. July 24: sec. 4, p. 17.
WILL, G. (1977a). "Shock of recognition." Newsweek, July 25:80.
_____ (1977b). "No halos for looters." New York Post (syndicated column), July 21:35.

Media
Contributions
to
Deviance

Part 4

10

SOCIAL CREATION OF CRIME NEWS
All the News Fitted to Print

SANFORD SHERIZEN

AUTHOR'S NOTE: *I wish to thank Yoram Neumann, Martin Sawzin, Lou Koch, Morrie Roth, Steve Boris, and Joan Sherizen for their comments on earlier drafts of this article. John Johnstone provided several excellent ideas for consideration. The students in a seminar on Mass Media and Crime, held at the University of Illinois, Chicago Circle, participated by discussing this project and providing aid in the content analysis of newspapers. I especially would like to thank George Bozich for his assistance.*

Our stated ideal for a murder story was that it should be so understood and told that the murderer would not be hanged, not by our readers. We never achieved our ideal, but there it was: and it is scientifically and artistically the true ideal for an artist and for a newspaper; to get the news so completely and to report it so humanly that the reader will see himself in the other fellow's place.

Lincoln Steffens, 1931

While researchers have intensively examined how people feel about crime, and found that the subject is very much on the minds of most Americans (Garofalo, 1977a), few researchers have empirically examined the sources of information from which people gain their ideas about crime or the nature of the impressions presented to them from which they select their opinions. Even though direct experience with crime informs the opinions of some, the majority of persons base their opinions about crime on more indirect derived forms of knowledge.

From the limited research available, it is clear that the mass

203

media play a major role in the creation and dissemination of beliefs about crime (Conklin, 1975). The average person is quite aware of a number of details about crime. These details provide them with an ability and a willingness to discuss the causes of, the nature of, and/or the solutions to the crime problem. For the audience of the mass media, crime becomes knowable. From the mass media, the problem of crime is readily available, certain reasons for criminality are offered, the effectiveness of governmental responses to crime can be measured, and personal ideas of safety can be judged.

The mass media provide citizens with a public awareness of crime, but this awareness is, at best, based upon an information-rich and knowledge-poor foundation. The level of interest people have about crime is not matched by the level of knowledge about crime which they are able to obtain from the mass media. Anyone interested in learning about crime from the mass media is treated to examples, incidents, and scandals but at such a level of description that it is impossible for them to develop an analytical comprehension of crime.

The nature of facts about crime found in the media limits rather than educates public opinion, acting as an important restriction on the public's ability to act as informed citizens. Public concerns, apprehensions, and reactions become part of the general response, which is based upon "cops and robbers" news stories.

In terms of its coverage of crime news, the mass media become an important part of the "complex nature of the screening and coding process whereby certain forms of rule breaking are picked out for attention" (Cohen, 1973). The mass media provide a distinctive social reality about crime (Quinney, 1970), identifying certain groups and their roles as crime fighters or crime doers. Meanings are provided for the populace by means of a body of sense-making elements, a structuring of "a common consciousness of what is, what is important, and what is right" (Gerbner, 1967).

Crime which is present in the mass media is not the same as crime-in-actuality. Printed crime stories are not a summary of all crimes which have occurred during the previous 24 hours. Nor do the mass media follow a priority listing of crime news by means of some inherent order, with the "most important" crimes getting major attention and lessor stories being buried or omitted. Rather, the mass media follow some rules which inform a selection of crime events.

The selection process from crime events to crime news is diagrammed in Chart One. It is true that the mass media cannot report all crimes that have been committed. Yet, the small number of crimes presented as crime news implies that some sorting out of the news takes place.

Chart One.

FROM CRIME EVENTS TO CRIME NEWS

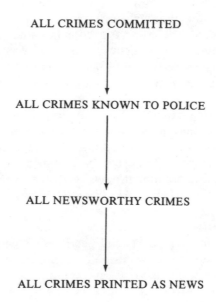

ALL CRIMES COMMITTED

ALL CRIMES KNOWN TO POLICE

ALL NEWSWORTHY CRIMES

ALL CRIMES PRINTED AS NEWS

This chapter contains an examination of the process by which crimes are selected from crime incidents and are reported as news. Specific attention will be paid to newspapers. This chapter will examine the omissions and commissions of crime news coverage, indicating the factors which structure decisions on crime coverage. By examining the production context (the ways by which crime events become newsworthy) rather than the audience context (the manner in which mass media information is received and used by the audience), we will suggest that crime news found in newspapers is a constructed reality. Only the crimes that meet the criteria established by bureaucratically and occupationally determined factors *as well as* meet the monopoly official sources have over primary information are considered for selection as crime news.

The newspaper reader is offered certain crime news-worthy events prepared as news stories about crime. These news stories contain specialized images of crime, images which have little to do with the realities or complexities of crime.

CRIME AS NEWS

Crime news differs from other news in terms of its relationship to the events which it represents. Newspaper accounts of sports, as a contrasting example, are quite thorough, offering several different forms of information to the reader. The sports section has some distinct relationships to the entire number of events which occur during a particular time period. Even though there is some selection as to what sports will be reported, the sports pages' readerships are able to expand their knowledge of sports.

Another contrasting example is that of international news. Newspapers capsulize the information about international news so that the reader is able to obtain the one or two facts which some consider the most significant. No attempt is made by the newspapers to create a full representation of all international news, with the exception of certain newspapers such as the *New York Times* (Galtung and Ruge, 1965; Cohen, 1973).

Crime news provides another category of representation of events. Crime does not appear in a special section but generally is found throughout a newspaper, except in smaller communities where a police report is given. It is unclear as to the representational order which crime news coverage characterizes. Obviously not all crimes can be reported, but those crimes reported tend to represent a very specific sample of crime events. News about crime found in newspapers represent a manufactured representation which is structured so that it appears to represent sufficient information for the reader.

The reader of crime news is provided with crime stories given as fact but, in reality, what they read are designed realities. Selected from a limited range of cognitive and evaluative elements, and mediated by organizational factors and information limitations (Elliott, 1972), the crime news is presented to the reader as "all the news worth knowing about."

The role of the mass media treatment of crime information can be viewed most fruitfully in the context of its influences on communicative behavior (Mueller, 1970). The manner in which crime is selected, treated, and distributed by the mass media influences the information level of the citizenry in its understanding of crime.

The role of the media has been one of limiting or repressing this level of understanding. By presenting a large volume of materials, particular world views on crime have been established in the public's mind. This world view is insufficient to provide for an understanding of crime in its larger context but sufficient to make the media audience concerned about crime. The world view or public belief system developed by the media limits the perspectives of the audience to certain limited aspects of the crime phenomena and, in the process of limiting its coverage, certain features of considerable importance are excluded from comprehension. The public may not only be immobilized by the violence found but the reasoning behind the media images being presented suggests a motivational explanation built upon individual decisions of good and evil, a nonpolitical explanation which minimizes societal factors (Murdock and Golding, 1973).

Thus, the mass media, particularly the newspapers, become sense-makers to the world, providing stocks of knowledge, available concepts (categories), and interpersonal rules (relations) by which individuals can classify and interpret crime events. The mass media audience becomes informed but not knowledgeable, interested about details but dulled by overstimulation, concerned about understanding but limited in comprehending.

Our concern in this chapter is with the account construction of crime news (Chibnall, 1975). What follows will be an examination of the rules which inform the selection of crime events. It will be found that the process of collecting news stories imposes gatekeeper-type constraints to a larger degree than suggested by other mass media researchers who have overemphasized the control of news by accepting a simplified model of gatekeeping based upon a group of news deciders (Breed, 1955).

THE IMPORTANCE OF CRIME IN NEWSPAPER DEVELOPMENT

When a tabloid prints it [crime and scandal], that's smut. When the [New York] *Times* prints it, that's sociology.

> Adolph Ochs, founder of the
> *New York Times.* Quoted in *Time,*
> August 15, 1977

Kai Erikson (1966) notes that the major changes which occurred in the nature of trials and punishment in England and colonial America "coincided almost exactly with the development of newspapers as a medium of mass information." The public's attraction to deviant behavior no longer required direct public involvement, since the mass media offered "much the same kind of entertainment as public hanging or a Sunday visit to the local gaol."

Newspapers are the most detailed purveyors of crime news of any of the media. At present, crime is the third largest category of subjects covered by newspapers, with local government and sports the only other topics receiving more coverage (Johnstone, private communication). Although there has been a decrease in the amount of crime and violence found in newspapers in recent years (Haskins, 1969), the large amount of such news still in existence is magnified in its impact by the high readership which crime items tend to have (Haskins, 1968). On the average, crime occupies from 2 to 7% of the total news space in the press (Haskins, 1968). Even outside of the United States, a similar pattern exists (Lenke, 1973).

Newspapers' relationship with crime has been constant from the days of the first newspapers in the United States. The first full time journalist in the U.S. was a crime and police reporter (Hughes, 1940). George Wisner came from London in 1833 to work for the *New York Sun*. This was a period of expansion for American newspapers beyond the party presses into a medium for the broad spectrum of the population. Wisner had become successful in his reporting of crime for British newspapers and he was hired to help increase the *Sun's* circulation by reporting on local crime. As the *Sun's* circulation did increase[1] other newspapers attempted to outdo each other by finding the most juicy crime and scandal stories for print (Steffens, 1931).[2]

Crimes occur daily, especially in large cities but even in smaller towns, where local incidents can be supplemented with national crime news available from the wire services. Crime is an event with periodicity, a characteristic which related perfectly with the "nonroutine" nature of news bureaucracies (Tunstall, 1972). The predictability of crime as a repeating event but with changes in participants and locations creates the same old story but with a newness every day.

Crime incidents are able to be structured into the format required by newspapers. Crime is one of the new media topics which is, or can be written as if it is, so fully people-centered.

If crimes are so easily available and moldable, the legitimizing nature of gaining information about crime situations adds an important factor to the usefulness of crime for newspapers. Crime is retrievable information which is available as a public event. Due to sources of information which reporters have developed, crimes become convenient to discover. Sources of information, mainly the police, provide notification of crimes occurring and serve as objective verifiers of events. Thus crime incidents can be changed into objective facts by means of the process of official encounters which represent public records and official sources of information.

The "expandability/shrinkability" factor of crime as a reportable event becomes even more important given the unpredictability of the amount of news available to fill in the day's space limits.

Finally, crime also serves as a "legitimate" topic for newspapers to cover. Crime is culturally relevant; a meaningful category for newspapers to report. By reporting crime, newspapers are fulfilling their responsibilities as dispensers of public information.[3]

In all, newspapers and crime are integrally related. Crime serves newspapers in a number of ways and in recognition of its usefulness, newspapers have accepted crime as a major topic of news today.

THE CRIME REPORTER

Social scientists have developed three perspectives on the primary controls over such decisions. Some view journalists as being controlled by other journalists, who are part of an autonomous occupation. Another perspective is that journalists choose according to the wishes of their employers, operating as employees in an occupational setting. Another view is that journalists are controlled by their news sources, determinations being made on stories by the process of newsgathering (Tunstall, 1972.)

Each of these controls operate within a framework which attempts to minimize conflicts between the dual roles of being a member of an organization and a profession. Tuchman (1972) has suggested that there are techniques available to a reporter which allow for certain strategies of objectivity to be used to construct accounts while minimizing the conflicts.

Crime reporters have similar approaches to their work. To a great degree, they serve as a conduit for official views of crime while presenting these views as objective reporting. By fulfilling their ability to gain sources of information, they serve to support a monopolization of information about crime. By accepting a particular mode of reporting, crime reporters make objective what is truly an official interpretation of criminality.

In many respects, crime reporters differ from their journalistic peers. Johnstone (private communication), in reporting on a major nationwide study of American journalists, found that 13.7% of the 70,000 full-time reporters in the United States cover crime or police, with another one or two percent of the reporters covering courts exclusively. The crime reporters tend to have less formal education than other reporters. Crime reporters tend to be older than other reporters, as well as having been on the job for a longer period of time. They tend to be more conservative in their political outlook and are oriented to their work in more traditional ways than their peers, especially the younger, liberal arts-background reporters. Of the 50 different areas or topics of coverage which newspapers present, only six were covered by less qualified persons, mainly measured by educational level and background experiences.

According to Tunstall (1972), British crime reporters have the lowest pay of any journalist and low status. Tunstall's study also points out that crime reporters have low story choice but high story use.

These personal characteristics cannot be separated from the working characteristics of the crime reporter's role, i.e., the nature of the work of reporting crime. While it is unclear whether pre-selection or socialization (Sigelman, 1973) play major roles in the development of the crime reporter, it is evident that the occupational requirements of reporting about crime distinguish the crime reporter from other reporters and have major consequences for the types of news which appear about crime.

Gathering the Facts: Contacting Sources of Information

For the crime reporter, there exists a number of *potential* persons who have information about crime. Only a few of these persons are turned to for stories. The crime reporter places limitations on where information is gathered, thus limiting the type of information which could ever be printed (Tuchman, 1972). The limitations stem from job-related requirements such as citing a creditable source of information so that the story is "objective" and writing the story with the least amount of work. To interview inmates as persons knowledgeable about problems in prison is to seek out "unofficial" comments which might be criticized as being from less than objective persons. Likewise, to seek out persons who are critical of some aspects of the criminal justice system is to have an unbalanced article, i.e., one that requires the right of reply for officials, a rebalancing act which requires more work than the simple filing of the more typical crime news report.

For the crime reporter, one major source of information meets the job-related requirements and provides other important gains. This major source is the police, who serve perfectly to provide the types of materials the reporters require. The relationship with the police is so well established that many newspapers have full-time reporters at police stations. In most cities, the report of the investigating officer was available to reporters in written form or over the phone (ABA, 1968).

Individual officers are able to offer on-the-spot information which others (victims or witnesses) who were present might provide but in less coherent form. Information which the officer is able to provide is official. The information is also "neutral" in that the officers are simply providing the press with information about public events. The wrong-doing is self-evident, not even necessarily noted by the officer in discussions with the reporter. Lastly, the information which the police provide the reporter is given as part of a relationship which has been established on a personal and institutional level. The reporter and the police officer have understandings about what information the police will give as well as how the reporter will handle the story.

The fact that the police serve as primary sources of information is only partially due to the official role of the police. They are available for informational purposes, *and* the symbiotic relationship which exists between the crime reporter and the police make their relationship even more feasible.

Crime reporters and lower level police officers share startlingly similar work experiences (Johnstone, private communication). Both are assigned to beats, where they are outside of the physical confines of the organization. By being "on the streets" as part of their job, they are in the position of being outside many major modes of socialization by which higher-ups establish control over their peer's behaviors and perceptions (Coser, 1961).

For the crime reporter, this relationship with the police appears to be more important than the working relationship with their supposed occupational peers. Crime reporters differ from other journalists by the time they spend with non-journalists as well as their socialization with and reliance upon the police. Crime reporters become more like the police than like other reporters while the police, to a large degree, remain constant to their police occupational identity.

The crime reporter gains sources of potential stories as part of a larger set of relationships. They are in the position of gaining their own monopoly over crime news, thus obtaining information which other reporters and citizens can only obtain through them. The relationships with the police is beneficial to the crime reporter. As a result, occupation and work become merged into new forms.

For the police, either as a department or for individual officers, crime reporters provide relationships with benefits. The police have a vested interest in crime news appearing in newspapers and other media. Their position as authorities on crime is reinforced as their views and opinions about crime develop from news reports on crime (Molotch and Lester, 1974). As crimes become more publicly known, the almost instinctive response of the public is to seek out more police. Thus, the more crimes which become known, the more aid the police may be able to gain in seeking increases in departmental budgets. Further, crime news results in a strengthening of the police view of the causes and solutions of the crime problem.

As a consequence of the police becoming a major if not the sole source of information about crime, both the police and reporter gain. A relationship of convenience becomes a matter of restriction of the crimes which become crime news.

Crime News as Police-Generated Information

The police act as "promoters" (Molotch and Lester, 1974) of crime news by helping to make crime occurrences available to crime reporters. The monopoly relationship which the police have with reporters provides the police with powerful event-creating and event-limiting influences.

One major limitation on the information provided to reporters is that it tends to come from lower ranking officers, because they are the police on the scene of crime incidents. These officers are able to provide materials on crime incidents, arrests, and preliminary information about the victims and offenders.

Post-arrest activities of the police are less seldom given to reporters since this information could only result from a change in the police-reporter relationship. Receiving such information would mean that a reporter's activities would generally be confined geographically to the police headquarters, higher ranking officers would automatically be involved, and, most importantly, the development and release of information would be under the bureaucratic control of departmental rules. These factors interfere with the type of reporting that many crime reporters perform, except in the instances where minor facts require verification.

A second major limitation of police-generated information is that, due to the details about crime given to reporters, the usual newspaper crime story is limited to police activities, generally the crime/arrest/charge periods of the criminal justice system. Seldom are there stories about the offender in court or in prision, except in the case of unique crimes, personages, or circumstances which make the case of interest.

A third limitation is that crime reporters depend upon their relationship with the police to such an extent that they are unable to report about the police when mistakes are made, when corruption is found, or when the crime fighters' image is not fulfilled. Such a story would be given to an investigative reporter or written without a byline (Rubinstein, 1973). This need to protect the police affects the basic working style of crime reporters. The reporter is an outsider whose access to the police is assured by his pledge not to reveal what he knows of police work.

A fourth limitation to crime news is related to the accuracy of the information which the police sources provide. Leaving aside purposeful inaccuracies, at least one report has found that police and other law enforcement agency information was inaccurate in some 88% of stories checked with the participants mentioned, exclusive of omissions, misquotes, and typographic errors. Court records were inaccurate in only 18% of the cases (Berry, 1967).

A final limitation is that crime reporters have been coopted by the police in the instances when they are willing to float certain stories which can help the police. This usually occurs when the police feel that a story in the newspapers about how close the capture is of a particular criminal may lead the person to come out of hiding and be more easily captured (Chibnall, 1975). Another instance of this cooptation is when the crime reporter is willing to print false information from the police about the amount of money stolen. By printing a higher amount than was actually taken, this information might cause suspicions and disagreements on the part of the criminals, leading them to think that one of their members is holding out more than the agreed share (Letkemann, 1973).

Thus, the nature of crime reporting incorporates a series of limitations on the information made available to the public. What passes for crime news is an ideological construct; that which is constructed out of the power of official versions of crime.

CONTENTS OF CRIME NEWS: THE END RESULT OF PROCESSING

We shall now look at the contents of crime news in one major American city. The contents provide an empirical picture of the selectivity of the news media. The contents of crime news will illustrate the nature of the information which occurs, at least in one city.

Chicago was selected because of it's large amount of crime as well as the fact that the city's newspapers[4] have made crime news a staple of their coverage. The findings, viewed as general patterns, have implications for other large American cities.[5]

An Empirical Study of Crime News

Selected students were provided with instructions on how to code newspaper articles.[6] They were assigned to code crime articles in four Chicago newspapers; the three main metropolitan papers and the black community paper. The final edition of each daily paper was chosen for all issues for every third month during 1975 (January, April, July, and October).

Ten coding categories were selected for the coding sheet, which were:

(1) newspaper and date,
(2) the crime reported,
(3) victim identification factors (name, address, age, sex, race, business, etc.),
(4) suspect identification factors (name, address, age, sex, race, business, etc.),
(5) area of the city in which the crime occured,
(6) source(s) of the information cited on the crime/victim/suspect,
(7) location of the article in the newspaper,
(8) number of column inches devoted to the article,
(9) presence of (and size and length of) any headlines, and
(10) presence of (and size and location of) any pictures.

Over 1,000 crime stories were coded for the time period. Since each article contained many items, the total number of items coded reached over 15,000. Categories excluded from consideration included Watergate, Lebanon, and foreign political assassinations. While these exclusions were decided upon in terms of coding clarity, it was clear that the remaining categories selected would result in a bias toward traditional crime activities. It can be argued that the omitted situations were not everyday affairs and should not be considered as the ordinary crimes generally written about in newspapers.

Findings

In terms of the vast number of crimes which occurred in Chicago each day, there is a clear shrinkage from all crime events found in official statistics as compared to all events reported as crime news. (See Table 1.) This shrinkage is even more evident if one considers the estimated truer rates of crime, which are those found in victimization studies, rather than official statistics, which are those reported by the police. For example, robbery has been estimated as being reported in only 53 out of every 100 occurrences (Garofalo, 1977b). Thus the shrinkage to be discussed is really second level (recognized by the police) or a third level (recorded by the police and provided to reporters) of selection.

An index of crime news shrinkage was constucted in order to compare the percentages of all crimes known to the police to those which were reported in the Chicago newspapers during the period under investigation. This shrinkage differed by crime, with the least shrinkage found for murder/manslaughter, where almost 70% of the crimes were reported (see Table 1). In terms of all other crimes known to the police, the shrinkage ranged from 5% reported for rape to less than 1% for almost all other crimes. The operating rule for shrinkage tended to be that the more prevalent the crime, the less it would be reported, with the exception of murder/manslaughter—seldom committed but serious—which captures the majority of attention. The only other crimes that appeared more frequently than expected were those which were (or could be written as) humorous, ironic, and/or unusual or in which the situation was sentimental or dramatic, especially in terms of the participants.

Not only was the least shrinkage for murder/homicides, but these stories were also the majority of the crime stories found in the newspapers. Almost half of all crimes reported were murder and manslaughter with another 35% involving other serious crimes. The notice given to murder and the lack of notice given to such other crimes as larceny and burglary is striking. Even though larceny/theft was 117 times more prevalent than murder, as reported by the police, homicides were presented in the newspapers almost ten times more often.

Even with these general findings, the selection process results in a particular image of crime being presented in the newspapers. Crimes are defined as that which happens in certain ways, by certain people, with certain consequences, and committed by individuals rather than institutions. Crimes are the most dangerous offenses, even though these incidents occur relatively rarely, especially to the majority of the readership. Crimes are that which occurs outside of the potential for the police to prevent, especially since homicides found in newspapers were presented as being "caused" by passions and insanities. For an individual reader who absorbs this imagery, crime appears to be violent, probably rampant, out of control, and likely to strike physically at any moment.

**Table 1. AN INDEX OF NEWS SHRINKAGE OF
            SELECTED CRIMES**

Selected Crimes	Reported by Police[1]		Reported by Newspapers		Index of Shrinkage of Crimes
	N[2]	% of Crimes	N	% of Crimes	% of Crimes
Murder/manslaughter	1109[3]	a	567	45	51
Forcible rape	1657	1	80	6	5
Robbery	22171	9	286	23	1
Aggravated assault	12514	5	178	14	1
Burglary/breaking & entering	47299	20	74	6	a
Larceny	117909	50	64	5	a
Motor vehicle theft	33484	14	a	a	a

1. F.B.I., *Uniform Crime Reports in the United States, 1975.* Table 6. Number of Offenses Known to the Police, 1975, Cities and Towns 10,000 and Over Population—Chicago, p.95.

2. Only the city of Chicago was selected. If the Chicago SMSA was selected, the number of crimes would be higher and even more shrinkage would be shown.

3. Nonnegligible manslaughter and manslaughter by negligence have been combined with murder for purposes of comparison with news stories where the categories were also combined in most instances.

a. Less than one percent or not available.

Not only were certain crimes emphasized, but also certain aspects of the criminal justice system were presented while others were not considered. The majority of the articles were limited to one particular stage of the criminal justice system, with over two thirds of the articles related to the beginning stages of the system. Crime incidents, arrests, captures, suspect followup, and/or charges placed against the suspect were the most prevalent responses to crime reported. The post-arrest stages of the criminal justice system were seldom mentioned.

Further emphasis on the action elements (the active nature of stopping crimes rather than punishing criminals) was found in the headlines and the tone of the stories. Commission of the crime represented the major details contained in the article. Little or no mention was made of how

Table 2. CRIME INCIDENTS REPORTED IN NEWSPAPERS

Arrest	347
Capture	199
Charge	340
Suspect followup	240
Indictment	93
Arraignment	54
Trial report	188
Appeal-plea	54
Verdict-decision	89
Sentence	63
Commitment	24
TOTAL	1691

many (or how few) of the crimes were solved or how many of the offenders were processed and in what ways.

A special case of this emphasis was found in the black community newspaper. The *Defender* concentrated nearly all of its crime stories on the first five pages of the paper. The majority of the crimes were homicides, presented in great detail and accompanied by banner headlines to draw the reader's attention. These articles, even more than in the metropolitan (white) press, were written with a concentration on the details of the crime incident. Few of the *Defender's* articles even contained an indication of whether the suspect had been arrested or, if so, whether charges had been placed by officials.

The imagery of this aspect of the crime news was that of crime running rampant, with the chances of becoming a victim quite high. Certain criminals were being arrested, especially after they had committed a crime. The police were doing all of the arresting but nothing else was happening in the criminal justice system to back the police up and make the streets safe.

Victims and Suspects

Victims of crimes were invisible, not appearing very often in the news account. Even when they did appear, they were presented only in terms of brief descriptions which give their name, age, sex, occupation, and/or injury. Once this basic information was presented, little else was mentioned. In fact, victims were mentioned as often as offenders; if details could be quantified, the invisibility of the victim would be even greater. Crime victims were quoted less often than were the police, but approximately the same number of times as witnesses to crimes and representatives of the suspect (defense attorneys and/or suspect's family) were quoted.

Ironically, even the brief mention of victims' names and addresses was not always in the best interest of the victims. This information has been used by criminals to further victimize the already victimized by robbing their homes while they are in the hospital recovering from the original incident *(New York Times,* 1975).

Table 3.
VICTIMS AND SUSPECTS REPORTED IN NEWSPAPERS

	Victims	Suspects
By name	892	903
By address	467	452
By area*	203	249
By age	628	763
By sex*	127	179
By race	62	114
By association	396	376
TOTAL	2775	3036

*May be understood from other categories, i.e., victim's sex can be known by victim's name.

The only newspaper of the four which presented the victim as a person in need of communal support in a time of plight was the *Defender.* Victims were highly visible with the crimes against them being portrayed as affecting their lives as well as the black community. Victims were portrayed sympathetically with great details often appearing about their lives prior to and after the crime. The newspaper also gave information on the victims' roles in their community, their relationships with others, and the social injustice resulting from crime. The metropolitan, "white" newspapers seldom if ever provided this type of treatment. In the rare instances when this did appear, the story often dealt with the insensitivity of public agencies in helping the victim.

Surprisingly, suspects were seldom described in detail. The typical information given about them was their name, age, and address. While certain sterotypes were found, such as "long hair," "ex-con," etc., there was less of this than expected. Of all suspects mentioned, the most information was given about homicide suspects. In these cases, the article tended to contain details which could serve as a framework for reasons why the crime occurred, i.e., information on the personality, background, and lifestyles of the suspects.

Information about suspects, as well as victims, was found in a more indirect description. While race was seldom mentioned in the news articles, a code of racial designation served some of the same purpose. In a way, the most overriding description of the suspects as well as the victims was that of race. It appeared to be the major master trait of the person, although this was mentioned in the news in the indirect fashion of the racial code.

The suspect's race, per se, was mentioned in only 114 of the articles, but certain areas of the city, known to be black in population concentration, were specified in 434 of the articles. A crime specified as taking place on the south side or by a suspect from the west side was to most Chicagoans clearly "black crime." When the crime occurred in the nonblack sections of the south side or the west side, some indicator usually was placed in the story to make it clear that this was another type of crime, e.g., Marguette Park or the Pullman area. Surprisingly, the south side is mentioned more than three times as often as the west side, although the west side is the poorer and more crime-ridden black section of the city. Especially in terms of homicides, the south side was mentioned more than any other section of town.[7]

Discussions of high status or famous persons who were suspects or victims also had its own geographical associational designations. Such terms as "Gold Coast," "Exclusive Suburb," and "Friend of Mayor Daley" were used to indicate another type of crime situation than the usual stories run in the newspapers. This was "unexpected" crime which was selected by the newspapers because it had a human side. These stories differed from the racial areas stories in their emphasis on the unusualness of the crime or situation. Stories appearing about the crime found in black areas of the city, and some found in white areas, tended to be written as if crime was a common occurrence rather than an exception.

Sources of Information

Most of the sources cited explicitly in the articles were directly or indirectly given as the police. These police sources were quoted in great detail and many facts which might be inadmissible in court, such as "there's no doubt about it, he did it," were printed. These "facts" were not limited to the suspect alone, but were also given about the victim and the victim's background as well as the possible motivations for the crime and the nature of the crime committed.

Table 4. INFORMATION SOURCES REPORTED IN NEWSPAPERS

Public records	615
Police	673
Prosecutor	154
Defense attorney or suspect's family	123
Victim	115
Witness	172
Corrections agent	84
Unofficial leak	35
TOTAL	1971

Very seldom were nonpolice sources quoted or even mentioned in the articles. Public records were found to be the second source given, although this seldom appeared. Victims were almost never guoted as the source of information. An occasional neighbor was quoted—"He was such a good boy. I never thought he would do something like this." Other more immediate sources of information, such as attorneys, witnesses, or relatives of the participants in the crime were rarely included. Interestingly, in the occasional article where one of the more immediate sources was used for information, the article contained much more detail and insight into the crime and its participants.

The sources of information also influenced the contents of the story, as mentioned in the other findings. The emphasis on the details of the crime appeared to be exclusively from the police view of the act. The emphasis on the capture often contained great detail and the names of the arresting officers were usually given.

Emphasis and Presentation of the Stories

Not all of the crime news could be examined as content. Another approach taken was to look at the uses of the crime news. One such use was as filler for the newspapers. The decision to print certain crime events not only depended upon the nature of the crimes and the availability of the information from a source. Independent of this was the fact that the number of crime stories and the length or detail of each story was dependent upon the amount of "hard news" available that day. During periods when other important events were in progress, such as Viet Nam, Watergate, mayoral or presidential campaigns, the amount of crime news printed was substantially less.

Crime news also varied by page, depending upon the need for filling in dead space. Crime news often appeared on the obituary page, a page which varied day by day in terms of length and coverage and where pre-planning is not possible more than just prior to print time. The impossibility of planning an obituary page more than a day in advance, some days being "slow" for death notices, as well as the ease by which crime news could be found by reporters and edited to fit page layout requirements, resulted in crime news being used to complete the page, a topping off of the advertisements, movie features, and death notices.

A final comment on the positioning of the crime news has to do with the location and length of crime articles. Crime stories were found most often in the most important sections of the newspaper. Over 50% of the articles were on the first three pages, usually on the top of the page. Almost 13% of the articles were on the front page and 33% were on the top of the page. A large majority of the stories, over 70%, had a banner 2- to 4-column inch headline, with the majority of the banner headlines related to homicide. Approximately 35% of the articles were from 8- to 13-column inches long with 10% larger, 13-column inches or longer. Clearly, crime news was an important part of the daily news.

SUMMARY AND CONCLUSION

Experienced bank robbers feel their work is made more difficult and the victim's situation more dangerous, by the tendency of the mass media to depict bank robberies as phony, 'toy gun stuff'. Robbers feel that they are now constrained first of all to convince their victims the event is 'not a joke'. This may require more brutal action on their part than they would otherwise need to use. They need to convince any potential 'heroes' among their victims that they cannot be subdued. TV dramas to the contrary. [Peter Letkemann, 1973]

The emphasis of this chapter has been on examining the process by which the information provided to people concerning crime is processed. It is the pool of information about crime from which people can select that has been highlighted.

It has been found that the process of gathering crime news restricts the types of crime-related information which appears as crime news. Crime news is a constructed reality, selected from a series of events which occur and, from which, crime-newsworthy events are written as crime news. Crime reporters are central to this process of restricting information. Viewing the nature of their relationship with the police, it becomes evident that gathering of crime news is based upon a monopolization of certain sources of information. Reporters support the police's version of crime. The police supply reporters with a constant stream of usable crime, and this information, fitting into the work requirements of the reporters, becomes the raw material from which crime news is written. As indicated in the analysis of crime news contents, crime news is limited in a number of serious ways, of which the readership is unaware. To build an understanding of crime and crime control from such information is to have the answers built into the presentation. The nature of crime is serious enough for citizens at large to question the role of the newspapers as adequate suppliers of information from which knowledgeable actions can be taken.

NOTES

1. While the population increased 32% in a decade (1830-1840), the total sale of newspapers increased 187% (Hughes, 1940:12 fn).

2. Newspapers have such a reputation for using crime news to increase their circulation that the British police for a time thought that the 1969 kidnapping of the wife of a newspaper executive was an attempt to create a front page story that would increase the paper's circulation. Reluctance to believe that the abduction was real delayed police efforts to solve the crime, possibly contributing to the woman's death. (Deeley and Walker, 1973).

3. Chevalier (1973) found that 19th-century Paris, the media and popular novels aroused public interest in crime while they fulfilled the public's demand for information about crime. This interest led to the collection of official crime statistics, which in turn fed public fears of crime.

4. Few differences were found between the newspapers, except in the instances mentioned in the text.

5. Similar findings were reported in Davis (1952), ABA (1968), Hauge (1965), and Roshier (1973).

6. The coding was open to the usual difficulties of coding selection compounded by the use of student volunteers. In a random spot check, some variation was found, mainly in terms of the exact category of coding reported. Some crime stories contained multiple crime descriptions, and this may have been recorded in different ways by different coders.

7. A study of the *Chicago Tribune* in 1973 found that only 51 of the 215 murders in the city were covered by the *Tribune* with 12 murders mentioned on the first five pages. While only 20% of the murder victims during this period were white (according to police statistics), nearly half of the murder stories concerned white victims. On the first five pages, where reader interest is highest, two thirds of the murder stories involved white victims (Blake, 1974).

REFERENCES

American Bar Association Project on Minimum Standards for Criminal Justice Standards Relating to Fair Trial and Free Press (The Reardon Report) (1968).

BERRY, F. (1967). "A study of accuracy in local news stories of three dailies." Journalism Quarterly, 44(3):482-490.

BLAKE, P. (1974). "Race, homicide and the news." The Nation, December 7:592-593.

BREED, W. (1955). "Social control in the newsroom: A functional analysis." Social Forces, 33(May):326-335.

CHEVALIER, L. (1973). Laboring classes and dangerous classes in Paris during the nineteenth century. New York: Howard Fertig.

CHIBNALL, S. (1975). "The crime reporter: A study in the production of commercial knowledge." Sociology, 9(1):49-66.

COHEN, S. (1973). "Mods and rockers: The inventory of manufactured news." Pp. 226-241 in S. Cohen and J. Young (eds.), The manufacture of news. Beverly Hills, Cal.: Sage.

CONKLIN, J. (1975). The impact of crime. New York: Macmillan.

COSER, R. (1961). "Insulation from observability and types of social conformity." American Sociological Review, 26(February):28-39.

DAVIS, J. (1952). "Crime news in Colorado newspapers." American Journal of Sociology, LVII(June):325-330.

DEELEY, P., and WALKER, C. (1973). Murder in the Fourth Estate. New York: McGraw-Hill.

ELLIOTT, P. (1972). The making of a television series: A case study in the sociology of culture. London: Constable.

ERICKSON, K. (1966). Wayward puritans. New York: John Wiley.

GALTUNG, J., and RUGE, M. (1965). "The structure of foreign news." Journal of Peace Research, (1):64-90.

GAROFALO, J. (1977a). Public opinion about crime: The attitudes of victims and non-victims in selected cities. LEAA, National Criminal Justice Information and Statistics Service. Washington, D.C.: U.S. Government Printing Office.

_____ (1977b). Local victim surveys: A review of the issues. LEAA, National Criminal Justice Information and Statistics Service. Washington, D.C.: U.S. Government Printing Office.

GERBNER, G. (1967). "Mass media and human communication theory." Pp. 40-57 in F. Dance (ed.), Human communication theory. New York: Holt, Rinehart and Winston.

HASKINS, J. (1968). "Stories of violence get high readership." Editor and Publisher, 101 (October 19):38.

_____ (1969). "Too much crime and violence in the press?" Editor and Publisher, 102(February 8):12.

HAUGE, R. (1965). "Crime and the press." Pp. 147-164 in Scandinavian Studies in Criminology (1). Oslo: Universitetsforlaget.

HOWITT, D. and CUMBERBATCH, G. (1975). Mass media, violence and society. New York: John Wiley.

HUGHES, H. (1940). News and the human interest story. Chicago: University of Chicago Press.

JOHNSTONE, J., et al. (1976). The newspeople. Urbana: University of Illinois Press.

LENKE, L. (1973). "Criminal policy and public opinion towards crimes of violence." Pp. 70-114 in Tenth Conference of directors of Criminological Research Institutes. Strasbourg: Council of Europe.

LETKEMANN, P. (1973). Crime as work. Englewood Cliffs, N.J.: Prentice Hall.

MOLOTCH, H., and LESTER, M. (1974). "News as purposive behavior: On the strategic use of routine events, accidents, and scandals." American sociological Review, (39):101-112.

MUELLER, C. (1970). "Notes on the repression of communicative behavior." Pp. 101-113 in H. Dreitzel (ed.), Recent Sociology No. 2. New York: Macmillan.

MURDOCK, G., and GOLDING, P. (1973). "For a political economy of mass communications." in R. Miliband and J. Saville (eds.), Socialist Register. West Orange, N.J.: Saifer.

New York Times (1975). "Information on crime victims a problem for papers." February 12.

QUINNEY, R. (1970). The social reality of crime. Boston: Little Brown.

ROSHIER, B. (1973). "The selection of crime news by the press." Pp. 28-39 in S. Cohen and J. Young (eds.), The manufacture of news. Beverly Hills, Cal.: Sage.

RUBINSTEIN, J. (1973). City police. New York: Ballantine.

SIGELMAN, L. (1973). "Reporting the news: An organizational analysis." American Journal of Sociology, 79(1):132-151.

STEFFENS, L. (1931). The autobiography of Lincoln Steffens. New York: Harcourt, Brace.

TUCHMAN, G. (1972). "Objectivity as strategic ritual: An examination of newsmen's notions of objectivity." American Journal of Sociology, 77(4):660-671.

_____ (1973). "Making news by doing work: Routinizing the unexpected." American Journal of Sociology, 73(1):110-131.

_____ (1976). "The news' manufacture of sociological data (comment on Danzger, ASR, October, 1975)." American Sociological Review, 41(6):1065-1067.

TUNSTALL, J. (1972). "News organization goals and specialist newsgathering journalists." Pp. 259-280 in D. McQuail (ed.), Sociology of mass communications. Harmondsworth, England: Penguin.

11

CHARACTER ASSASSINATION IN THE PRESS

GERALD CROMER

In their relentless search for new angles, reporters always seem to fall back on the old staples. An indefinable but much vaunted news sense has apparently led them to the conclusion that "the basic interests of the human race are not in music, politics and philosophy, but in things like food and football, money and sex, and crime—especially crime" (Chibnall, 1977:ix). But while the press can now take this situation for granted and simply "give the public what it wants," scholars of various disciplines are still trying to understand the underlying reasons for these preferences.

A growing number of sociologists are of the opinion that our seemingly insatiable desire for "law and order news" cannot simply be explained in terms of an interest in the out of the ordinary. In fact "the reason why deviant behavior occupies so much media space is not because it is intrinsically interesting, but because it is intrinsically instructive" (Box, 1971:40). The normative contours of a society are most clearly drawn during the different types of confrontations with its deviant members. Whether they take the

form of legal proceedings or psychological examinations, these degradation ceremonies (Garfinkel, 1956) provide the most effective way
of delineating the border between right and wrong.

In order to perform this function, however, the deliberations, or at least
the decisions reached, must be brought to the attention of society as a
whole. Hence, the long standing tradition of administering penal sanctions in places highly visible to the public.

The termination of this practice coincided almost exactly with the
rise of mass circulation newspapers. While this may be an accident
of history, it is undoubtedly true that the press coverage of crime tends
to fulfill the same function as these "hanging matches." "Newspapers
make redundant the need for large gatherings of persons to witness
punishments; instead individuals can stay at home and still be morally
instructed" (Box, 1971:40).

Surprisingly little attention has been paid to this aspect of the
interaction between crime and media. Only recently have sociologists
begun to turn their attention to the different ways in which they act as
agents of social control rather than as a major threat to the social order.
All the studies (Chibnall, 1977; Cohen and Young, 1973) so far,
however, are concerned with the type of coverage given to different
groups of criminals and deviants; the portrayal of individual offenders is
not touched upon at all. The whole question of prejudicial publicity, for
instance, has only been discussed from a legal point of view. In contrast to
a constant stream of articles on the judicial aspects of trial by the press,
nothing has yet been written on its sociological implications.[1] This
chapter forms the first part of a large-scale study designed to bridge this
gap in our knowledge.

PREJUDICIAL PUBLICITY

In the legal literature, the problem of prejudicial publicity is invariably
discussed within the framework of the free press—fair trial debate.
Particular attention is paid to three questions: the types of material that
should be considered as prejudicial (Jaffe, 1965:5-7; LeWine, 1971:946-
948), the extent to which they influence actual or potential jurors
(Wilcox, 1970:63-73), and the different ways of dealing with the problem
(Friendly and Goldfarb, 1967:95-157, 237-256; Jaffe, 1965a:8-17).
Although they are all of potential interest to the sociologist, this chapter is
almost totally concerned with the first and most basic question of what
constitutes prejudicial publicity. However, before analyzing the problem

from a sociological perspective, it is necessary to give at least a brief description of the legal consensus on this particular point.

One of the major analyses (Friendly and Goldfarb, 1967:11) pointed out two ways in which news coverage can preclude the possibility of a fair trial.

> One comes from the bringing to the attention of the actual or potential jurors, outside the courtroom, information and opinions that are "nonjudicial" (or "extra-record" or "extra-judicial), namely, material that they are not allowed to consider under procedures society has designed to govern the fair adjudication of a defendant's guilt or innocence. The second comes from creating an overall atmosphere in the community by the sheer volume or sensationalism of publication about a case.

Nonjudicial material covers a multitude of sins. Although usually divided into a large number of categories, it can very conveniently be considered under three broad headings:

(1) Inadmissable evidence, i.e., material that would not be accepted in open court because of the content matter (e.g., details of past convictions) or the manner in which it is obtained (e.g., involuntary confessions, illegal search and seizure);

(2) Unsubmitted evidence, i.e., material that would be accepted but is in fact not presented in open court; and

(3) Opinionated statements, i.e., pronouncements on such issues as the reliability of evidence, credibility of witnesses and even the guilt of the defendant himself.

Each of these types of nonjudicial material is considered a "clear and present danger" to the defendant's right to be tried on the basis of evidence presented in open court alone, and must therefore be defined as prejudicial. The situation regarding sensational publicity, on the other hand, appears to be much less clearcut.

Despite the fact that sensationalism is both as varied and widespread as nonjudicial material, it is usually discussed under one broad heading and referred to only in passing. Most analyses of the free press—fair trial debate tend to include all examples concerning the general "tone and character" of reports under a single heading such as "inflammatory publicity" (LeWine, 1971:948), or "miscellaneous inflammatory material which may sway a jury's sympathy against a defendant" (Jaffe, 1965a:7).

This lack of attention is due, to a large extent at least, to the highly pragmatic nature of the free press for trial debate. Participants of all shades of opinion are interested in solving the problem of prejudicial news reporting, rather than reaching a deeper understanding of its internal dynamics. But since inflammatory material is assumed to be less harmful than nonjudicial publicity, the need to deal with it is thought to be less acute (Jaffe, 1965b:162). In addition, the task of doing so is widely regarded as more difficult because of problems involved in deciding what types of material should in fact be classified as inflammatory (Jaffe, 1965b:162). The dubious nature of both these propositions will be pointed out later in this chapter.

STATUS DEGRADATION CEREMONIES

The secularization of the legal process has not been accompanied by any changes in its basic functions. Erikson's (1966:103) observations of church trials in Puritan Massachusetts are still apposite today. "When the whole affair is seen as a ceremony and not a test of guilt, as a demonstration rather than as an enquiry, its accents and rhythms are easier to understand." Thus while legal scholars continue to debate whether the search for truth is best expedited by the inquisitional or advisory system, sociologists are in no doubt that the latter is most suited to the court's denunciatory role. The Anglo-Saxon procedure provides the ideal setting for a morality play between the forces of good and evil.

Even today, long after the public trial and punishment of offenders has been abandoned, crowds may "greet" the more infamous defendants on their arrival at and departure from court. On some occasions, those present in the spectators' gallery also tend to get caught up "in the spirit of a gladiatoral display" (Cohen, 1973:107). This is due, to some extent at least, to the drama of the trial itself—the costume, language, and staging that together constitute the majesty and paraphernalia of the law. The court has been referred to as "the perfect stage for acting out society's ceremonies of status degradation" (Cohen, 1973:106).

These public rites are designed to effect the alteration of total identities. Degradation ceremonies therefore take the form of a "publicly delivered curse that the denounced is not as he appears to be but is otherwise and *in essence* of a lower species." If successful, they culminate in the ritual destruction of the person concerned (Garfinkel, 1956:420-422).

"Face to face contact," Garfinkel (1956:424) points out, "is a different situation from that wherein the denunciation and reply are conducted by radio and newspaper." The communicative tactics employed must be selected accordingly. The essential nature of the ceremony, however, remains the same. Thus, while legal scholars have rightly condemned the press for encroaching on the province of the court, they are mistaken in their estimation of the extent of the problem. By focusing attention on the ways in which newsmen try to prove that the suspect committed the crime in question, jurists tend to overlook the fact that the press is also at pains to point out that he is the type of person capable or even likely to have done so. What has hitherto been referred to as prejudicial publicity is in fact just one stage of a much more comprehensive process of character assassination.

This type of press coverage can therefore be viewed as an example of status degradation. But Garfinkel does not only define the aim of this type of denunciation, he also enumerates the conditions that must be met in order for it to be successful (1956:422-423). It is therefore necessary to investigate both these aspects of degradation ceremonies with special reference to our particular case of character assassination. In order to do so, the role of the denouncer (the press) and the coverage of the denounced (the suspect) must be analyzed in detail. But before undertaking these tasks, we must briefly turn our attention to what Garfinkel refers to as the "witnesses to the denunciation work," i.e., those in front of whom the ceremony is performed. Besides being of interest in its own right, this will, it is hoped, shed a new light on the nature of the degradation process as a whole.

WITNESS FOR THE PROSECUTION

The mass media, Boorstin (1962:7-44) has argued, are one of the most effective ways of creating "the thicket of unreality which stands between us and the facts of life." As their rather limited role of newsgathering has ceded pride of place to the more enterprising one of newsmaking, reporters have found themselves under increasing pressure to actually create news. They can only meet these demands by creating a flood of "pseudo-events." Consequently, we are not presented with a true picture of reality. The media are no longer (if indeed they ever were) a window on the world. Perhaps a more apposite image would be that of a distorting mirror.

Boorstin's (1962) analysis is based almost exclusively on the activities of the Washington press corps. It is equally applicable, however, to the work of crime correspondents. The awareness of editors and reporters alike that law and order news is particularly popular puts them under a great deal of pressure to keep coming up with a story. In fact this desire to give the public what it wants not only affects the amount of copy that they are expected to produce, it also influences the way in which it is presented. Young (1974:241) argues that the press "selects events which are atypical, presents them in stereotypical fashion and contrasts them against a blackcloth of normalcy that is overtypical."

This type of coverage is thought to be particularly influential because contemporary society is characterized by an extremely high degree of social segregation, or what Wilkins (1964:62) has somewhat cryptically referred to as "selective living." Knowledge of remote groups tends to be very limited. In many cases the media provide the only antidote to this "pluralistic ignorance." Quinney (1970:281-285) was one of the first to point out the effects of this situation as far as crime is concerned. The image presented in the media, he argued, is diffused throughout society and becomes the "public view of reality." Other studies (Cohen, 1973; Young, 1971) have since analyzed this process in greater detail and described how it affects the social reaction to crime and, in turn, the offenders themselves. They came to the conclusion that a self-fulfilling prophecy is set in motion: the fantasy conjured up by the media is translated into reality.

An increasing amount of quantitatively oriented research,[2] however, has reached very different conclusions concerning both the amount and effects of law and order news. In addition, at least some of the most frequent charges of sensationalism (e.g., those concerning the overpresentation of sex offenses and young offenders) appear to be unfounded. Of particular importance to our analysis, however, are the inconclusive results concerning the influence of the press or the public image of crime. "Theories that the mass media determine public perceptions and beliefs are shown to be unsupported by empirical evidence" (Cumberbatch and Beardsworth, 1976:72).

These findings need not necessarily set our minds at rest as far as the problem of prejudicial publicity is concerned. The press could conceivably wield a much greater influence in this particular respect. Causes célèbres are, after all, accorded front page treatment over a long period of time and covered in the most intricate detail. In addition, the effect only has to last for a limited period of time (i.e., until after a verdict is reached) to be considered harmful. Once again, however, there does not seem to be much cause for alarm. "If a tentative conclusion may be ventured at this point it is that there is no empirical evidence to support a view that extensive, or even irresponsible, coverage of a court case destroys the ability of jurors to decide the issue fairly" (Gillmor, 1965:176).

An increasing number of media analysts are therefore of the opinion that up till now "those involved with evaluating the role of the mass media are so overwhelmed by its size and scope that they seek such powerful effects." Given the lack of effects, they argue, "the question is rather why the mass media do *not* seem to influence public behaviour and beliefs" (Cumberbatch and Beardsworth, 1976:86). In order to tackle this problem, however, it is necessary to adopt a wider perspective of the situation. Attention must be paid not only to the content of the media, but to the nature of the audience as well.

Advocates of the uses and gratifications approach (Katz et al., 1974) have argued that the effects of the media are themselves "mediated through the expectations and needs of audience members." There is no reason to assume that the situation concerning the portrayal of crime and deviance is an exception to this rule. These images, in common with other messages of the media, are accepted or rejected according to the psychological dispositions and social circumstances of those to whom they are directed.

Even if the press can meet all the conditions of successful degradation ceremonies and it employs the appropriate communicative tactics, there is no guarantee that the ritual destruction will be accomplished. The mediatory role of the "witnesses to the denunciation work" must also be taken into account. A negative response, or even a lack of one, on the part of the reading public would after all preclude the possibility of achieving the desired results. This point must be borne in mind since the analysis that follows is limited to an examination of the status of the press and the type of coverage given to the person being denounced. The public response and, therefore, the question as to whether character assassination is effective or not remains unanswered.

This argument is, in fact, of relevance to status degradation ceremonies in general. A complete picture of any public denunciation can only be arrived at if the response of the witnesses is taken into consideration. Since Garfinkel's paper is limited to an analysis of the role of the denouncer and the reconstitution of the person being denounced, the conditions he enumerates constitute the necessary rather than the sufficient ones for successful degradation.

THE VOICE OF THE PEOPLE

The denouncer has to meet two major conditions if the degradation is to prove successful. He must (1) act in his capacity as a public figure, and (2) speak in the name of the supra-personal values of the tribe (Garfinkel, 1956:423). The press, it is argued, can fulfill both these prerequisites. An analysis of its various roles, major sources of information, and framework of values will indicate why this is the case.

Roles

A free press has long been regarded as a sine qua non of democracy. This belief finds its clearest expression in Thomas Jefferson's oft quoted assertion that (Ford, 1904:69):

> The basis of the government being the opinion of the people, the very first object should be to keep that right: and were it left to me to decide whether we should have a government without newspapers or newspapers without a government, I should not hesitate a moment to prefer the latter.

All the liberal philosophers, however, were at pains to point out the crucial role of the press as both a source of public enlightenment and a check on all three estates of the realm. While there is still widespread agreement as to the need for providing the general public with this opportunity both to criticize the government and take an active part in it, the ability of an unfettered press to do so is increasingly open to question. As a result of changing perspectives or the nature of both man and society, libertarianism has ceded pride of place to what is generally referred to as the doctrine of social responsibility.

"Freedom of the press," Felix Frankfurter (Pennekamp v. Florida, 1946) argued, "is not an end in itself, but a means to the end of a free society. The scope and nature of constitutional guarantees of freedom of the press are to be viewed and applied in that light." Hence, a long series of attempts to draw up codes setting ethical standards for the press and other mass media. There is a large body of opinion, however, that believes reporters and editors alike are not living up to their responsibilities and only more stringent legislative measures will ensure that they do. But these misgivings about the present situation do not signify a retreat from libertarianism as regards the role of the press. On the contrary, the concern arises out of a continuing belief in its centrality.

The experience of muckrakers at the turn of the century illustrated a problem facing the press in its capacity as a public watchdog. "After a period of time," Tebbel (1974:287-288) pointed out, "the public was unable to face any bad news and wanted to hear good news again." In its more general crusading role, however, the press seems to be faced with, or perhaps to have created, a seemingly insatiable desire for bad tidings. Hence, the constant flow of moral panics about various forms of youth culture or other types of behavior regarded as a threat to the existing order of things (Cohen, 1973:9-10). Even if the press and other media are not "self-consciously engaged in crusading or muckraking, their very reporting of certain facts can be sufficient to cause alarm, anxiety, indignation or panic" (Cohen, 1973:15). However, the relationship is a reciprocal one. Not only does the fact that "it's in the paper" serve as an indication of the severity of the problem, acting as the guardian of the public conscience also invests the press with an additional source of credibility.

Sources

The public stature of the press derives, to a large extent at least, from "establishmentarian bias" of the vast majority of newspapers. Particularly important in this respect is the overwhelming reliance on "authoritative sources." Sigal (1973:69) has argued that "as the press increasingly organized the newsgathering practices around government institutions, authoritativeness began to vary with distance from position of formal responsibility for public policy. Today the higher up in government a man is, the better his prospects to make news." In his analysis of the "professional imperatives of journalism," Chibnall (1977:22-45) added, "certified experts who are looked to to provide impartial comment and evaluation" to the list of "accredited spokesmen." But while this may lead to a slight increase in the number of people who have access to the press, it by no means reduces its conservative bias. In fact, exactly the opposite may be the case. The citing of expert opinion is likely to lend further credence to the official view and in turn enhance the stature of the press. This bias is particularly marked in the case of law and order news (Chibnall, 1975:51-54). The history of crime reporting is characterized by an increasing reliance on one major institutional source—the police. Official press releases, however, are regarded as highly inadequate by crime correspondents. Most of their information is culled from informal contacts with highly placed officers. Nevertheless, the picture presented by the press is a completely establishment-oriented one.

Research studies of both political and crime correspondents (Chibnall, 1975; Sigal, 1973) have shown that reporters are subject to a process of absorption or assimilation as a result of overdependence on official sources. Thus, not only is an inordinate amount of space devoted to the official view on the order of things; the "party line" tends to engulf the newsmaking process as a whole.

The highly structured access to the press seems to conflict with the journalistic practice of "writing it down the middle." In actual fact, however, this is not the case because of the very restricted way in which the professional canon of objectivity is interpreted. While the "structure of balance" requires the admission of an opposing point of view, they too must come from "accredited alternative sources" (CCCS, 1976:75). "The variation which occurs is all within the limits of certain permitted discourse areas or models of interpretation" (Young, 1974:230). In practice, this means from others who share the "shared perspective of the liberal concensus." Those who do not subscribe to this particular paramount reality are regarded as beyond the pale and, therefore, as having foregone the right of espousing their cause. As Becker (1967:241) has pointed out, "credibility and the right to be heard are differentially distributed through the system."

Those opposed to the dominant world view find themselves caught up in a typical "Catch 22" situation. Chibnall's (1977:104-105) observations concerning the experience of the Angry Brigade in this respect are applicable to other extra-parliamentary critics of the status quo.

> The only way to attract media attention to a cause was to commit sensational acts, but once appropriated by the media nothing could prevent the form and style of the protest being used as a criterion for the evaluation of both the cause and its promoters . . . Once the apparently irrelevant ideas had been successfully swept aside, the whole thing could be simplified into a variation of conventional crime news format. 'Cops and Robbers' could be transformed into the new spectacle of 'Cops and Bombers', Good vs. Evil in a fresh guise.

Values

The fact that the press is "structured in dominance" in this way is therefore closely related to the second of Garfinkel's conditions vis à vis the denouncer. Both the authoritative sources and the accredited alternatives are granted the right to be heard because they speak in the name of the supra-personal values of the tribe or, in slightly less prosaic terms, "set themselves up as the guardians of consensus" (Young, 1974:244). In fact, the stature of the press itself is similarly based. In their role as public watchdogs, newsmen represent the electorate vis à vis the ruling elite. As moral entrepreneurs, on the other hand, they speak out on behalf of this "silent majority" against the threat of deviance. In both cases, however, the press assumes the mantle of the voice of the people and takes up the cudgels on its behalf.

A closer analysis of this role will show that not only can the press meet the conditions enumerated by Garfinkel, but they are in fact interrelated. Its public stature is based on a complete identification with and constant advocacy of the supra-personal values of the tribe. Paradoxically, however, the widespread acceptance of the fact that everyone else believes in these ultimate values is largely the result of the press' own endeavors. Society is characterized by conflict rather than consensus.

The voice of the people consists of what Young (1974:238) has referred to as "a bricollage of contrary opinions and positions." However, the press and other mass media tend to "reinforce the consensural part of their consciousness, castigating other tendencies as irrational and regrettable." Consequently "the major sphere of media power is creating a consensus that there is a consensus" (Young, 1974:254). Newsmen create the image of society on which their own credibility is based.

RITUAL DESTRUCTION

For a degradation ceremony to be successful, Garfinkel (1956:423) argues, the denounced person must be "ritually separated from a place opposed to it. He must be placed outside, he must be made strange." Another of the conditions enumerated hints as to how this can be achieved (1956:422-423):

> Both event and perpetrator must be placed within a scheme of preferences that show the following properties
> A. The preferences must not be for event A over event B, but for event of
> The preferences must not be for event A over event B, but for event of type A over event of type B. The same typing must be accomplished for the perpetrator. . . .
> B. The witness must appreciate the characteristics of the typed person and event by referring the type to a dialectical counterpart. Ideally the witness should not be able to contemplate the features of the denounced without reference to the contraconception.

This condition is quoted in detail because both typification and comparison are particularly common in the press coverage of law and order news. One of the essential elements in the creation of a "consensual monolith" is the exaggeration of the differences between conformity and deviance. A distorted image of the criminal is pitted against an equally exaggerated one of the apocryphal "man in the street."

The paradigm that follows is not designed to measure the extent to which the press meets the conditions of successful degradation ceremonies. The major aim is to show that character assassination, in common with other public denunciations of this genre, is concerned with the ritual destruction of the person concerned. This can be most clearly shown by dividing the communicative work into three stages: behavior, personality, and panic. Although they are closely interrelated, the process as a whole will be most clearly understood if each type of news coverage is analyzed separately. It is to this task that we now turn our attention.

Behavior

The fact that the person must be referred to as a "motivational type" by no means obviates the need for coming to terms with his behavior. In fact, in order to alter his total identity it is necessary to concentrate on those actions regarded as symptomatic of the "new person." In our particular case of character assassination, therefore, the press devotes a great deal of attention to the imputation of criminality itself. This type of coverage can be divided into three areas: evidence, motive, and pronouncement of guilt.

It has already been pointed out that legal scholars are almost exclusively concerned about the ways in which the press tries to show that the suspect is in fact guilty of the crime in question. Not surprisingly therefore, they enter into great detail about the different types of evidence that are published in order to achieve this aim. From a sociological point of view, however, both the general dichotomy between admissible and inadmissible evidence and the more intricate distinctions between one kind of material and another are of little relevance. All forms of press coverage designed to show that the person denounced committed the crime under investigation can, and in fact should, be included under a single heading. Together they constitute the first step in the process of character assassination.

Criminal law manuals tend to emphasize the advantage gained by the prosecution if it can prove that the suspect had a reason for perpetrating the crime of which he is accused. Smith and Hoggen (1969:48), for instance, argue that:

> as evidence motive is always relevant. This means simply that if the prosecution can prove that D had a motive for committing the crime, they may do so since the existence of a motive makes it more likely that D in fact did commit it. Men do not usually act without a cause.

It is therefore particularly surprising that legal scholars make no reference to this point in their analyses of prejudicial publicity. In actual fact, however, newsmen are also intent on backing up their argument that the suspect committed the crime in question by showing that he had a reason for doing so. Only in the case of certain economic offenses is the motive regarded as too obvious to require further elucidation.

"It is not unusual," Lofton (1966:149) has pointed out, "for news-paper headlines to indirectly pronounce guilt solely on the basis of police assertions." In some cases the press itself "acts as though it were a prosecutor or a jury sitting in judgement" (Lofton, 1966:154). But whether the reporter or his police source acts as the proof object (Wilcox, 1970:60), the end product is exactly the same. Besides being confronted with a series of facts about which he can make up his own mind, the reader is also faced with the considered opinion of those "in the know." Even this, however, is likely to fall on deaf ears unless accompanied by a comprehensive attack on the character of the person concerned.

Personality

The various allegations concerning the suspect's behavior constitute only the first stage of his ritual destruction. In order to ensure a complete degradation, the misdemeanor of which he is suspected must be portrayed as indicative of his personality as a whole.

As Strauss (1962:84) has pointed out, however, "the awareness of constancy of identity is in the eyes of the beholder rather than in the behaviour itself." It is in fact the highly ambiguous nature of human actions and personality that leaves the press with so much room for maneuver. The imputation of criminality presents newsmen with the opportunity of reconstructing both the character and biography of the person being denounced. Although these processes are closely inter-related, it is possible to analyze them under separate headings. The first will be referred to as stereotyping, the second as retrospective interpre-tation.

"Stereotyping involves a tendency to jump from a single cue or a small number of cues in actual, suspected, or alleged behaviour to a more general picture of the kind of person with whom one is dealing" (Schur, 1971:52). It is therefore particularly common in the case of crime and deviance because both are widely regarded as a master status (Becker, 1963:33-34). Just the imputation of criminality provides the press with sufficient grounds to set this process in motion. The alleged misdemeanor serves as the behavioral basis for what Lofland (1969:124) has referred to as a "pivotal category" that defines "who the person is."

Having taken this step, however, "there can begin the reverse game of scrutinizing Actor for the degree to which his other categories are appropriately consistent with the category taken to be pivotal" (Lofland, 1969:125). Thus after ferreting out all the information available on the suspect, crime correspondents tend to emphasize those aspects of his personality that clearly confirm what they now regard as his "essential nature."

The "rite of consistency" not only influences the portrayal of the suspect's present state of mind, it also affects the coverage of his past. "As we remember the past we reconstruct it in accordance with our present ideas of what is important and what is not. . . . This means that in any situation with its near infinite number of things that could be noticed we notice only those things that are important for our immediate purposes. The rest we ignore" (Berger, 1963:70). Because, in the case of character assassination, it is the imputation of criminality that provides the starting-off point for any excursion into the suspect's past, all biographical details are chosen with this in mind.

Crime correspondents adopt Lofland's (1969:150) rule of thumb that "the present evil of current character must be related to past evil that can be discovered in biography." Once again, therefore, they emphasize or ignore different features of the suspect's life-history according to whether or not they are in harmony with what is now looked upon as his "core being." However, this retrospective interpretation (Kitsuse, 1962:253) always seems to provide sufficient evidence to support the conclusion that the person being denounced has been of unsavory character all the time. As Garfinkel (1956:422) succinctly puts it, "the former identity stands as accidental; the new identity is the basic reality. What he is now is what after all he was all along." The ritual destruction is accomplished, the degradation complete.

Panic

The press coverage of the suspect's personality is undoubtedly the central aspect of character assassination. There is, however, one further stage that remains to be considered. Inferences concerning the crime situation in general tend to form an integral part of trial by the press. Although by no means a condition of successful degradation, they should therefore be included within the paradigm of this type of communicative work.

Prejudicial publicity can have repercussions far beyond the particular case in question. This is not altogether surprising since it is often portrayed as just the "tip of the iceberg" or "a sign of the times." In this way, character assassination tends to create either a discrete moral panic about the extent and seriousness of the particular type of crime of which the suspect is accused or a more diffuse concern about the question of law and order as a whole. In a crusading panic of this sort, there is a tendency to "map together increasing numbers of problems as constituting one single threat" (CCCS, 1976:76-78). By engaging in this process of convergence, the press urges its readers to orient themselves "not just to an incident, a type of behaviour or even a type of person, but to a whole spectrum of problems and aberrations" (Cohen, 1973:54).

The "rite of consistency" is obviously an integral part of this process. As in the preceding stage of character assassination, newsmen engage in both stereotyping and retrospective interpretation. Offenders are referred to "not just as in terms of particular events or particular disapproved forms of behaviour but as distinguishable social types" (Cohen, 1973:9-10).

The relationship between these two types of press coverage (i.e., of individual cases and the crime situation in general) is, however, a reciprocal one. This very brief description of how moral panics are often created on the basis of a single cause célèbre covers only one aspect of the situation. Of particular importance to us, in fact, is the way in which they in turn provide further momentum to the ongoing process of character assassination.

The over-reporting (Cohen, 1973:31-32) or "shotgun approach" (Knopf, 1970:17) that is so characteristic of the press during periods of moral panic tends to reinforce the more individually oriented aspects of character assassination. The personal degradation of the suspect is compounded by his portrayal as an example, or even the apogee, of a much wider social problem. Paradoxically, therefore, any panic that is generated by a case of prejudicial publicity becomes in turn an integral part of it. The vicious circle is completed.

CONCLUSION

At the risk of appearing trite, this chapter concludes with the almost traditional call for further research. Rather than talking in very general terms, however, attention will be drawn to just one area of study that arises directly out of the paradigm presented in the last section of this article.

The analyses of the different stages of character assassination give a rather distorted picture of the research project on which it is based. The propositions put forward are in fact discovered from Israeli data and not logically deduced from a prior assumption.[3] Together they constitute what Glaser and Strauss (1967) have referred to as a grounded theory. Although the point of theoretical saturation seems to have been reached as far as the Israeli press is concerned, the analyses of examples of character assassination in other countries may still lead to a refinement of the emergent categories (Glaser and Strauss, 1967:61). Their presentation will hopefully stimulate others to find out whether this is in fact the case.

NOTES

1. To the best of my knowledge the sole exception is a brief reference in Lofland (1969:150-151).

2. A large proportion of the research studies are still unpublished, however, a comprehensive review of this literature can be found in Cumberbatch and Beardsworth (1976).

3. The author is at present engaged in writing up the case studies on which this theoretical analysis is based. Details concerning their publication are available from the Department of Criminology, Bar Ilan University, Ramat Gan, Israel.

REFERENCES

BECKER, H.S. (1963). Outsiders. Studies in the sociology of deviance. New York: Free Press.

_____ (1967). "Whose side are we on." Social Problems, 14(3):239-247.

BERGER, P. (1963). Invitation to sociology. Harmondsworth: Penguin.

BOORSTIN, D.J. (1962). The image. New York: Atheneum.

BOX, S. (1971) Deviance, reality and society. London: Holt, Rinehart, and Winston.

CCCS Mugging Group (1976). "Some notes on the relationship between the societal control culture and the news media: The construction of a law and order campaign." Pp. 75-79 in S. Hall and T. Jefferson (eds.), Resistance through rituals. London: Hutchinson.

CHIBNALL, S. (1975). The crime reporter: A study in the production of commercial knowledge. _Sociology,_ 9(1):49:66.

_____ (1977). Law-and-order news. London: Travistock.

COHEN, S. (1973). Folk devils and moral panics. London: Paladin.

_____ and YOUNG, J. (eds.) (1973). The manufacture of news. Deviance, social problems and the mass media. London: Constable.

CUMBERBATCH, G., and BEARDSWORTH, A. (1976). "Criminals, victims and mass communications." Pp. 72-90 in E.L. Viano (ed.), Victims and society. Washington: Visage.

ERIKSON, K.T. (1966). Wayward puritans. New York: Wiley.

FORD, P.L. (ed.) (1904). The writings of Thomas Jefferson. New York: Putnam.

FRIENDLY, A., and GOLDFARB, R.L. (9167). Crime and publicity. New York: Twentieth Century Fund.

GARFINKEL, H. (1956). "Conditions of successful degradation ceremonies." American Journal of Sociology, 61(5):420-424.

GILLMOR, D.M. (1965). "Free press and fair trial: A continuing dialogue. Trial by newspaper and the social sciences." North Dakota Law Review, 41(2):156-176.

GLASER, B.G., and STRAUSS, A.L. (1967). The discovery of grounded theory. London: Wiedenfeld and Nicholson.

JAFFE, C. (1965a). "The press and the pooressed—A study of prejudicial news reporting in criminal cases. Part I: The problem, existing solutions and remaining doubts." Journal of Criminology, Criminal Law, and Police Science, 56(1):1-17.

_____ (1965b) "The press and the oppressed—A study of prejudicial news reporting. Part II: Some speculations and proposals." Journal of Criminology, Criminal Law, and Police Science, 56(2):158-173.

KATZ, E., BLUMLER, J.G., and GUREVITCH, M. (1974). "The utilization of mass communications by the individual." Pp. 19-32 in J.G. Blumler and E. Katz (eds.), The uses of communications. Beverly Hills, Cal.: Sage.

KITSUSE, J.I. (1962). "Societal reaction to deviant behavior: Problems of theory and method." Social Problems, 9(3):247-257.

KNOPF, T.A. (1970). "Media myths on violence." Columbia Journalism Review, 9(1):17-23.

LEWINE, J.M. (1971). "What constitutes prejudicial publicity in pending cases." American Bar Association Journal, 6(10):942-948.

LOFLAND, J. (1969). Deviance and identity. Englewood Cliffs, N.J.: Prentice-Hall.

LOFTON, J. (1966). Justice and the press. Boston: Beacon Press.

Patterson v. Colorado (1907). 205 U.S. 454, 462.

Pennekamp v. Florida (1946). 329 U.S. 331, 354-355.

QUINNEY, R. (1970). The social reality of crime. Boston: Little Brown.

ROCK, P. (1973). Deviant behavior. London: Hutchinson.

SCHUR, E. (1971). Labelling deviant behavior. New York: Harper and Row.

SIGAL, L.V. (1973). Reporters and officials: The organization and politics of news-making. Lexington: Lexington Books.

SMITH, J.C., and HOGGEN, B. (1969). Criminal law. London: Butterworths.

STRAUSS, A.L. (1962). "Transformations of identity," Pp. 63-85 in A.M. Rose (ed.), Human behavior and social processes. Boston: Houghton Miflin.

TEBBEL, J. (1974). The media in America. New York: Crowell.

TURNER, R.H., and SURACE, S.J. (1956). "Zoot suiters and Mexicans: Symbols in crowd behavior." American Journal of Sociology, 62(1):14-20.

WILCOX, W. (1970). "The press, the jury and the behavioral sciences." Pp. 49-105 in C.R. Bush (ed.), Free press and free tiral. Athens: University of Georgia Press.

WILKINS, L.T. (1964). Social deviance. London: Travistock.

YOUNG, J. (1971). The drugtakers: The social meaning of drug-taking. London: Paladin.

_____ (1974). "Mass media, drugs and deviance." Pp. 229-259 in P. Rock and M. McIntosh (eds.), Deviance and social control. London: Travistock.

TRANS-SEXUALISM
Legitimation, Amplification, and Exploitation of Deviance by Scientists and Mass Media

EDWARD SAGARIN

AUTHOR'S NOTE: *I am deeply indebted to Dr. George L. Kirkham for collaboration and assistance in studies on this subject. Parts of this chapter were inspired by his field notes, which he made available to me, and by our lengthy exchange of correspondence.*

For many years, it has been contended that some diseases come into being because the members of a society either become aware of a state that had hitherto been unknown to them, or they define as a disease a condition that had theretofore been ignored or had been defined in other terms (as sin, witchcraft, crime, or simply as nonconformism). However, not only can a disease be discovered, but it can be created or invented, and dissemination of information about it can serve to amplify as well as reduce its frequency. The process of discovery involves locating and recognizing an entity that was present before, labeling it, describing such features of it as symptoms and possible remedies, investigating its etiology, incidence, and epidemiology, and distinguishing both the pathology and the afflicted from other closely related states and persons. Invention, on the contrary, involves a process whereby a pathological condition is brought about by the belief that it exists, by statements from authoritative persons that it is a very definite entity unto itself, and this belief, firmly held by both medical scientists and patients, as well as the latter's family and friends, creates the state that was supposedly already in existence. Amplification is a process that can follow invention and/or discovery, in which the increased incidence results from the publicity and the legitimation of the symptoms, manifestations, or behavior as qualifying for the label of illness.

If transsexualism is an invention, it is one in which the diagnosis is used to relieve the element of stigma; in that respect, it may be more like kleptomania or pyromania: medical or quasi-medical terms utilized to explain unacceptable behavior in such a manner as to mitigate anticipated sanctions.

EARLY REFERENCES TO TRANSSEXUALISM

Despite a great deal of publicity to the effect that transsexualism has its roots in antiquity, there is only sparse record of occasional instances that can properly be given this label until the 1950s. Green (1969a:22) writes of the "long-standing and widespread pervasiveness of the transsexual phenomenon," after citing instances in Greek mythology, biblical cases, and Roman history, as well as anthropological evidence, particularly from the American Indians. However, many of Green's citations involve homosexuality, institutionalized transvestism, or change of sex as *punishment*.

Transsexualism has been defined in a variety of ways. On the one hand, it is a state of a person with the anatomy of one gender who believes that he (or she) is "really" of the other sex, that the anatomy is a "mistake," that the sex organs are "deformities," and that surgery can correct this error of nature. On the other, many writers define it as the desire to be of the other sex, and report that a male patient, for example, will state that, as long as he could remember, "I wanted to be a girl."

Between these two definitions, there is a cleavage, to the point where they are irreconcilable. A transsexual who believes that "he is a female," despite anatomical evidence to the contrary, cannot "want to be a girl" and cannot want "to change sex." He already is (in his own mind) a female, and if he changed his sex, he would become a male.[1] Thus, if one accepts the definition of Benjamin (1953) describing "anatomic males feeling themselves to be women and wanting to be women," one must note that Benjamin is talking about two different persons or groups of persons. In the first definition, one is close to the "official" statement of Green and Money (1969:487) quoted below in full:

TRANSSEXUALISM: behaviorally, it is the act of living and passing in the role of the opposite sex, before or after having attained a hormonal, surgical, and legal sex reassignment; psychically, it is the condition of people who have a conviction that they belong to the opposite sex and are driven by a compulsion to have the body, appearance, and social status of the opposite sex.

It is rather doubtful if many male transsexuals believe they are females "trapped in a man's body," as the saying would have it. Stoller (1968) contends that each person has a core gender identity, always consistent with the anatomic sex. If this is so, who, then, are the transsexuals? Omitting from this definition for the moment the postoperative persons (who can be defined as postoperative transsexuals, male castrates, conversion females, or in other fashions), should the category consist of those people who have a strong desire to be of the other sex but who *know* they are not of that other sex? Not exactly. For it is possible that, when subjected to enough popular and technical propaganda as well as mass media communications, in which they are told that there is such an entity as transsexualism wherein a male is trapped in a female's body, they come to believe that such a thing can be. When this is reinforced by statements coming from prestigious scientists, they come to believe not only that such an entity exists, but also that they are such examples. A male who formerly wanted to be a female, but knew that he was not, first learns that he can become a female, and then that there are people with bodies like his who *really* are females, and from this point it is not a difficult step to believe that he is just such a person.

One therefore begins with the hypothesis that, as Stoller points out, there are no men and women who genuinely believe they are of the sex other than that assigned to them, or almost none; then, one bombards the popular and medical literature with the assertion that there are such persons, hundreds and thousands of them, and impressionable and susceptible people become convinced that there are such cases, that they are themselves examples, and the entity comes into existence. This is not a discovered disease, but an invented one.

GENDER AS DICHOTOMY AND CONTINUUM

Gender, according to Pauly (1969), is a continuum, not a dichotomy. Pauly goes on to suggest two terms: pseudotranssexual and true transsexual, as a further differentiation among those harboring this extreme form of gender disorientation. "In the small percentage [of the transsexuals] who appear to seek the operation as a means of rationalizing or justifying their primary homosexual desires, the term pseudotranssexual might be considered" (1969:43). In these particular individuals, it would be most important to document the history of life-long gender reversal from other family members. Certainly the strength of their denial of homosexuality, and their abhorrence of this, Pauly writes, suggests the possibility of an underlying motive in some. On the other hand, he states, "evidence suggests that the true transsexual, as distinct from the pseudotranssexual, demonstrated marked and persistent gender role reversal long before he ever know what homosexuality or genital sexuality of any kind was."

The terminology is unfortunate because it postulates without specifically stating that "true transsexualism" is an entity with an existence outside of the mind or control of the individual, and that it may have biological roots.

Putting aside the phenomenon of the relatively small number of pseudohermaphrodites, a more useful distinction might be made among several states: homosexuality, effeminacy, transvestism, and two versions of transsexualism (the conscious and articulated desire to be of the other sex, and the belief that one is of the other sex). The first might be called anticipatory transsexualism, the second delusionary transsexualism.

There are sequences, degrees, and overlappings among these entities. The male with homosexual interests may or may not be effeminate; the effeminate male may or may not have homoerotic desires (although strong effeminacy is seldom not accompanied by conscious homosexuality); the transvestite may or may not be homosexual, frequently denies it, but there seems to be a good deal of evidence that he usually has conscious homosexual interests; furthermore, the transvestite may or may not be effeminate, particularly in that he may have the ability to assume feminine mannerisms and gestures when he wishes, especially when "dressed," and to doff them at other times; the transsexual, including the anticipatory one, is always effeminate, and seems overwhelmingly to be homosexual (Pomeroy, 1969), although by defining himself as a female, he can define the erotic interest and the erotic activity with males as heterosexual. This last definition of one's situation should not be accepted by others except as a window on the mind of a schizoid or near-schizoid individual, or as the mechanisms of a great put-on.[2]

The most common itinerary followed on this map starts with effeminate homosexuality, goes to transvestism, to anticipatory transsexualism, then to transsexualism. In this voyage, the way stations can be skipped, two stations condensed, and two identities simultaneously embraced.

SELF, GENDER, MEMORY, AND CHILDHOOD

A distinction among transsexuals is frequently made on the basis of memory of gender disorientation. The memory test is of course unreliable, because on both a conscious and unconscious level, the transsexual is likely to repress information about times in the past when he did not believe that he was a girl, or was not cross-dressing and acting as a girl. Memory screening can be a powerful factor, but it has been discounted as a distortion factor by some researchers (Pomeroy, 1969). There are no doubt male children who show considerable signs of effeminacy very early; reports go back to approximately 18 months, while others vary from two to seven years (Green, 1969b, 1974). Not all such children turn out to have gender identity problems; many of them go through stages, which is particularly true of tomboys, who often outgrow their cross-gender behavior. The ability of such a large number of prepubertal and adolescent tomboys to develop into ostensibly normal females, and the inability of large numbers of males in the corollary position to make corresponding adjustments, suggests the social roots of gender disorientation in the attitudes taken by others toward violation of sex-role behavior. The continuity of stigmatized and negatively viewed behavior, seen as encapsulation or imprisonment in a role, may result from the belief that the pattern is a condition, an identity, and is immutable (Sagarin, 1975:144-154, 1976, 1977).

At present, there is no evidence which empirically supports the conclusion of a biological etiology (endocrinological, chromosomal, or other), although it has been defended by Benjamin (1969), and such a putative etiology is in the final analysis based upon a reification of transsexualism to the point where it is given existence and an entity in its own right, outside of the imagination, fantasy, or mind (the "feeling") of the patient. The transsexuals are, in terms of all known biologic sex criteria (chromosomal, gonadal, genital, and others) normal males. They are not hermaphrodites. The designation of these persons as "psychic hermaphrodites" is misleading because it introduces a misnomer having no scientific referent. Hermaphroditism is a physical condition that does not have its analogue in such vague areas of the individual as the personality, mind, "soul," "psyche," or even brain.

THE NEWLY DISCOVERED TRANSSEXUALS

Who are these new transsexuals? They are recent converts. In their own words, they "found out about themselves" or "discovered what they were." As the publicity about the operation increases, as it is given the imprimatur of legitimacy by men and women of scientific standing and by impeccable institutions, more and more homosexuals and transvestites are going to discover their transsexual identities.

Whatever evidence may be brought up from a rare book or document, from anthropological studies, and from rather doubtful imterpretations of mythology, it is indubitably true that transsexualism has increased at a remarkable pace during the last quarter of a century. Before 1952, when an obscure GI underwent an operation in Denmark which was reported by a medical team shortly thereafter (Hamburger et al., 1953), transsexualism was virtually unheard of, even in the deviant subcultures of homosexuals. There is hardly mention of it or anything that can suggest it in the lengthy discussions of homosexualism, transvestism and numerous paraphilia and bizarre entities and behavioral patterns found in the work of Krafft-Ebing (1886). Only Havelock Ellis (1936), writing at the turn of the century, described, in a section of his work dealing with transvestism (or eonism, as he preferred to call it), a number of men who had fantasy wishes of being or becoming women, but even these were rare instances, as compared to the phenomena of homosexuality and other clinical entities. There is little to suggest that clinicians of the 1940s and early 1950s who were specializing in sexual disorders were encountering such instances (Allen, 1951; Karpman, 1954).

The announcement of the Jorgensen operation, the publication of the Hamburger report and the subsequent publicity given to it, and the coining of the word transsexual by Cauldwell (1949) and later, more successfully, by Benjamin (1953), the publication of a book (Benjamin, 1966) that rapidly became the Bible of true believers (and perhaps of converts), and the announcement by reputable scientists of belief in the entity and of faith in surgery as the answer to the dilemma (with dismissal of psychotherapy as patently hopeless), all served to create transsexualism by implanting in the minds of many impressionable and suggestible people that that is what they were, and the transsexual identity might be a better mechanism for the management and eventual conquest of stigma than effeminacy, homosexuality, and transvestism. Hamburger (1953) alone, following the Jorgensen story, received applications from almost 500 persons who suddenly recognized that their problems derived from this newly publicized malady.

While it is possible to imagine that there were thousands of concealed transsexuals, unwilling to acknowledge their secret feelings and inner longings at a time when professionals were unreceptive and a way out of their dilemma still unknown, this is an unlikely explanation for the sudden rise in this phenomenon. For if the secret transsexual always existed and in considerable numbers, why is the psychiatric and psychoanalytic literature almost completely devoid of such instances? The most bizarre and unusual phenomena are described, but almost never a case that fits into the framework of transsexualism. As a matter of fact, Stürup (1969), in an effort to show that transsexualism in Denmark has a long history, goes back to a 1924 case, which on careful reading involves only transvestism and lesbianism.

The new transsexuals are highly discredited effeminate homosexuals and compulsive transvestites, whose tenacious pursuit of the transsexual label is explicable in terms of secondary deviation (Lemert, 1967). If homosexuality is stigmatizing and discrediting, effeminate mannerisms combined with homosexual interest and behavior are even more so. As pointed out by Green (1967), even the "ordinary" homosexual shows disdain for the "swish."

The concept of oneself as a transsexual is buttressed by an ideology based on several highly debatable contentions: that transsexualism is a clinical entity: that it is not amenable to psychotherapeutic, psychoanalytic, or psychiatric treatment; that the operation does result in the transformation of a person from male to female (or reverse), that is, one can become a "real female"; and that overwhelmingly those operated on are better adjusted to the problems of life than they were before surgery. The media exploited the story of Christine, the Cinderella of the transsexual movement. There is also reading, exposure to, and willingness to believe selected sectors of the scientific literature. Little is written of those transsexuals who commit suicide, institute lawsuits, or become prostitutes following the operation; little is understood of the enormous stigma following surgery. Few have expressed more strongly than Allen (1961:809) the view that sex change is not accomplished by the transsexual surgery, but many authorities agree with that view:

> It is, of course, absolutely impossible to have one's sex changed (except in some instances of hermaphroditism). Sexual differences penetrate even to the bones, and one can tell the sex of a skeleton of someone who lived some seven thousand years ago.

SECONDARY DEVIANCE AS LEGITIMATION

Lemert (1967) suggests that deviance becomes secondary when the deviant begins to employ his deviance, *or a role based upon it,* as a means of attack, defense, or adjustment to the overt and covert problems caused by societal reaction to his behavior. Following the Lemert formulation, the deviance of effeminate homosexuals and of compulsive transvestites is sufficiently bizarre, highly visible, and violative of the most thoroughly ingrained sex-role concepts of the society, as to be deeply discrediting and to result in the labeling of the person as a deviant and in the constant view of him, by others and by himself, in this deviant capacity.

These deviants have in common with some others not only the inability to conceal their stigmatizing trait, but an inability to compartmentalize their lives so that other roles can be pursued without calling attention to this special one. It can be said that their discrediting stigma taints every aspect of identity, every corner of life space, both in the eyes of self and others. Such persons face the formidable task of "managing a spoiled identity" (Goffman, 1963), which is common to those who must daily confront a negative looking-glass self, and must constantly grapple with strong feelings of guilt and shame attendant upon having attitudes and pursuing behavior that are culturally defined as either "immoral" or "sick," if not both.

It will be argued that it is paradoxical to suggest seriously that such persons would actually seek what is ostensibly an even more discredited status (transsexual), as a mechanism for the management of the present ones (effeminacy, homosexuality, transvestism, or combinations thereof). However, there are perceived or fantasied psychosocial gains of such anticipated magnitude as to convince one to initiate a career movement on the part of the homosexual or transvestite toward becoming, or proclaiming oneself, a transsexual; that is, toward "discovering" that transsexualism is a malady that one has, and that a properly trained physician can diagnose. The anticipated defensive, self-insulative, and conflict-resolving gains attendant upon validation and legitimation of the transsexual status provide the discredited homosexual or transvestite an impetus toward embracing the transsexual career by discovering what he "was" all along. W.I. Thomas has stated, in the oft-quoted dictum, that "when men define situations as real, they are real in their consequences." When men of scientific standing define the sex reassignment surgery as the only way out for some people with problems of gender disorientation, such people will ignore the warnings and difficulties described by these same scientists and the body of literature to the contrary. When the scientists restrict this solution to problems of inner distress, turmoil, gender disorientation, and the like in which the condition has been diagnosed as being transsexualism, this will set in motion strong conscious and unconscious forces within many deviants to redefine themselves in such a way as to obtain the elusive solution. Here, screen memory begins to play an important part, but one should not overlook the possibility of a deliberate put-on, in which reputable scientists are fooled by persons of no training and little understanding, who repeat, "Yes, I've always felt that I was a girl," and "I started to wear girl's clothes as long ago as I can remember." A superb example of such a put-on has been described by Garfinkel (1967); a person using the name of Agnes, with little sophistication or education, deceived medical men highly learned in the matters under study. Surely this betrays, on the part of the deceived, an extraordinary will to believe.

CHOICES AND CAREER CONTINGENCIES

Why should discredited effeminate homosexuals and compulsive transvestites move toward a transsexual career? What gains are consciously and unconsciously anticipated? The members of the three groups (effeminate homosexuality, compulsive transvestism, and transsexualism) all face the similar problem of management of spoiled identity (Goffman, 1963). The activity of all three generally produces strongly negative societal reaction from normals, including significant others; and here, too, the transvestite and transsexual (both pre- and postoperative) can handle this in several ways. One method is the creation of a new identity among people who remain ignorant of the true anatomic sex or, if it has been effected, of the operation.

Transsexuals make great effort to deny their homosexuality, although overwhelming evidence of that homosexuality has been noted by the most sympathetic observers. For example, Pauly (1969) describes an anatomic male, living as a female, as "a young, attractive woman, about the female status of whom there was no question"!

The negative reactions of others, according to Lemert (1967), lead to defensive maneuvers, attempts to neutralize the social malaise and personal shame and anxiety which follow the transformation of a discreditable into a discredited stigma (Goffman, 1963). Among the defensive mechanisms employed by persons with gender stigma, one can list a redefinition of oneself as a heterosexual female, and a person with a legitimate illness. This legitimation is supported by a body of scientific literature.

Nevertheless, the literature is by no means one-sided. If one carefully reads the Green-Money (1969) collective volume, which is probably the most thorough study of the subject to date althouth it carries a strong bias in favor of surgery as the only answer, one notes much in it that would discourage a person from embarking on the next stage in a transsexual career, much that can be considered a deglorification of the surgical process. Pauly (1969) describes the postoperative transsexual as constantly being dissatisfied, always wanting more and more operations, repairs, new surgical work, breast development, corrections here and there. The late Henry Guze (1969), who was by no means an ideologue of the transsexual faith, and who even suggested, against all the canons of the followers, that psychotherapy might be effective, emphasized the schizoid and psychotic nature of many of the patients whom he examined. Sherwin (1969) urges that everything be done to keep the knowledge that one was not always a female from the world, implying although never so stating that the postoperative transsexual carries the burden of stigma: the discredited has become discreditable.

FROM IDEOLOGY TO RECRUITMENT

The ideology of transsexualism contains the manifest promise of relief from a lifetime of suffering, and even couched in the language of doubt and chance, of gamble and irreversibility, for the gender-disoriented individual this will be overlooked in favor of a glimmer of hope. And why not, since he is told by these medical authorities over and over again that psychotherapy is hopeless and useless, which is exactly what he wants to hear and believe. But the ideology also contains a subliminal enumeration of component psychosocial gains, the most important of which is self-esteem. Effeminacy and transvestism are self-denigrating images, and homosexuality has been such for centuries, although this may be changing; transform them into a clinical entity that is devoid of moral condemnation, and one in which there is interest by professionals and defense on social and moral grounds, and the shattered ego can be reconstructed. The stamp of respectability from eminent scientists and the universities and hospitals with which they are associated, and the strategically documented references in talk shows on television and other mechanisms of mass communication to a handful of "happy transsexuals" who marry perfectly normal men, become a body of beliefs for many deeply distressed effeminate homosexuals and transvestites, who see a possible answer to their previously unanswerable problems, and who flock to "gender identity clinics" for confirmation of a belief that they really are, and in fact were all along (but did not know it) transsexuals.

THE GAINS OF THE NEW LABEL

In sociology, the process of labeling the deviant has been assumed to be a totally undesirable event from the perspective of the deviant; it is forcibly foisted upon him by the moral entrepreneurs and their agents, the moral enforcers, to use the words of Becker (1963). It is possible, however, that certain deviants may actively pursue another deviant status as a mechanism by which they can manage their life patterns and escape (or hope to escape) from the orginal or primary deviance. By traveling from effeminate homosexual to transsexual, they do not go, in their own view, from a lesser to a greater stigma, or even from one stigma to another; rather they go from a degrading, discrediting, stigmatizing status to the status of one who has a legitimate and "respectable" illness, unfortunate only in the sense that victims of any illness can be so regarded. Their own contempt for homosexuals betrays not so much self-hate, but a reinforce-ment of their view of that status as degrading.

Thus, for the embryonic transsexual, the new recruit, there are mutually defensive gains in securing validation of a transsexual status, and the recognition of such gains produces a reciprocal reinforcement of the new definition of the situation. At this point, family members may become anxious to contribute information, to remember childhood incidents likely to support the diagnosis, and to screen out information tending to invalidate it. The transsexual and those who know him, and who might be called upon by labeling agents to attest to his transsexual-ism, become locked in a symbiosis born of common interest, and often adulterated by a component of compassion. What biases all reports further is that family members that would invalidate the story are seldom encountered; they are systematically excluded, or have excluded them-selves. Neither Garfinkel (1967) nor the physicians with whom he was working (see Stoller, Garfinkel and Rosen, 1960) ever met the mother or brother of the transsexual they were studying, although both entered into the story and the failure to meet them assisted in the deception of the scientists by the patient.

This family situation becomes further complicated by the frequent threat of suicide that is made by the person aspiring to validation of the transsexual status. Whether these persons do actually represent a sector of the population that is highly suicide-prone (more so, for example, than people with variously diagnosed psychological and psychosexual prob-lems) is not known. The aspiring transsexual soon learns that the threat of suicide ("If I don't get the operation, I'll kill myself") is a potent weapon to frighten and control significant persons around him, including particu-larly any family members who have retained a close tie and do not want to gamble on the possibility that this threat might be carried into actuality. In this manner, the transsexual aspirant assists family members in the process of selective memory and other techniques that will validate his status. In the course of obeying the mandate, the family members playing this game come more and more to believe what they started out by doubting: namely, the child is indeed a transsexual.

Whatever the etiology of severe gender disorientation, the validation of transsexualism as a clinical entity of a medical nature exculpates the individual from the egregious stigma which follows the imputation of "free will" as the cause of effeminate homosexuality and other stigmatized behavior violative of ascriptive sex roles. Given the stigma attached to mental illness, it would seem clear that the validation of a sick role is more difficult for those whose claimed illness is psychological in nature; the converse is true: this validation becomes infinitely easier when the problem is organic or physical. An ailment which defies psychotherapeutic treatment despite the psychological origin imputed to it, and which once diagnosed becomes subject to treatment by chemotherapy (estrogens), surgery, and physiological change approved by physicians even when not carried out by them (electrolysis, epilation, or depilation), all conspire to conjure up an image of the transsexual as legitimate actor in the sick role.

The element of revulsion on the part of normals toward "men who dress like women to get queer kicks" is correspondingly attenuated. The task here becomes, however, that of getting others to redefine one as a woman, at which point the long history of gender dissonance becomes sociologically nonexistent. Psychotherapy, or perhaps one might say sociotherapy, becomes an instant process; one is "cured" of gender dysphoria the moment one is defined as being that which is consonant with feeling and behavior. Since others will, it is expected, reflect a less hostile image, this will reinforce the self-image of oneself as a "real" female, and the ego bolstering that accompanies this. But what of those who do not reflect this lesser hostility and greater compassion? Because of the medical validation, they can be dismissed as biased and prejudiced on the one hand (bigot, in fact, in a land in which this is a highly pejorative term), and just uninformed and ignorant on the other. How easy it is for those with gender disorientation problems to adopt this mentality can be seen by reading the Green and Money volume and noting that men of science use these very terms against their opponents.

THE SELF ON STAGE

There is a good deal of game-playing in these events. One must reconcile prostitution with the good woman image, which is an asexual image. This can be done by denying the pervasiveness of prostitution, and at the same time pointing out the difficulties facing these individuals in their pursuit of earning a living and noting that prostitution with normal men is a validation of their female status. The carrying of estrogen may be more of a show than a reality; this does not necessarily mean that one is taking it. And pursuit of sex reassignment surgery was easy to handle when there was little danger that it would result in the surgery; it fed a fantasy life without resulting in the operation. But the game then develops a dynamic of its own, and in the course of this mass pursuit, the "enemy," in the form of the world of bias and respectability, begins to capitulate: the hospital doors open and surgery can no longer be demanded without the real possibility that the offending organs will be removed, never to be returned.

The presentation of a credible transsexual self is a complex and sequentially unfolding event, aided by the surgery-prone transsexual authorities. This self-presentation is promised upon adequate learning of the role expectations of the transsexual status, which may be likened to a form of anticipatory socialization as described by Merton (1957:265-270), from whom I have borrowed the language. Following initial exposure to the ideology of transsexualism, and recognition of the potential psychosocial gains likely to trail closely after the validation of such a status, the burgeoning recruit to transsexualism must acquire sufficient information about the phenomenon to be able to carry off this credible self-presentation. He must learn the behavior, responses, and activities so that he can convince himself, significant others, and the scientific authorities that he really is a transsexual, because he knows they lack any biological, physiological, or chemical tests that will validate his being "a woman," although there are plenty of such tests that demonstrate he does have a man's body. That does not mean he is trapped therein, except insofar as each human, and for that matter each animal organism, is trapped in its own body.

The responses are learned by cues, by reading the literature, by interaction with other transsexuals, and are even picked up in interaction with medical scientists. One learns to insist that one "always felt this way," to state that one's own genitals are abhorrent and always have been, and that the only way out, other than validation as a woman, is suicide.

Caught up in the game, some of these deviants come to believe so strongly in the new status, and in the beckoning of happiness awaiting them if it is brought to its ultimate conclusion, that they do undergo the surgery. Whether at that point they are women is more than a semantic problem involving the question of what label should be placed on a given individual. It is a conceptual problem involving how people view reality, a legal one involving the manner in which that view is interpreted by governmental bodies, and an ideological one involving the uses to which the label of "women" is being put for the further recruitment into the ranks of the newly invented malady.

The primary reason why late recruits to transsexualism often slip through the elaborate clinical mesh of gender identity clinics and secure validation of their status as transsexuals may be due to the dramaturgical surroundings and the very conscious role-playing of those seeking the validation, as well as the investment of the scientists in the existence of the malady that they have created. Here, psychological, medical, and even sociological personnel are viewing the individual in a "staging area"—a place where the would-be transsexual is "on" in the most meaningful sense of the word. By the time such persons reach gender identity clinics, seeking status validation, they are very well "prepped" (and "propped") on the problems of presenting themselves as trans-sexuals, and are finely attuned to the tasks of giving the right answers to acquire the desired validation. This is neither mendacity nor put-on; rather it is the subtle process of coming to believe what has been suggested to the person, coming to know what one is supposed to be, and presenting what one has come to believe and to know will enable passage of the test. It can be compared to the self-presentation at an interview for a job; not an interview in which an ex-convict, for example, might straight-facedly say no when asked if he has an arrest record, but one in which the applicant, asked if he can be patient working with large numbers of mentally deficient people, places himself in a state of mind in which he answers in the affirmative and so believes, although he has an interest, rather than a reason, in so believing.

Like the applicant for the job, the transsexual at the gender identity clinic has a strong and vested interest, often on an unconscious level, in believing that he really is what he presents himself as being. Therefore, in addition to consciously withholding certain information which might discredit the definition of the situation presented for validation, he will engage in considerable repression and selective distortion of reality, utilizing particularly the techniques of selective memory in order to make his history congruent with the image being presented for the benefit of self and others. For example, he will not only deliberately refuse to tell the interviewing clinicians about how he often enjoys orgasmic release in clothing of the opposite sex (for he has learned by grapevine and by reading that such a delict will immediately end the game and discredit his claim to being a real transsexual), but he will also delude himself into believing that he really has always felt, and he emphasizes to himself and others the "always," like a real woman. Over and over again, the same statements appear in the literature, reported by such scientists as Pauly (1969) and others, but known and learned, even memorized, by the aspirant for the transsexual status. For example: "As long as I can remember, I always felt like a girl," (but note: the statement stops short of saying: I always felt I was a girl, which would be the ultimate in transsexualism, but might expose the entire symptom as being a psychotic flight from reality). Another example: "I've always hated homosexuals," which is not interpreted as an indication by the gender clinicians that they are dealing with people deeply involved in almost or fully pathological self-hate or in what has come to be called homophobia; rather it shows that they are not like other homosexuals (who obviously do not hate one another, because they form organized groups and cliques together, cavort with each other in bars and clubs, and make love together). And finally, "I have always loathed my penis." As for the statement of a male that he has "always felt like a woman," there is an inherent illogicality in such a sentence. Unless the speaker is a woman, there is no possible way for him to know what it is like to feel like a woman.

The role of the media in the amplification of deviance started with the George (later Christine) Jorgensen case. In New York, the Daily News proclaimed a front-page headline: "EX-GI BECOMES BLONDE BEAUTY—OPERATIONS TRANSFORM BRONX YOUTH."

Books, articles, and other information sources have come forth, actually sponsored by a foundation which was ostensibly seeking to assist people with gender disorientation problems, but which propagandized unceasingly that surgery and "change of sex" was the only answer and would produce magnificent results. At least two famous persons were paraded before the public as males-turned-into-females: a highly regarded journalist and a professional tennis player. The people who came on TV after an operation told glowing reports of their new lives: the failures were never mentioned. Some ex-males who married were reported to be living in such marital bliss with a heterosexual husband that one suspected that these were the only happy marriages left in a country where breaking up has become part of the commonly accepted life cycle.

In a recent publication, in which the transsexual operation is presented on the cover of the journal with the inticing headline:"The quest for sexual identity," Shaffer (n.d.) reports that some doctors who were once enthusiastic about the transsexual operation are having second thoughts and a change of heart. But the statement was at the end of an article in which the major thrust has been a glorification of the surgery.

The media, in the freedom to choose the material for presentation, seize upon the sensational, and a successfully transformed man-into-woman is more newsworthy than the lonely, forlorn, psychotic, or suicide-prone eunuch. However, the effects of such selective presentation on impressionable people already having problems of gender dysphoria have not as yet been investigated.

The legitimation of transsexualism as a clinical illness separate from homosexuality was explained by Benjamin (see Jorgensen, 1967:3), who was able to make the distinction by simply denying that Jorgensen had been a male, even before the operation:

> Since a psychological status of a transsexual male is that of a female, it is natural that sex attraction centers on a male. Christine makes this point so pathetically clear when he (at that time, he was still George) realizes that there was in him a woman's love for a man, not that of a homosexual.

THE WORD AND THE THING

It has frequently been contended that the untrained layman, particularly one with neurotic predelictions, when reading about symptoms of mental and emotional disorders, easily imagines that he has these symptoms, recognizes them in himself, and then begins to suffer as if he had them. But he would not have the underlying ailment of which the manifestations were symptomatic.

What if, however, the ailment consists of the symptoms? The disease is transsexualism, and it consists of (note: consists of, not manifesting itself in the symptom of) a person believing that he feels he is (or feels as if he were) a member of the other sex, or having so strong a desire to be a member of the other sex that he would rather die than not have this desire fulfilled. It is a symptom that for some people can be implanted, particularly when, given other disturbances and unsatisfying life patterns, it appears to offer rewards. The symptom becomes implanted in the individual who hears that there is such an entity, and the symptom or the feeling is the malady.

One of the contributing factors in this development of the transsexual phenomenon was the coining of the word transsexual itself. This is not to suggest that a thing cannot exist without a word or label that identifies it. A person lacking completely in language, or not knowing any word for the problem, can have hunger or pain (as witness infants, for example). A disease can exist without a name for it; people undoubtedly died of uremia, for example, without anyone knowing what the source of the difficulty was; and once discovered and named, this did not increase the number of cases, but only the number of known cases, although it may have increased the number of people imagining that they had the malady, were frightened of it, or had other related manifestations.

Transsexualism is, however, a "feeling"; a feeling that one has the "mind" of one sex and the body of another. This feeling has no existence outside of the person's mind or imagination. While there would be many people with gender-dissonant behavior without the awareness of the existence of the word and entity, transsexualism, the existence of the word, and the development of the ideology of respectability surrounding it, suggested the feeling to many who could not have had the creative imagination to recognize in themselves a condition that had no existence.

The witches of the Inquisition were likewise inventions, manufactured and believed in, even by the victims themselves. However, they did not become witches, possessed by devils or animal spirits. Transsexualism is not a discovery but an invention; once the word was coined and the disease invented, the condition came into existence. At this point, it appears that it will take on the form of a minor epidemic, in which further recruits will discover that they are transsexuals, and further scientists will validate that status.

NOTES

1. There is a great deal of difficulty in writing about transsexuals, or even transvestites, in deciding the proper pronouns to be used. The writers whose thesis I dispute in this chapter do not encounter this difficulty, because they accept the fact that a new sex is achieved by the sex reassignment operation. Thus, Christine Jorgensen, or any other postoperative former male, can be called "she," not only in deference to the wishes of the subject and to appearance, but as a statement that accepts a new definition of what constitutes maleness and femaleness. But these scientists go much further, and use the feminine pronoun for preoperative anatomic males. In my own writing, wherever possible, I avoid the gender-identifying pronoun. Few reputable scientists speak of a change of sex; they in fact prefer the concept of sex assignment. If one were concerned only with the social and legal implication, then a feminine pronoun might be useful for a male-to-female postoperative individual. However, the pronomial implications involve what one putatively is, not what one is living as if one were. From this vantage point, the pronoun corresponding to the original anatomic sex should always be used in scientific writing, not only when referring to the preoperative, but also to the postoperative transsexual.

Nevertheless, in interactional transactions with the transsexuals, a pronoun may be used that best suits a situation and its goals. For example, the sociologist may use the adopted-gender pronoun, in order not to disrupt the social interaction at a gathering, whereas the psychotherapist may refuse to use it because he may be seeking to reorient a preoperative candidate for surgery to accept the ascribed and anatomic sex.

Incidentally, the pronoun corresponding to original anatomic sex was used in the official "Statement on the Establishment of a Clinic for Transsexuals at the Johns Hopkins Medical Institutions" (Green and Money, 1969:267-269). Note, for example: "The male transsexual looks, dresses, and acts exactly like a woman, and the same is true for his female counterpart." Furthermore, nowhere in this statement is there a hint that the Johns Hopkins scientists believe that there is such a thing as change-of-sex surgery, nor even what has been called sex-reassignment surgery. Note: "The staff has seen a few dozen patients, **has completed surgery to change the external manifestations of sex** in a small number of patients, and has initiated the surgical procedures in several additional patients" [emphasis added]. For a psychiatric approach to transsexualism, see Socarides (1969).

2. I write here, and elsewhere in this article, about effeminate homosexuals, transsexuals, transvestites, and others. Elsewhere, I have sought to show that the language imputing an identitiy to people who have characteristics, traits, attributes, and behavior patterns can be seriously misleading (Sagarin, 1975, 1976, 1977, 1978). People dress in the clothes of the other sex, but this is not an identity. It is the voluntary choice of a free person who can decide to continue or not to continue to dress in this manner. One imputes a continuing identity to such a behavioral pattern when one calls that individual a transvestite. The same can be said for other conduct that is linguistically translated from doing to being. This theme is suggested by many authors; see particularly Kinsey et al. (1948, 1953).

REFERENCES

ALLEN, C. (1951). The sexual perversions and abnormalities. London: Oxford University Press.

(1961) "Perversions, sexual." Pp. 802-811 in A. Ellis and A.Abarbanel (eds.), The encyclopedia of sexual behavior. New York: Hawthorn Books.

BECKER, H.S. (1963). Outsiders: Studies in the sociology of deviance. New York: Free Press.

BENJAMIN, H. (1953). "Transvestism and transsexualism." International Journal of Sexology, 7:12-14.

(1966). The transsexual phenomenon. New York: Julian Press.

(1969). "Introduction," Pp. 1-10 in R. Green and J. Money (eds.), Transsexualism and sex reassignment. Baltmore: Johns Hopkins Press.

CAULDWELL, D. (1949). "Psychopathia transsexualis." Sexology, 16:274-280.

ELLIS, H. (1936). "Eonism." Pp. 1-110 in Studies in the psychology of sex. Vol. II, Part II. New York: Random House.

GARFINKEL, H. (1967). Studies in ethnomethodology. Englewood Cliffs, N.J.: Prentice-Hall.

GOFFMAN, E. (1963). Stigma: Notes on the management of spoiled identity. Englewood Cliffs, N.J.: Prentice-Hall.

GREEN, R. (1967). "Sissies and tomboys." In C. Wahl (ed.), Sexual problems: Diagnosis and treatment in medical practice. New York: Free Press.

(1969a). "Mythological, historical and cross-cultural aspects of transsexualism." Pp. 13-22 in R. Green and J. Money (eds.), Transsexualism and sex reassignment. Baltimore: Johns Hopkins Press.

(1969b). "Childhood cross-gender identification." Pp. 23-25 in R. Green and J. Money (eds.), Transsexualism and sex reassignment. Baltimore: Johns Hopkins Press.

———— (1974). "The behaviorally feminine male child: Pretranssexual? Pretransvestic? Prehomosexual? Preheterosexual?" In R.C. Friedman, R.M. Richart, and R.L. Vande Wiele (eds.), Sex differences in behavior. New York: John Wiley.

————, and MONEY, J. (eds.) (1969). Transsexualism and sex reassignment. Baltimore: Johns Hopkins Press.

GUZE, H. (1969). "Psychosocial adjustment of transsexuals: An evaluation and theoretical formulation." Pp. 171-181 in R. Green and J. Money (eds.), Transsexualism and sex reassignment. Baltimore: Johns Hopkins Press.

HAMBURGER, C. (1953). "Desire for change of sex as shown by personal letters from 465 men and women." Acta Endrocrinologica, 14:361-375.

————, STURUP, G.K., and DAHL-IVERSEN, E. (1953). "Transvestism: Hormonal, psychiatric, and surgical treatment." Journal of American Medical Association, 152:391-396.

JORGENSEN, C. (1967). Christine Jorgensen: A personal autobiography. New York: Paul E. Eriksson. Introduction by Harry Benjamin.

KARPMAN, B. (1954). The sexual offender and his offenses. New York: Julian Press.

KINSEY, A.C., POMEROY, W.B., and MARTIN, C.E. (1948). Sexual behavior in the human male. Philadelphia: Saunders.

KINSEY, A.C., POMEROY, W.B., MARTIN, C.E., and GEBHARD, P.H. (1953). Sexual behavior in the human female. Philadelphia: Saunders.

KRAFFT-EBING, R. von. (1886). Psychopathia sexualis (in German). Stuttgart. English language editions, 1906, 1922, 1965.

LEMERT, E.M. (1967). Human deviance, social problems, and social control. Englewood Cliffs, N.J.: Prentice-Hall.

MERTON, R.K. (1957). Social theory and social structure. Rev. ed. New York: Free Press.

PAULY, I.B. (1969)."Adult manifestations of male transsexualism." Pp. 37-58 in R. Green and J. Money (eds.), Transsexualism and sex reassignment. Baltimore: Johns Hopkins Press.

POMEROY, W.B. (1969). "Transsexualism and sexuality: Sexual behavior of pre- and postoperative male transsexuals." Pp. 183-188 in R. Green and J. Money (eds.), Transsexualism and sex reassignment. Baltimore: Johns Hopkins Press.

SAGARIN, E. (1975). Deviants and deviance: An introduction to the study of disvalued people and behavior. New York: Praeger.

———— (1976). "The high personal cost of wearing a label." Psychology Today, 9(March):25ff.

———— (1977)."Doing, being, and the tyranny of the label." Et cetera, 34:71-77.

———— (1978). "Judicial power and the tyranny of the label." Unpublished working paper.

SHAFFER, H.B. (n.d.). "Transsexualism: New attitudes." The Press, 5(28):13-15, 38.

SHERWIN, R.V. (1969). "Legal aspects of male transsexualism." Pp. 417-430 in R. Green and J. Money (eds.), Transsexualism and sex reassignment. Baltimore: Johns Hopkins Press.

SOCARIDES, C.W. (1969). "The desire for sexual transformation: A psychiatric evaluation of transsexualism." American Journal of Psychiatry, 125:1419-1425.

STOLLER, R.J. (1968). Sex and gender: On the development of masculinity and femininity. New York: Science House.

————, GARFINKEL, H., and ROSEN, A. (1960). "Sexual identification in an intersexed person." Archives of General Psychiatry, 2:379-384.

STURUP, G.K. (1969). "Legal problems related to transsexualism and sex reassignment in Denmark." Pp. 453-460 in R. Green and J. Money (eds.), Transsexualism and sex reassignment. Baltimore: Johns Hopkins Press.

NONVOTING
The Media's Role

GARRETT J. O'KEEFE
HAROLD MENDELSOHN

AUTHOR'S NOTE: *The research reported here was funded in part by grants from the committee for the Study of the American Electorate and the University of Denver Faculty Research Fund. The authors thank Donna Carlon for assistance in data processing.*

Recent evidence testifying that mass media may exert significant influences on American voting behavior has led to a comprehensive re-examination of the nature of political communication behavior per se, as well as its functional antecedents and potential consequences. One emerging and promising area of inquiry focuses on the role communication behavior may play in political participation, particularly with regard to voter turnout.

Voter abstention has of course become a popular topic of late, given that the proportion of eligible citizens actually casting ballots in national elections has steadily declined in recent years, dropping to 53% in 1976. Blame for this has been popularly attributed to various forms of public alienation, presumably resulting from perceptions of rising corruption in government, declining morality, reduced communication between government and governed, as well as "negatively biased" portrayals of politics in the press. Actually, a more empirically based view shows that much of the drop in turnout is readily explained by population dynamics, mosy notably by the rapidly expanding proportion of 18- to 35-year-olds within our society, an age segment traditionally above the norm in abstention, coupled with the recent enfranchisement of 18- to 21-year-olds.

However, neither the popular "alienation" view nor the population-based explanation tells much about how and why citizens decide to vote or not, or about the role of a host of additional factors, including communicatory ones, in affecting turnout.[1]

Traditional thinking has typified nonvoters as likelier to be young, less educated, less affluent, single, female, geographically mobile, generally more socially and politically uninvolved, more alienated from political institutions and processes, and less likely to attend to news and other public affairs-related media content. In gross descriptive terms this across-the-board prognosis is probably not too wide of the mark. It follows from a somewhat simplistic yet logical assumption that non-voters, for a variety of underlying reasons, are less integrated into the political system and see themselves as having less at stake in the outcome of elections.

However, recent literature on political as well as communication behavior presents a number of more sophisticated models based upon either systemic or individual-level factors aimed at explaining turnout.

Systemic factors obviously include registration and residency re-quirements as well as the actual procedures involved in voting. Also, degree of electoral competitiveness has been shown to be significant: "close" elections typically provide higher turnouts (Key, 1951; Burn-ham, 1965). Kim, Petrocik, and Enokson (1975), utilizing a unique multi-variate design, compared the relative weight of legal, competitive and aggregated individual factors on voter turnout across states, and found each factor yielding independent and important contributions to turnout.

However, of greater import here are individual-level predictors of turnout, the most direct of which appear to be psychological and social orientations, including communicatory ones, toward voting and politics as well as social participation in general.

For example, Olson (1972) reports empirical support from a survey of Indianapolis residents for what he terms a "social participation" theory of voting behavior. Moderate associations were found between prior membership in nonpolitical social organizations—e.g., voluntary associ-ations, community and church groups—and voter turnout when age, education level, political interest, party identification, and mass media and interpersonal communication behaviors were controlled for. Olson hypothesizes a causal flow in which higher education level leads to greater involvement in voluntary organizations, resulting in higher voter turnout.

More revealing from a communication perspective was a cross-cultural study of eligible voters (Nie, Powell and Prewitt, 1969), which found that the direct impact of socio-economic characteristics on political participation, including voting, was attenuated by five "attitude sets" held by individuals toward the political system: sense of citizen duty, political efficacy, political knowledge, perceived importance of political outcomes, and attentiveness to mass media political content. Organizational membership and labor force participation also showed a substantial independent effect on participation.

Moreover, Burstein (1972) presents data in support of a causal model of political participation based more on requisites of social structure. The best predictors of overall participation, including voting, were those locating the individual in social networks, primarily organizational involvement and attention to political media content. Socioeconomic status predicted participation less well, and demographics predicted least of all. Burstein argues that his individual-level data support what other aggregate level studies have found—that when communication behavior is included, it is typically the best predictor of political participation. Lovin-Smith (1976), in examining a respecification of both the Nie et al. and Burstein models, found media use to affect participation positively, and also found the relationship to be nonrecursive, in that among females participation had a return effect on media use. No significant return effect was found among males, however.

While the above appear to relegate age and other demographics to a secondary role of serving as descriptive locators of turnout, they should not be readily dismissed. Age becomes a particularly important variable in this regard if we assume that political socialization is not a process that ends in late adolescence, but rather continues over the life cycle. Circumstances, agents of socialization, and the context and content of learning may change, but the basic processes of coping with changing social and physical environments remain. The growing emphasis on socialization as a lifetime process (Brim and Wheeler, 1966; McLeod and O'Keefe, 1972; Jennings and Niemi, 1974; Chaffee, 1977) has brought less concern for age per se as a critical variable and more concern with the differentiated variable of life-cycle position pertinent to a given set of behaviors and roles. After one leaves adolescence, age may become less relevant that the differing lifestyles and demands associated with marriage, changing occupations, childraising, etc. Nonetheless, age level may serve as a ready indicator of these positions.

There are also increasing arguments for looking at age groups as strata much in the sense of social class. Glenn and Grimes (1968) employed both cross-sectional and cohort data to find that political interest increased from middle to advanced age, and voter turnout remained almost constant when sex and education were controlled for. They argue that their findings go against the so-called "disengagement" hypothesis that transition to old age is marked by a progressive disengagement of citizens from social interactions, possibly leading to less awareness of issues confronting the society. Rather, Glenn and Grimes postulate that political interest and activity may be in part a function of freedom from more pressing duties of life. Campbell et al. (1960) suggest that strengthened party identification over the years makes voting more likely as a result of increased loyalty.

Hout and Knoke (1975) used multivariate techniques to identify effects of age, cohort and time period on voter turnout, finding each an important influence when education, religion, sex, occupation, region, race and class were controlled for. Voter turnout was decidedly low below age 33 and over age 73 when the above factors were accounted for.

In terms of political attitudes, a cohort analysis by Cutler and Kaufman (1975) suggests that increased ideological conservatism is not necessarily a function of aging, but rather that older cohorts started out with more politically conservative views, and have tended to stick with them. Agnello (1973) found that feelings of political powerlessness decrease between age 21 and the mid-forties, and then begin to increase again with age.

Changes in patterns of political behavior, including communication behavior and voting, deserve to be examined more cohesively over the life cycle, particularly in the context of asking which of the factors described in the studies above influence voting at which stages. Further light can be shed on the viability of the above models by investigating factors associated with turnout within life cycle stages. A crucial factor for our purposes is that of media usage.

Mass communication behaviors themselves also may be assumed to change over the life cycle. As people grow in age and experiences, their needs for news, information, and entertainment change, as do the media forms they pursue in satisfaction of these needs. The consequences of media usage are also likely to change over the years. Yet there is scant empirical evidence directly supporting such seemingly obvious assumptions.

The impact of prior communication behavior on voter turnout has been perhaps most cogently explored from a socialization perspective by

Blumler and McLeod (1974) in a study of the behavior of young first-time electors during the 1970 British General Election. The authors found that measures of interpersonal and mass media communication orientations of young eligible voters during the campaign accounted for between 13 and 28% of the variance in turnout, depending upon respondents' party preferences. Dispositional, attitudinal and motivational variables accounted for between 12 and 17%. When young eligibles were compared against old, media use, interpersonal communication, and dispositional variables accounted for more variance in turnout among the former. Structural factors, including socio-economic status, marital status, and sex accounted for more variance among older voters. Blumler and McLeod conclude that, at least among firt-time eligible voters, "communication matters just as much as anything else does," and argue that the traditional "limited effects" model of communication influence (Klapper, 1960) simply does not hold up insofar as the impact of communication on turnout, and probably other political orientations, is concerned.

In a similar vein, O'Keefe (1976) presents data from a 1972 Ohio study suggesting that associations between turnout and other factors, including communication, vary across the life cycle. Within the 18- to 24-year-old group, political media orientations explained the largest share of variation in voter turnout (6.3%), and within that set reliance on newspapers and magazines as decision aids contributed the most variance. Mass communication orientations thus emerged as a primary predictor of turnout among the young, much as it did in the Blumler-McLeod study. The next most powerful set of factors was political disposition (5.5%).

Among 25- to 34-year-olds, the dominant role of media was replaced by that of political dispositions. Media ranked second, accounting for 3.1% at the variance. More substantial changes occurred among the 35- to 64-year-olds, with the main predictors of turnout being political disposition (12 to 15% of variance explained), followed by structural and status characteristics. Clearly, changes in predictors of turnout, and presumably reasons for voting, occurred between the young adult years and the middle years, when the decision to vote may become more dependent upon already-formed dispositions. Turnout among those over 65, on the other hand, was most accounted for by political disposition (14.1%), followed by media orientations (6.1%). The rise in association between media orientation and turnout among those 65 and over may in part be a consequence of greater social isolation of this group. The elderly, with greater interest in politics, whether for reasons associated with politics serving as a functional substitute for other activities or not, may find greater political stimulation from media use than from social contacts. The media may become more prominent in the lives of older persons, replacing activities and social contacts more common in earlier years.

Thus, what the young eligible voter has learned from the media and parents, combined with his trust in politicians, may be more important in determining turnout than other factors. The middle-aged and older voters may act more in line with dispositions formed over the years as a result of previous voting and other political experiences, and may rely less on media. Voting in later years also appears more tied to status within the community.

The above research substantiates a view that not only does voter turnout vary across the life cycle, but that different demographic, sociological and psychological variables are related to turnout at specific life-cycle stages. Mass communication behavior appears a more important factor early in political life, and again in later years. To obtain a more complete picture of the relationship between communication and turnout, it seems necessary to examine also communication behaviors within both voter and nonvoter groups over stages of political life. The research on mass media uses by voters, and the consequences of such, is quite extensive (see, for example, Berelson, Lazarsfeld and McPhee, 1954; Klapper, 1960; Converse, 1966; Blumler and McQuail, 1969; Atkin, 1973; McLeod, Becker and Byrnes, 1974; Mendelsohn and O'Keefe, 1976). Also, some of the more recent research has shown concern with age differences in voting and communication behavior, particularly in terms of comparing young first-time voters to older ones (see, for example, Blumler and McLeod, 1974; O'Keefe, Becker, and McLeod, 1976; Chaffee and Becker, 1975; McLeod, Brown, Becker, and Ziemke, 1977). However, scant attention has been given to describing communication or more general characteristics of the nonvoting population. One landmark volume, *Voting and Nonvoting* (Lang and Lang, 1968), is incisive in its discussions of media use and nonvoting, but places the issue into the somewhat limited context of the impact of election result forecasts prior to poll closings on abstention.

This chapter attempts to extend and elaborate upon the above research by taking as its point of departure the investigation of motivations and media uses underlying nonvoting behavior. The aim is to examine nonvoters as a population subgroup in terms of the motivations these individuals may have for their inactivity and to associate those motivations with media orientations over the life cycle.

If reasons for not voting and media orientations do vary with age, the problem becomes one of investigating the relationship between media orientations and nonvoting reasons within age categories. Such investigation also requires the control of certain variables which might be expected to affect both media orientations and nonvoting reasons within age groups, and which more importantly may affect the relationship between the two within age groups. For these preliminary analyses, two such control variables will be considered: political interest and level of education. Both have emerged as important predictors of both media use and nonvoting in the previous research cited above.

METHODOLOGY AND RESULTS

The data reported below were generated from a national survey of nonvoters conducted in July 1976 by the polling firm of Peter Hart and Associates. Multi-stage area sampling techniques, combined with interviewee screening procedures, were used to arrive at a final sample of 1,486 respondents identified as nonvoters in the sense of their either: (1) having failed to vote regularly for reasons other than legal requirements in the previous four national elections, or (2) indicating that there was a 50-50 chance or less that they would vote in the 1976 presidential election. While there is a problem of validity in that the study relied completely upon respondents' self-assessments of their past voting history and 1976 election behavior, there is no reason to suspect that the sample as a whole does not reflect a representative group of individuals less likely to participate in politics through voting. A demographic profile of the sample is presented in Table 1.

For the purposes here, analyses will be limited to a series of items ascertaining respondents' reasons for not voting and certain characteristics of their mass media behavior, in addition to age, political interest, and education.

Reasons for not voting were assessed by asking respondents to rate the importance of each of 11 items culled from a larger list of 18 items on the basis of their face validity, variance, and a cluster analysis. The items reflected the following rationales for not voting: (1) cynicism toward candidates; (2) inability to discriminate between candidates; (3) distrust of candidates; (4) distrust of government; (5) general lack of concern with politics; (6) inefficacy of voting; (7) lack of objective information about candidates; (8) feeling generally unqualified to vote; (9) difficulty in registering to vote; (10) inconvenient poll hours; and (11) inconvenient poll locations. Specific items appear in Table 2.

Table 1: AN OVERVIEW OF THE SAMPLE (N=1486)

Sex

Men	48%
Women	52

Race

White	73%
Black	17
Oriental	1
Hispanic/Chicano	8
Other	1

Age

18-24	21%
25-34	34
35-49	20
50-64	14
65+	11

Marital Status

Married	60%
Single	40

Income

Under $10,000	51%
$10,000–14,999	23
$15,000 and over	25

Education

0–8 years	21%
9–12 years	61
College	19

Party Identification

Democratic	43%
Independent	28
Republican	29

Generally, the first six can be classified as "substantive" reasons for not voting largely involving negative reactions against candidates, government, and/or the political system. Perceived lack of information or general qualifications reflect a more neutral stance based in part on inability to attain and/or process information. The last three center on "technicalities," or matters of convenience, regarding the actual voting process.

The most important reasons for abstention over the sample as a whole were those associated with distrust and cynicism toward candidates, lack of concern with politics, and lack of information about candidates, while those least important had bearing on hardships encountered in registering or getting to the polls (Table 2). With respect to age, the emphasis given substantive reasons and lack of information declined steadily from young to old. Eighteen- 24-year-olds consistently rated these reasons as more important than did any other cohort. Nonvoters aged 65 and over, however, rated candidate cynicism and inefficacy more important than did the middle-aged, and emphasized lack of qualification and, as expected, inconvenience of polling places moreso than any other age group.

Table 2. MEAN SCORES FOR REASONS FOR NOT VOTING BY AGE

	18-24 (n=307)	25-34 (n—505)	35-64* (n=508)	65+ (n—158)	Total Sample (n=1486)
Candidate cynicism[1]	1.93	1.82	1.72	1.80	1.81
Candidate indiscrimination[2]	1.85	1.73	1.67	1.64	1.73
Candidate distrust[3]	2.20	2.16	2.08	2.07	2.14
Government distrust[4]	1.81	1.76	1.62	1.56	1.70
Political unconcern[5]	1.79	1.75	1.77	1.75	1.77
Innefficacy of voting[6]	1.75	1.72	1.66	1.69	1.71
Information lack[7]	1.83	1.80	1.68	1.65	1.75
Unqualified to vote[8]	1.49	1.45	1.38	1.53	1.45
Registration difficulty[9]	1.31	1.28	1.32	1.30	1.30
Poll hours inconvenient[10]	1.28	1.21	1.28	1.30	1.26
Poll place inconvenient[11]	1.23	1.16	1.22	1.30	1.21

* 35- to 49-year-olds and 50- to 64-year-olds were combined for these analyses.
1. "Watergate proved that elected officials are only out for themselves."
2. "All candidates seem pretty much the same."
3. "Candidates say one thing and then do another."
4. "The government seems to act too secretly."
5. "I just don't bother with politics."
6. "One person's vote really won't make any difference."
7. "It is hard to find reliable and unbiased information on the candidates."
8. "I don't feel qualified to vote."
9. "The registration rules make it difficult for people to register."
10. "I couldn't get to the polls during voting hours."
11. "The location of the polling place is inconvenient."
All items scored 1 = "Not very important;" 2 = "Somewhat important;" 3 = "Very important."

One might have expected the young to place more weight upon registration requirements than the old, but that was not found. Perhaps registration campaigns aimed at making the process as simple as possible, primarily with the young in mind, at least made the point that the process was a relatively easy one.

In sum, the young, followed somewhat distantly by the elderly, attached greater importance to items reflecting a general disaffection with electoral processes. Whether this is more a function of youth itself or of generational differences cannot be properly addressed with the data here. However, surveys of voting populations over the years have generally found the young to have lesser feelings of political trust and efficacy than older voters, suggesting maturational influence. Quite the same phenomenon may be taking place among nonvoters, albeit perhaps to a greater degree. The rank orders of mean scores of the reasons were quite consistent within each age cohort.

Table 3. MEDIA ORIENTATIONS, POLITICAL INTEREST AND EDUCATION, BY AGE

	18-24 (n=307)	25-34 (n=505)	35-64 (n=509)	65+ (n=158)	Total Sample (n=1486)
Television fairness[1]	1.84	1.92	1.95	1.87	1.91
Hi int.	1.71	1.86	1.98	1.71	1.86
Hi ed.	1.63	1.85	1.83	1.71	1.79
Television exposure[2]	2.00	2.16	2.30	2.50	2.21
Hi int.	2.32	2.31	2.64	2.69	2.47
Hi ed.	2.13	2.28	2.43	2.50	2.29
Television attention[3]	1.82	1.97	1.99	2.03	1.95
Hi int.	2.41	2.58	2.53	2.42	2.52
Hi ed.	1.98	2.27	2.18	2.23	2.18
Television helpfulness[4]	2.11	2.20	2.18	2.16	2.17
Hi int.	2.14	2.27	2.37	2.55	2.32
Hi ed.	2.05	2.26	2.39	2.25	2.25
Newspaper fairness[5]	1.81	1.81	1.84	1.93	1.83
Hi int.	1.69	1.66	1.76	1.74	1.71
Hi ed.	1.62	1.58	1.61	1.86	1.61
Newspaper exposure[6]	1.95	2.05	2.20	2.32	2.10
Hi int.	2.16	2.08	2.34	2.42	2.23
Hi ed.	2.27	2.08	2.45	2.36	2.20
Newspaper attention[7]	1.63	1.68	1.70	1.69	1.68
Hi int.	2.22	2.08	2.10	2.18	2.12
Hi ed.	1.87	1.91	1.89	1.87	1.88
Newspaper helpfulness[8]	2.20	2.25	2.22	2.15	2.22
Hi int.	2.37	2.30	2.29	2.46	2.32
Hi ed.	2.30	2.38	2.25	2.18	2.32
Education[9]	2.18	2.18	1.79	1.39	1.96
Hi int.	2.31	2.41	1.97	1.58	2.15
Hi ed.	——	——	——	——	——

Table 3. MEDIA ORIENTATIONS, POLITICAL INTEREST AND EDUCATION, BY AGE (Cont'd)

	18-24 (n=307)	25-34 (n=505)	35-64 (n=509)	65+ (n=158)	Total Sample (n=1486)
Political interest[10]	1.88	2.01	2.00	1.91	1.97
Hi int.	——	——	——	——	——
Hi ed.	2.14	2.26	2.33	2.50	2.26

1. Generally speaking, would you say that the information about politics you get from television is biased and slanted, or that it is objective and fair? (3 levels, 1 = "biased.")

2. The national network news is on TV in the early evening. National network news is shown five days a week, Monday through Friday. In a typical five-day week, how many days do you usually watch at least one of these newscasts? (3 levels, 1 = low.)

3. When you are watching the news on television, and stories about national politics come on, do you usually pay very close attention to the story, pay some attention to find out what it is about, pay a little attention, or pay no attention to it at all? (3 levels, 1 = low.)

4. Has the presentation of this year's presidential campaign on television made it easier or harder for you to understand what the candidates stand for? (3 levels, 1 = "harder.")

5. Generally speaking, would you say that the information about politics you get from the newspapers is biased and slanted or that it is objective and fair? (3 levels, 1 = "biased.")

6. In a typical seven-day week, how many days would you say you get a chance to read the daily newspaper—if any at all? (3 levels, 1 = low.)

7. When you come across stories about politics in your newspaper, do you usually read the complete story, read enough of the story to know what it is about, read a little of it, or read none of it? (3 levels, 1 = low.)

8. Has reading about this year's presidential campaign in the newspapers made it easier, or harder, for you to understand what the candidates stand for? (3 levels, 1 = "harder.")

9. What is the highest grade or year of regular school or college you have attended? (3 levels, 1 = low.)

10. How interested are you in national politics and national affairs—are you very interested, somewhat interested, only slightly interested, or not interested at all? (3 levels, 1 = low.)

The profile of nonvoters' mass media orientations does not differ markedly from that regularly found for voters (Table 3). Exposure to newspapers and television news and attention to political news content generally increases with age, education, and political interest.

Eighteen- to 24-year-old nonvoters and those 65 and over saw both television and newspapers as less helpful and television as less fair than other respondents. Political interest increased over the life cycle among nonvoters, as it has been found to do among voters.

Within each age group, the more educated and politically interested indicated greater newspaper and television news exposure, attention to political news, and perceptions of being helped by news media in better understanding the candidates. However, they rated both newspaper and television as being less fair in treatment of political matters than did the overall sample.

Television emerges as by far the prime political information medium for nonvoters. Half or more of the nonvoters in all age groups listed television as their main source of political information (Table 4), and newspapers were listed by less than a quarter of the respondents, barely edging out radio. This finding goes against results obtained from past samples of voters in which newspapers are usually ranked only slightly below television. Television appears especially relied upon by nonvoters over age 50. Eighteen- to 24-year-olds indicated greater preference for magazines than older respondents, a result consistent with research on voters.

Table 4. MAIN SOURCE FOR POLITICAL INFORMATION BY AGE[1] (N=1486)

	18-24 (n=307)	25-34 (n=505)	35-64 (n=508)	65+ (n=158)
Magazines	7%	7%	3%	1%
Other people	14	11	9	11
Television	50	49	56	57
Newspapers	9	16	20	13
Radio	15	11	9	10
None	5	6	3	7

1. "Which one of these sources do you count on most for news and information about national politics— magazines, talking with people, television, newspapers, or radio?"

In order to assess the relationships between media orientations and reasons for not voting, the media orientations along with education and political interest were inserted into a multiple linear regression analysis of their impacts on each of the nonvoting reasons.[2] These analyses were repeated within each of the four age groups.

Over the sample as a whole, interest in politics emerges as the most consistent predictor of substantive reasons for abstention (Table 5). The more politically interested nonvoters were, the less import they attached to candidate cynicism and indiscrimination, distrust of candidates and government, inefficacy of voting and lack of political concern, regardless of education level or media orientations. Highly interested nonvoters are thus unlikely to be classifiable as a congregation of concerned-yet-disenchanted citizens who choose not to vote out of contempt for general malaise with electoral processes.

On te other hand, the data do not quite so firmly dispell the argument that the news media "alienate" citizens into modes of lesser political involvement. While the results for newspaper orientations square some-what with the familiar hypothesis of mass media usage supporting positive political inclinations, the data for television are quite divergent. Most striking is the finding that increased attention to televised political

Table 5. REGRESSION ANALYSES OF NONVOTING REASONS, BY EDUCATION, INTEREST AND MEDIA ORIENTATIONS (Base N=1486)

	Television				Newspapers				Educa-tion	Polit. Int.	R²
	Fair-ness	Expo-sure	Atten-tion	Help-ful	Fair-ness	Expo-sure	Atten-tion	Help-ful			
Candidate cynicism	-.07[a] (-.02)	-.03 (-.01)	-.03 (.04)	-.02 (.03)	-.08[a] (-.09)[a]	.03- (.03)	-.03 (.01)	-.06 (-.06)	-.09[b] (-.07)[a]	-.18[b] (-.18)[b]	.05
Candidate indiscrimination	-.06 (-.02)	-.09[b] (-.05)	-.08[a] (.01)	-.08[a] (.01)	-.05 (-.05)	-.05 (-.02)	-.12[b] (-.06)	-.14[b] (-.12)[b]	-.07[a] (-.04)	-.14[b] (-.10)[b]	.05
Candidate distrust	-.09[b] (-.09)[a]	-.10[b] (-.08)[a]	-.02 (.08)[a]	-.04 (.04)	-.05 (-.01)	-.03 (-.01)	-.08[a] (-.05)	-.11[b] (-.10)[b]	-.06 (-.04)	-.13[b] (-.12)[b]	.05
Government distrust	-.04 (.02)	-.07[a] (-.07)	.03- (.09)[a]	-.06- (.00)	-.08[a] (-.09)[a]	-.04 (-.03)	-.01 (.01)	-.11[b] (-.10)[b]	-.03- (-.02)	-.07[a] (-.08)[a]	.03
Political unconcern	.05 (.09)[a]	-.11[b] (-.04)	-.22[b] (-.09)[a]	-.05 (.01)	.00 (-.09)[a]	-.08[b] (-.04)	-.22[b] (-.11)[b]	-.09[b] (-.05)	-.17[b] (-.11)[b]	-.27[b] (-.17)[b]	.12
Inneficacy of voting	-.02 (-.02)	-.07[a] (-.04)	-.06 (.04)	-.04 (.01)	-.00 (-.01)	-.04 (-.02)	-.11[b] (-.05)	-.08[a] (-.06)	-.12[b] (-.08)[a]	-.19[b] (-.17)[b]	.05
Information lack	-.14[b] (-.04)	-.04 (-.04)	.05 (.08)[a]	-.17[b] (-.08)[a]	-.16[b] (-.11)[b]	-.07[a] (-.06)	.00 (.00)	-.19[b] (-.14)[b]	.04 (.02)	.02 (.00)	.08
Unqualified to vote	.06 (.07)	.00 (.04)	-.10[b] (-.08)[a]	-.01 (.00)	.03 (-.07)[a]	-.08[a] (-.07)[a]	-.09[b] (-.04)	-.03 (-.02)	-.08[a] (-.05)	-.07[a] (-.01)	.03
Registration difficulty	.02 (.01)	-.02 (-.02)	-.01 (.02)	-.07[a] (-.03)	.03 (-.03)	-.05 (-.03)	-.02 (.01)	-.10[b] (-.09)[a]	-.09[b] (-.07)[a]	-.03 (-.00)	.02
Poll hours inconvenient	.00 (.02)	-.04 (-.06)	.06 (.06)	-.03 (-.06)	-.01 (-.02)	-.04 (-.04)	.04 (.02)	.01 (.04)	-.03 (-.04)	.06 (.05)	.02
Poll place inconvenient	.04 (.03)	-.00 (-.01)	-.01 (.01)	.01 (.02)	.04 (.01)	-.00 (.01)	-.01 (.00)	-.01 (-.03)	-.09[b] (-.09)[b]	.01 (.04)	.01

[a] p .05   Upper value in each cell represents zero-order Pearson r.
[b] p .01   Lower value (in parenthesis) represents standardized regression coefficient.

news is *positively* associated with nearly all substantive reasons for not voting. The greater attention viewers paid to stories about national politics, the higher they rated candidate cynicism and indiscrimination, distrust in candidates and government, and inefficacy of voting. While only the standardized regression coefficients for candidate and government distrust were significant, the overall consistency of these results is marked. Moreover, perceived helpfulness of television in understanding candidates maintains low, yet positive, associations with all substantive reasons. Fairness of television in political matters is more troublesome, yielding coefficients mixed in directionality with the substantive rationale, e.g., a negative and significant relationship with candidate distrust but a positive and significant relationship with political unconcern.

On the other hand, level of exposure to network television news and newspaper exposure and attention were quite consistent in yielding low order negative coefficients with substantive reasons. And, the more fair and helpful readers found newspapers to be, the less important they rated substantive reasons, a finding that was statistically significant in several cases.

In general, then, expectations of newspapers as being fair, and the perceived effect of newspapers in terms of their helpfulness, were associated with decreased importance of political disaffection and malaise. However, the activity of greater attendance to televised political news was associated with an increased importance of negative attitudes toward politics. A partial explanation for this discrepancy may well lie, of course, in the divergent natures of the two news media. Even a high level of attention to television news is apt to provide only a surface view of often complex political issues and personalities, emphasizing "blacks and whites" at the expense of thoughtful shades of gray. Such superficiality, accompanied by the obvious fact that bad news is more interesting than good, may promote and/or reinforce negative feelings toward politics.

Media orientations were paramount in predicting the importance of lack of objective information as a criterion for not voting, following much the same pattern as described above. However, level of education emerged as the key predictor of "convenience" reasons for not voting, with the more educated significantly less likely to rate registration difficulties or inconvenience of polling places as important.

The results of the regression analyses within each age cohort (Tables 6 through 9) generally match those for the sample as a whole. However, the relative impact of media orientations on reasons for abstention varies with age. For instance, political interest emerged as a quite weak

Table 6. REGRESSION ANALYSES OF NONVOTING REASONS, BY EDUCATION, INTEREST AND MEDIA ORIENTATIONS AMONG 18- TO 24-YEAR-OLDS (BASE N=307)

	Television				Newspapers				Educa-tion	Polit. Int.	R^2
	Fair-ness	Expo-sure	Atten-tion	Help-ful	Fair-ness	Expo-sure	Atten-tion	Help-ful			
Candidate cynicism	.01 (.00)	−.01 (−.03)	.06 (.11)	.02 (.01)	−.02 (−.02)	.12 (.12)	.03 (.04)	.03 (.01)	.02 (.02)	−.10 (−.17)	.04
Candidate indiscrimination	−.01 (−.02)	−.04 (−.03)	−.01 (.05)	−.03 (.01)	.03 (.06)	−.03 (−.01)	−.06 (−.03)	−.11 (−.11)	−.01 (.03)	−.08 (−.08)	.02
Candidate distrust	−.12 (−.14)	−.14 (−.12)	.03 (.16)[a]	.02 (.08)	−.05 (−.00)	.02 (.04)	−.10 (−.07)	−.07 (−.07)	−.08 (−.06)	−.16[a] (−.18)[a]	.08
Government distrust	−.10 (−.07)	−.10 (−.08)	−.10 (−.05)	−.13 (−.07)	−.10 (.11)	.05 (.08)	−.02 (−.15)	−.18[a] (−.10)	−.07 (−.10)	−.13 (−.10)	.08
Political unconcern	.07 (.10)	−.04 (.02)	−.30[b] (−.10)[a]	−.04 (.02)	−.01 (−.04)	−.01 (.04)	−.27[b] (−.16)[a]	−.14 (−.11)	−.14 (−.11)	−.21[b] (−.02)	.15
Innefficacy of voting	−.05 (−.02)	−.09 (−.07)	.02 (.14)	−.10 (−.04)	−.04 (−.03)	.04 (.09)	−.15[a] (−.14)	−.13 (−.13)	−.10 (−.11)	−.09 (−.04)	.07
Information lack	−1.12 (−.04)	−.04 (−.07)	.17[a] (.16)	−.17[ab] (−.10)	−.13 (−.08)	−.10 (−.08)	.10 (.03)	−.13 (−.09)	.08 (.04)	.13 (.08)	.10
Unqualified to vote	.07 (−.00)	.09 (.09)	−.07 (−.10)	−.03 (−.04)	.15[a] (.17)[a]	−.05 (−.03)	−.02 (.03)	−.05 (−.05)	−.05 (−.03)	−.04 (−.01)	.05
Registration difficulty	.05 (.01)	−.02 (−.02)	−.02 (.03)	.00 (.05)	.01 (.02)	−.00 (.04)	.01 (.07)	−.13 (−.16)[a]	−.05 (−.04)	−.11 (−.11)	.04
Poll hours inconvenient	.08 (.10)	−.07 (−.11)	.09 (.12)	−.01 (−.01)	.00 (−.02)	.07 (.11)	.09 (.10)	.04 (−.09)	−.03 (−.02)	−.06 (−.11)	.05
Poll place inconvenient	.05 (.01)	.01 (−.01)	.03 (.05)	.03 (.05)	.07 (.08)	.16[a] (.21)[b]	.05 (.09)	−.09 (−.19)[a]	−.11 (−.12)	−.08 (−.10)	.08

[a] p .05   Upper value in each cell represents zero-order Pearson r.
[b] p .01   Lower value (in parenthesis) represents standardized regression coefficient.

Table 7. REGRESSION ANALYSES OF NONVOTING REASONS, BY EDUCATION, INTEREST AND MEDIA ORIENTATIONS AMONG 25- TO 34-YEAR-OLDS (BASE N=505)

	Television				Newspapers				Education	Polit. Int.	R^2
	Fairness	Exposure	Attention	Helpful	Fairness	Exposure	Attention	Helpful			
Candidate cynicism	-.09 (-.04)	-.07 (-.04)	-.08 (.02)	-.02 (.04)	-.09 (-.11)	.00 (.01)	-.05 (.01)	-.07 (-.08)	-.17[b] (-.16)[b]	-.18[b] (-.16)[b]	.07
Candidate indiscrimination	-.05 (-.05)	-.01 (.04)	-.14[a] (-.04)	-.10 (-.01)	-.03 (-.03)	-.11 (-.10)	-.15[b] (-.07)	-.17[b] (-.13)	-.14[a] (-.08)	-.15[b] (-.11)	.08
Candidate distrust	-.10 (-.17)[a]	-.02 (.01)	-.06 (.03)	-.05 (.02)	-.00 (.07)	-.07 (-.07)	-.09 (-.05)	-.10 (-.07)	-.13[a] (-.09)	-.14[a] (-.13)[a]	.06
Government distrust	-.08 (-.06)	.00 (.02)	.01 (.07)	-.05 (.06)	-.04 (-.03)	-.02 (-.02)	.00 (.04)	-.16[b] (-.19)[b]	-.06 (-.04)	-.12[a] (-.16)[a]	.06
Political unconcern	.07 (.04)	-.10 (-.04)	-.27[b] (-.14)[a]	-.02 (.01)	.06 (-.03)	-.08 (-.07)	-.20[b] (-.07)	-.05 (-.02)	-.19[b] (-.10)	-.26[b] (-.15)[a]	.12
Innefficacy of voting	-.03 (-.10)	-.02 (.01)	-.02 (.05)	.03 (.07)	.05 (.08)	-.03 (-.05)	.02 (.08)	-.03 (-.06)	-.13[a] (-.11)	-.17[b] (-.19)[b]	.06
Information lack	-.17[b] (-.08)	-.02 (.00)	.02 (.02)	-.16[b] (-.03)	-.19[b] (-.13)	-.14[a] (-.13)[b]	-.01 (.01)	-.24[b] (-.21)[b]	.01 (.01)	.02 (-.03)	.11
Unqualified to vote	.05 (.08)	.02 (.05)	-.14[a] (-.15)[a]	.01 (.02)	-.01 (-.07)	-.07 (-.06)	-.08 (-.02)	.01 (.01)	-.03 (-.00)	-.04 (.02)	.03
Registration difficulty	.00 (-.05)	-.04 (-.00)	-.10 (-.11)	-.09 (-.02)	.07 (.10)	-.06 (-.06)	.00 (.08)	-.15[b] (-.13)[a]	-.03 (.02)	-.05 (-.03)	.04
Poll hours inconvenient	-.11 (-.14)	-.00 (-.01)	.07 (-.00)	-.04 (-.08)	-.05 (.08)	-.11 (-.13)[a]	.07 (.03)	.04 (.09)	.07 (.05)	.14[a] (.11)	.05
Poll place inconvenient	.03 (-.06)	-.00 (.02)	.06 (-.13)	-.00 (.03)	.08 (.12)	-.15[b] (-.14)[a]	-.01 (.03)	-.06 (-.06)	.00 (.03)	.09 (-.13)[a]	.05

[a] p .05   Upper value in each cell represents zero-order Pearson r.
[b] p .01   Lower value (in parenthesis) represents standardized regression coefficient.

Table 8. REGRESSION ANALYSES OF NONVOTING REASONS, BY EDUCATION, INTEREST AND MEDIA ORIENTATIONS AMONG 35- TO 64-YEAR-OLDS (BASE N=508)

	Television				Newspapers				Educa-tion	Polit. Int.	R²
	Fairness	Exposure	Attention	Helpful	Fairness	Exposure	Attention	Helpful			
Candidate cynicism	-.06 (.03)	.00 (.05)	-.05 (-.02)	.02 (.08)	-.10 (-.14)a	.06 (.10)	-.05 (-.03)	-.04 (-.07)	-.11 (-.13)a	-.13a (-.13)a	.06
Candidate indiscrimination	-.08 (.02)	-.19b (-.14)a	-.12a (-.05)	-.07 (.03)	-.11 (-.13)	-.01 (.04)	-.13a (-.07)	-.15b (-.12)	-.08 (-.08)	-.07 (-.01)	.08
Candidate distrust	-.08 (.01)	-.13a (-.10)	-.05 (.03)	-.04 (.08)	-.10 (-.10)	.00 (.03)	-.09 (-.05)	-.13a (-.15)a	-.05 (-.05)	-.09 (-.06)	.05
Government distrust	-.05 (.16)a	-.05 (-.09)	.13a (.15)a	-.04 (-.03)	-.09 (-.19)b	-.06 (-.04)	-.00 (-.03)	-.06 (-.06)	-.08 (-.09)	.06 (.04)	.06
Political unconcern	.00 (.11)	-.17b (-.06)	-.20b (-.08)	-.08 (-.03)	.03 (-.14)a	-.12a (-.07)	-.22b (-.10)	-.08 (.00)	-.13a (-.06)	-.28b (-.20)b	.13
Inefficacy of voting	-.00 (.10)	-.09 (-.00)	-.17b (-.10)	-.07 (-.03)	-.04 (-.14)a	-.08 (-.04)	-.18b (-.10)	-.08 (-.02)	-.10 (-.06)	-.18b (-.12)a	.07
Information lack	-.13a (-.01)	-.01 (-.00)	.03 (.04)	-.14a (-.06)	-.16b (-.14)a	.03 (.03)	.01 (.01)	-.19b (-.15)a	.00 (-.02)	.03 (.02)	.06
Unqualified to vote	.03 (.11)	-.03 (.02)	-.10 (-.08)	-.01 (-.01)	-.03 (-.12)	-.12a (-.08)	-.11 (-.06)	-.02 (.00)	-.11 (-.08)	-.05 (-.00)	.04
Registration difficulty	.03 (.03)	.02 (.00)	.08 (.09)	-.08 (-.08)	.02 (-.01)	-.03 (.01)	-.04 (-.08)	-.06 (-.02)	-.16b (-.17)b	.09 (.12)	.06
Poll hours inconvenient	.04 (.05)	-.04 (-.08)	.10 (.10)	-.04 (-.09)	.02 (-.01)	-.03 (-.01)	.04 (.03)	.01 (.05)	-.12a (-.13)a	.05 (.06)	.04
Poll place inconvenient	.06 (.10)	-.03 (-.05)	.02 (-.00)	-.01 (-.04)	.00 (-.07)	-.01 (.01)	.00 (-.00)	.06 (.08)	-.11 (-.12)a	.04 (.06)	.03

a p .05   Upper value in each cell represents zero-order Pearson r.

b p .01   Lower value (in parenthesis) represents standardized regression coefficient.

Table 9. REGRESSION ANALYSES OF NONVOTING REASONS, BY EDUCATION, INTEREST AND MEDIA ORIENTATIONS AMONG 65+-YEAR-OLDS (BASE N=158)

	Television				Newspapers				Educa-tion	Polit. Int.	R²
	Fair-ness	Expo-sure	Atten-tion	Help-ful	Fair-ness	Expo-sure	Atten-tion	Help-ful			
Candidate cynicism	-.08 (-.02)	-.06 (.00)	.14 (.20)	-.24ᵃ (-.07)	-.10 (.04)	-.12 (-.14)	-.01 (.10)	-.25ᵃ (-.17)	-.11 (.01)	-.39ᵇ (-.41)ᵇ	.27
Candidate indiscrimination	-.04 (.01)	-.04 (-.00)	.14 (.27)ᵃ	-.12 (.02)	-.05 (-.07)	.00 (.05)	-.14 (-.11)	-.11 (-.04)	-.15 (-.03)	-.43ᵇ (-.44)ᵇ	.25
Candidate distrust	-.04 (-.03)	-.04 (-.03)	.20 (.26)ᵃ	-.19 (-.13)	-.03 (.02)	.01 (.03)	.02 (.02)	-.12 (-.06)	-.13 (-.11)	-.21 (-.18)	.14
Government distrust	.05 (.21)	-.08 (-.10)	.23ᵃ (.36)ᵇ	-.06 (-.06)	-.02 (-.20)	-.11 (-.08)	-.06 (-.15)	.04 (.09)	-.13 (-.04)	-.15 (-.12)	.16
Political unconcern	.11 (.29)	-.14 (-.08)	-.02 (.16)	-.13 (.02)	-.03 (-.26)	-.11 (-.02)	-.21 (-.18)	-.19 (-.17)	-.33ᵇ (-.22)	-.37ᵇ (-.22)	.27
Innefuacy of voting	-.02 (.05)	-.20 (-.14)	.04 (.21)	-.09 (.10)	.03 (-.05)	-.14 (-.03)	-.22ᵃ (-.15)	-.13 (-.12)	-.25ᵃ (-.06)	-.46ᵇ (-.40)ᵇ	.28
Information lack	-.08 (.14)	-.13 (-.15)	.10 (.22)	-.30ᵇ (-.25)ᵃ	-.14 (-.22)	.04 (.11)	-.12 (-.17)	-.14 (.01)	-.08 (-.16)	-.16 (-.05)	.17
Unqualified to vote	.15 (.32)	-.09 (-.05)	-.09 (.03)	-.03 (.04)	.01 (-.26)	-.07 (.00)	-.19 (-.17)	-.08 (-.07)	-.21 (-.12)	-.22ᵃ (-.11)	.13
Registration difficulty	.00 (-.02)	-.12 (-.04)	.04 (.13)	-.13 (-.13)	.05 (.04)	-.14 (-.08)	-.10 (-.06)	.02 (.06)	-.18 (-.12)	-.17 (-.08)	.08
Poll hours inconvenient	.06 (.25)	-.04 (-.06)	.07 (-.01)	-.01 (-.07)	-.04 (-.25)	-.04 (-.02)	-.10 (-.17)	.08 (.13)	-.00 (.01)	.08 (.15)	.07
Poll place inconvenient	.05 (.20)	.00 (-.02)	.02 (.11)	.05 (.01)	-.06 (-.27)	.11 (.18)	-.12 (-.25)	.11 (.15)	-.15 (-.17)	-.03 (.05)	.12

ᵃp .05   Upper value in each cell represents zero-order Pearson r.
ᵇp .01   Lower value (in parenthesis) represents standardized regression coefficient.

predictor among 18- to 24-year-olds while attention to televised political news was generally the strongest. Again, the more attention to television news, the greater the importance attached to candidate distrust, inefficacy of voting, and lack of information. Not only does it appear that media usages are intrinsic in predicting voting versus nonvoting among young voters, but also in explaining motivations for abstention. This is particularly noteworthy given that the young scored lowest among all age groups in exposure and attention to television and newspapers. Perhaps in the absence of other political stimuli, including years of experience to draw from, even a modest amount of media encounter yields significant impact.

Political interest regains its status in predicting nonvoting reasons among older respondents. Media orientations are only sporadically well-associated with abstention reasons among 25- to 34-year-olds, and within the 35- to 64-year-old group newspaper fairness is the only media variable consistently and significantly related to nonvoting rationales. However, importance of government distrust over the middle years appears less a function of interest or education than of media orientation. Among age 65 and over nonvoters, television attention shows markedly high positive coefficients with substantive nonvoting reasons, particularly those pertaining to distrust. These results bear out the increased predictability of turnout by media usages among both the young and the elderly found in earlier research, and point to a potentially critical role for attention to televised news vis a vis reasons for abstention.

DISCUSSION

Recent literature on political behavior suggests several models attempting to account for variation in voter turnout. Individual level predictors which have been among the most successful in explaining voter participation and abstention include age and political communication behavior. When appropriate controls are introduced, voter turnout increases linearly with age, and higher levels of politically relevant mass media usage typically correlate positively with turnout. Recent findings also indicate media usage to be a particularly powerful predictor of turnout among first-time eligible voters, and to a lesser but nonetheless sizable extent among citizens age 65 and over. While previous investigations have to some extent explored media use characteristics of the voting population, a more complete understanding of turnout and communication processes may evolve from inspection of media use among nonvoters over the life cycle, particularly as related to motivations for not voting. Reasons for abstention and media use patterns were found to vary with age in this study, as did the nature of the relationship between media orientations and specific reasons for not voting.

Specifically, media orientations were more predictive of abstention reasons among 18- to 24-year-olds and those age 65 and over than for middle-age groups. Moreover, greater attention to televised political news was found positively associated with political distrust and other forms of disaffection as abstention reasons. However, the more fair and helpful vis a vis politics newspapers were perceived as being, the less import nonvoters gave to such reasons.

This study is of course limited in using a cross-sectional design; cohort and longitudinal analyses would enhance the inferences to be made from these data. It is clear, however, that development of political orientations such as turnout over the life cycle deserves much closer attention than it has received in the past.

The often-supported generalization that greater public affairs media use encourages voting particularly deserves a closer look. Finer delineation between such orientations as exposure and attention, as well as credibility and helpfulness, with each medium may provide a clearer picture of precisely what kinds of usages are associated with specific influences.

Greater clarification may well also be found in examining the various gratifications sought by nonvoters, particularly the young and the elderly, in their political communication usages, and the extent to which they rely on mass media for assistance in forming political beliefs, values and behaviors.

For instance, one key distinction in terms of information seeking between newspapers and television centers around selectivity. The regular newspaper reader can more easily pick and choose content consistent with existing interests and views. For the regular television news attender, however, such selectivity is cognitively more difficult. The politically disinterested viewer who wants to "keep up with the news" in general may find political content hard to avoid. Cognitively tuning out one uninteresting story on a well-paced news program often leads to missing the next as well. Thus the heavy viewer disinterested in and/or disaffected with politics is likely to get a fair dosage of it regardless, particularly during peak campaign periods, and perhaps with disagreeable effects. More politically interested news viewers attempting to evaluate candidates may find themselves in much the same situation: potential voters with a preferred candidate and seeking reinforcement are likely to also view content favorable to the opposition; and, those literally undecided not only receive candidate comparisons on attributes of importance to them, but on other attributes as well, perhaps in some cases hindering discrimination between candidates.

In addition, nonvoters holding negative views toward candidates and government may seek out televised political news for its relative simplicity of presentation which allows them to seek reinforcement and justification for their views. In addition, the aim for balanced coverage of political personalities and issues may give an appearance of blandness, leading to viewer perceptions of "all candidates being alike." Similarly, time allocated by the networks to extraneous campaign events and "hoopla" (Patterson and McClure, 1976) may lessen in viewers' eyes the critical import of voting and elections. This is not to say that newspapers necessarily exhibit continuous studied insight into the workings of politics, but most observers, including network news producers, would agree that print media do provide greater depth and insight into the complexities of politics.

The findings with respect to attention to televised news are quite compatible with evidence offered by Robinson (1976) that citizens who depend more on television in general for political information during presidential campaigns exhibit a greater sense of political inefficacy, as well as cynicism and distrust. Robinson attributes this relationship to what he terms "videomalaise" resulting from unique factors he perceives in the makeup of contemporary television journalism and the audience it serves.

Continuing research in this realm should focus more on those groups for whom communication seems to matter the most vis a vis abstention. The lifecycle approach used here has identified two such segments—the young emerging electorate and the oldest, and presumably most politically experienced, citizens. While at first blush they appear as quite disparate cohorts, commonalities have been found here. However, the reasons underlying the similarities may be quite different. For example, among the young, media may be sought out in a limited way as a readily available agent of political learning, particularly during campaigns, and specific gratifications may result. For the age 65 and over cohort, increased social isolation may lead to greater reliance on media as a source of political interaction, increasing the relevance of mass communications in their political participation. Among nonvoters in each of the two age groups, the markedly positive relationship between attention to televised political news and political disaffection and malaise may result from the differences in television and newspaper presentation formats discussed above. In particular, consider that most campaign media presentations aim at the largest block of voters—the 25- to 64-year-olds—and emphasize issues pertinent to them. The young and the elderly viewing the campaign in broad strokes on television news may perceive that others are the main ones being addressed and courted, adding to disenchantment. Greater attention to newpapers may allow these "out-groups" more selectivity in choosing stories speaking to their immediate concerns, and lead to greater satisfaction.

Some interesting consequences for future study of the political system may result, whether the trends here are primarily generational or a result of aging processes. For instance, if the association between media use and turnout among young voters is mainly a function of young inexperienced citizens seeking out readily available sources of political information and influence, it is important that we acknowledge the role of the media as a political learning device and investigate the specific uses made of media in that regard, and the consequences which derive. If, on the other hand, the media use-turnout relationship is based more upon generational differences, we may expect the role of the media to increase as present-day young voters mature. Presumably, this might be coupled with a decline in the role of social and organizational involvement, value-oriented political commitments, party affiliations and the like in affecting turnout. The media in a literal sense could become a foundation for a "new politics." One suspects, however, that the trend may reflect both cohort and generational changes; subsequent research should turn to unravelling the relative impacts of each within particular circumstances.

NOTES

1. It is admittedly difficult to address abstention as an operational form of political deviance, if for no other reason than that in terms of the proportions of citizens involved, nonvoting typically appears as statistically normative behavior. Nonetheless, abstention can ususally be assumed to reflect underlying disaffection or anomie vis a vis integrative democratic process in contemporary society, ranging from extreme deviation from political norms to more moderate protuberances. While research on political deviance has generally concentrated more on exhibition of political activism on the extreme ideological right or left related to alienation and anomie (Yinger, 1973), closer investigation of political nonparticipation in line with those same factors appears highly warranted.

2. The appropriateness of multiple regression analysis as a tool for the type of inquiry being pursued here has of course been the subject of considerable debate. However, it is felt that the technique is optimum for the purpose of describing relative contributions in terms of variance explained each of the factors considered, sequentially controlling for the other factors. A parametric strategy of regression analysis was used, following arguments of Kim (1975) and others that use of Person's r adequately meets the requirements of multivariate

analysis given the ordinal nature of the measures used here. Multicollinearity does not appear to be a problem, since the highest correlations between any two independent predictors are below .60. Inspections of cross-tabulations revealed no distinct curvilinear relationships between the independent predictors and voter turnout. A problem remains in that interaction effects between or more independent variables on the dependent variable may occur, with a resultant loss in variance explained by the set of independent predictors. However, the total proportions of variance explained by the sets of independent predictors below appear substantial enough to allow provisional inferences to be made. Interactions between predictor variables will be examined in subsequent analyses.

REFERENCES

AGNELLO, T.J. (1973). Aging and the sense of political powerlessness." Public Opinion Quarterly, 37:251-259.

ATKIN, C.K. (1973). "Instrumental utilities and information seeking." Pp. 205-242 in P. Clark (ed.), New models of communication research. Beverly Hills, Cal.: Sage.

BERELSON, B., LAXARSFELD, P., and MCPHEE, W. (1954). Voting. Chigago: University of Chicago Press.

BLUMLER, J.G., and MCLEOD, J.M. (1974). "Communication and voter turnout in Britain." In T. Leggatt (ed.), Sociological theory and survey research. Beverly Hills, Cal.: Sage.

BLUMLER, J.G., and MCQUAIL, D. (1969). Television in politics: It uses and influence. Chicago: University of Chigago Press.

BRIM,O.G., and WHEELER, S. (1966). Socializaiton after childhood: Two essays. New York: John Wiley.

BURNHAM, W.D. (1965). "The changing shape of the American politiacal universe." American Political Science Review, 59:7-28.

——— (1974). "Theory and voting research." American Political Science Review, 68:1002-1023.

BURSTEIN, P. (1972). "Social structure and individual political participation in five countries." American Journal of Sociology, 77:1987-1110.

CAMPBELL, A., CONVERSE, P.E., MILLER, W.E., and STOKES, D.E. (1960). The American voter. New York: John Wiley.

CHAFFEE,S. (with M. Jackson-Beeck, J. Lewin and D. Wilson) (1977). "Mass communication in political socialization." In S. Reshon (ed.), Handbook of political socialization. New York: Free Press.

CHAFFEE, S.H., and BECKER, L.B. (1975). "Young voters' reasctions to Watergate issues." American Politics Quarterly, 3:360-385.

CHAFFEE, S.H., and WILSON, D. (1975). "Adult life cycle changes in mass media use." Presented to Association for Education in Journalism, Ottawa, Canada.

CONVERSE, P.E. (1966). "Information flow and the stability of paritsan attitudes." In E. Dreyer and W. Rosenbaum (eds.), Political opinion and electoral behavior. Belmont, Cal.: Wadsworth.

CUTLER, S.J., and KAUFMAN, R.L. (1975). "Cohort changes in political attitudes: Tolerance of ideological nonconformity." Public Opinion Quarterly, 39:63-81.

DOWNS, A. (1957). Economic theory of democracy. New York: Harper.

FONER, A. (1974). "Age stratification and age conflict in political life." American Sociological Review, 33:187-196.

GLENN, N.D., and GRIMES, M. (1968). "Aging, voting and political interest." American Sociological Review, 33:563-575.
HOUT, M., and KNOKE, D. (1975). "Change in voting turnout, 1952-1972." Public Opinion Quarterly, 39:700-713.
JENNINGS, M.K., and NIEMI, R.G. (1974). The political character of adolescence. Princeton: Princeton University Press.
KEY, V.O. (1951). Southern politics in state and nation. New York: Knopf.
_____, PETROCIK, J.R., and ENOKSON, S.N. (1975). "Voter turnout among the American states: Systemic and individual components." American Political Science Review, 69:107-123.
KLAPPER, J.T. (1960). The effects of mass communication. New York: Free Press.
LANG, K., and LANG, G.E. (1968). Voting and nonvoting. Walthan, Mass.: Blaisdell.
LOVIN-SMITH, L. (1976). "Individual political participation: The effects of social structure and communication behavior." Presented to Association for Education in Journalism, College Park, Md.
MCLEOD, J.M., BECKER, L.B., and BYRNES, J.E. (1974). "Another look at the agenda setting function of the press." Communication Research, 1:131-166.
MCLEOD, J.M., BROWN, J.D., BECKER, C.B., and ZIEMKE, D., (1977). "Decline and fall at the White House: A longitudinal analysis of communication effects." Communication Research, 4:3-22.
MCLEOD, J.M., and O'KEEFE, G.J. (1972). "The socialization perspective and communication behavior." Pp. 121-168 in F.G. Kline and P.J. Tichenor (eds.), Current perspectives in mass communications research. Beverly Hills, Cal.: Sage.
MENDELSOHN, H. and O'KEEFE, G.J. (1976). The people choose a president: Influences on voter decision making. New York: Praeger.
NIE, N.H., POWELL, G.B., and PREWITT, K. (1969). "Social structure and political participation: Developmental relationships. Parts I and II." American Political Science Review, 63:361-378, 808-832.
O'KEEFE, G.J. (1976). "Voter turnout over the life cycle." Presented to Midwest Association for Public Opinion Research Annual Conference, Chicago, Ill.
_____, BECKER, L.B., and MCLEOD, J.M. (1976). "The youth vote in 1976: Implications of research on 1972's first-time voters." Presented to Midwest Association for Public opinion Research Annual Conference, Chicago, Ill.
OLSON, M.E. (1972). "Social participation and voting turnout: A multivariate analysis." American Sociological Review, 37:317-333.
PATTERSON, T.E., AND MCCLURE, R.D. (1976). The unseeing eye: New York: Putnam.
RILEY, M.S., and FONER, A. (1968). Aging and society. Volume one: An inventory of research findings. New York: Russell Sage Foundation.
RILEY, M.S. JOHNSON, M., and FONER, A. (1972). Aging and society. Volume three: A sociology of age stratification. New York: Russell Sage Foundation.
ROBINSON, M.J. (1976). "Public affairs television and the growth f political malaise: The case of 'The Selling of the Pentagon.' " American Political Science Review, 70:409-432.
SEARS, D. (1969). "Political behavior." G. Lindsey and E.Aronson (eds.), Handbook of social psychology, Vol. 5. Reading: Addison-Wesley.
VERBA, S., and NIE, N.H. (1972). Parictipation in America: Political democracy and social equality. New York: Harper and Row.
YINGER, J.M. (1973). "Anomie, alienation and political behavior." In J.N. Knutson (ed.), Handbook of political psychology. San Francisco: Jossey-Bass.

STUDYING VIOLENCE AND THE MEDIA
A Sociological Approach

JAMES D. HALLORAN

There is enormous interest in the connection, if any, between mass media and the specific kind of deviance represented by violence. In recent years there has been abundant evidence, ranging from government-sponsored enquiries and research to expressions of concern in the media and elsewhere and the information of pressure groups, that the alleged, although ill-defined, relationship between the mass media and violence is considered by many people to be important and problematic. The problem as popularly perceived is not a new one. Much of what is now being said about television has been said before about the other media, and throughout history innovations in communication technology have frequently been blamed for producing social disruption. Nevertheless, the protrayal of violence by the media, particularly by television, is increasingly seen as a major social problem, particularly in Western Europe and North America.

The concern is expressed in a variety of ways. People complain, they group together, they attend meetings, they exert pressure and plan collective action in the hope that this will lead to a solution, usually a censorious one, to the problem as they see it. Whether or not the concern is justified is a different matter. The evidence suggests that the process of influence, the role of the media and the nature of violence are not understood and that consequently the problem is inadequately defined. In view of this, the solutions put forward are not likely to be appropriate, and in fact the whole debate is characterized by inconsistencies and internal contradictions.

As far as the media/violence issue is concerned, the general tendency— which applies to much of the research as well as to the media and the public debate—is to oversimplify grossly the problem. People often talk about media violence and violent behavior almost as though there were no other sources of violence in society. They seek neat, convenient, uncomplicated answers which illustrate simple causal relationships. Once having identified a fixed point of evil, external to self, they use this as a scapegoat, which helps them to maintain their own particular view of self and society.

Assuming the media/violence relationship is worth examining, the first thing to do is remove the media from center stage. The main focus of our examination is violence or violent behavior in society and our interest in the media—at least as far as this problem is concerned—is what, if any, is the relationship between the media on the one hand and violent behavior on the other.

Violence may be categorized in several ways. For example, we may make a distinction between collective or political violence and personal or individual violence. If we accept this distinction and look at collective violence from an historical perspective, we shall see that it is much more normal, central and historically rooted than many would have us believe. Tilly has written (Graham and Gurr, 1969:788):

> Historically, collective violence has flowed regularly out of the central political processes of western countries. Men seeking to seize, hold or realign the levers of power, have continually engaged in collective violence as part of their struggles. The oppressed have struck in the name of justice, the privileged in the name of order, and those in between in the name of fear.

Much of what we now accept, take for granted, and enjoy are the outcomes of violent action in the past, although this will now have been fully legitimated with the aid of the media together with educational and other institutions. Certain important aspects of our history offer a tempting model of violence for those with a sense of grievance who might seek to solve their problems and achieve their goals by emulating their illustrious forebears.

It is important to stress that research and discussion on media violence should not be confined to "illegitimate violence" as this is defined by most of those who express concern about media violence. Many of these people, who feel they have a firm stake in the established system, loudly condemn "illegitimate violence" but urge the use of what they regard as legal or "legitimate violence" to protect the existing order and therby their own position or vested interest. There is, of course, a difference between legitimate violence and legal violence. The former depends on consensus. Legal violence is not necessarily legitimate.

As with the definition of the concept, neither the sources nor the roots of violent behavior can be adequately studied outside the appropriate national, historical, cultural, and economic contexts. The roots obviously differ from country to country. For example, in the U.S.A. it has been suggested that the "frontier factor," the patterns and extent of immigration, the War of Independence, the industrial revolution, urbanization, rapid social change and mobility, unprecedented prosperity and affluence, the class system and relative deprivation—some of which are unique to the U.S.A. and some common to several countries—have all played a part in contributing to the present situation in that country.

The media are not mentioned in the above list and it is worth noting that in the U.S.A. and elsewhere few of those who have systematically and scientifically studied violent behavior have cited the media as a major cause. They find the roots of such behavior elsewhere, as we shall see. However, we shall also see that quite a few researchers, particularly in the U.S.A., whose approach to the problem has been via media and communication studies have been more inclined to indict the media. The reasons for these differences make an interesting study in themselves. It all depends on how the problem is defined and on what questions are asked.

Even allowing for the aforementioned national and cultural differences, it is still possible, albeit in general terms, to make suggestions about some of the main sources of violent behavior which will be done here without referring to peculiarities in biological makeup. In a report on the history of violence in America to the National Commission on the Causes and Prevention of Violence in the U.S.A.—claimed to be "the most comprehensive, authoritative study of violence ever published"—we may read that, although many factors impinge on what is a complex process, there is considerable evidence supporting the assumption"that men's frustration over some of the material and social circumstances of their lives is a necessary precondition of group protest and collective violence," and that (Graham and Gurr, 1969:803-804):

Probably the most important cause of major increases in group violence is the widespread frustration of socially deprived expectations about the goods and conditions of life men believe theirs by right. These frustratable expectations relate not only to material well-being but to more intangible conditions such as security, status, freedom to manage ones own affairs, and satisfying personal relations with others.

It has also been suggested that the situation could be exacerbated when a country (e.g., Great Britain) experiences a period of "sharp relative decline in socio-economic or political conditions after a prolonged period of improving conditions." The repercussions would be widespread and take several forms, for "people whose dignity, career expectations, or political ambitions are so frustrated are as likely to rebel as those whose pocket-books are being emptied" (Graham and Gurr, 1969:807). A further problem occurs when people in such situations "believe that they cannot make their demands felt effectively through normal, approved channels and that 'the system' for whatever reasons has become unresponsive to them" (National Commission, 1969:291).

The above passages from the report to the National Commission are couched mainly in terms of group or collective protest or political behavior, but they are applicable mutatis mutandis to individual behavior as well. Studies of the violent behavior of delinquents and criminals show that in many cases there is a lack of appropriate or legitimate ways of problem-solving at a variety of levels. In addition to the economic level, these include the search for identity and satisfactory interpersonal relationships. Those whose opportunities to respond to the demands of life are severely limited and who can visualize no other solution may resort to violence. Violence may come to be regarded as —perhaps the only— alternative road to success, achievement, and status, which they have been led to believe society values so highly.

The above comments are not meant to provide a comprehensive explanation of violent behavior. There are several other approaches, each with its own emphasis. The main intention is to place the media/violence problem in perspective, to draw attention to the complexity of the situation and to the many factors involved, and—above all—to provide a wider, more relevant framework than is normally used, within which the problem may be examined and discussed.

It should be noted that the report of the U.S. National Commission quite rightly does not absolve media institutions and practitioners from their responsibilities. Although television is not regarded by the Commission as a principal cause of violence in society, both the nature and amount of violence on the small screen are roundly condemned. However, in the way they address the problem, the members of the Commission—like so many before and after them—do not always ask the right questions. But this is not surprising in view of the fact that they appeared to rely so heavily on the research results from those who oversimplify the problem and think of causal relationships in terms of initiation, increased aggressive drives, attitude change, and so on. Unfortunately, the Commission did not really face up to the media implications of its own conclusions about relative deprivation and frustration, which were referred to earlier, although there was a reference in the report to "additional complications (which might) arise from the hish visibility of both violence and social inequalities" (National Commission, 1969:292).

Clearly violence is not unrelated to frustration even though the relationship is not as direct and simple as some psychologists seem to have indicated. Consequently, it is certainly worthwhile asking the question: What, if anything, do the media contribute to frustration in our society, and, through this, aggression and violence.

As we have seen, the situation will vary from country to country and will clearly be influenced by a variety of factors, media and nonmedia, including advertising, degree of urbanisation, and so on. But let us assume we are dealing with a commercially oriented, industrialized, urban society in which advertising plays an important part in media operations and in the economy generally. The main goals, aims, and objectives of this kind of society will be closely related to the achievement of material prosperity, and a great deal of effort, time and money (not just through advertising) will be expended on the promotion of these goals. We know that one of the tasks of advertising is to make people dissatisfied with what they have and to stimulate them to want more, irrespective of their economic circumstances. Society places far greater stress on materialistic goals than on the legitimate ways of achieving these, and the media reflect this imbalance. For the poorer, deprived sections of the community this would exacerbate feelings of frustration and discontent.

In these circumstances, deprived groups in society are reminded, by a daily bombardment, of what is available to others, what is said to be theirs for the asking, yet what they certainly do not possess, and moreover are not likely ever to achieve. There are of course other powerful agents of frustration operating at a variety of levels from the interpersonal to the environmental, but it would be foolish to ignore the possibility that the media, in their normal day-to-day operations, by the presentation of these norms and values, may increase expectations unrealistically, aggravate existing problems, contribute to frustration, and consequently to the aggression and violence that may stem from this.

This, however, is not the sort of relationship people normally have in mind when they speculate or pontificate about the link between the media and violence. This type of relationship is certainly not central to those who vociferously condemn media violence.

As might be expected, the condemnation of media content is highly selective. Not all forms of media violence are condemned any more than are all forms of violent behavior. In passing it is interesting to note that quite a number of those who regard media violence as a serious problem not only tend to be aggressive in the way they express this but also adopt a somewhat negative and punitive approach to several other social issues. They favor the death penalty, corporal punishment, and tougher discipline generally. They also exhibit racist tendencies, and oppose penal and other social reforms. Overall, they tend to be conservative, conformists and authoritarian.[1]

Just as violence is defined selectively, so research results are used selectively. This is particularly true in the case of some of those just mentioned, that is, in so far as they find it necessary to refer to research at all in support of their claims.

Earlier it was stated that, although those researchers whose work centered on violent behavior and violence in society had not found the media to be a major source of violent behavior, others—those whose main focus had been the media and violence—had been more inclined to indict the media. On the whole most of these researchers are psychologists who have addressed themselves directly to some form of hypothesized relationship between the media's portrayal of violence on the one hand and violent or aggressive behavior on the other. In many cases their work has been commissioned and is financially supported for this specific purpose.

The U.S.A. Surgeon General's one million dollar, 23 project research program on television violence represent the biggest and most expensive, if not the most sophisticated and coordinated, exercise in this area. Because the findings and interpretations of this research program are frequently quoted by those who claim a causal link (media violence = violent behavior) has been established, and despite the many criticisms levelled against the individual projects, we must obviously look at what the report has to say (Surgeon General's Scientific Advisory Committee, 1972).

In view of the way it has been used to prove a case against television, it is surprising to find that the Surgeon General's Report is really quite cautious in its conclusions. It refers to *a preliminary and tentative indication* of a causal relation between viewing violence on the television and aggressive behavior *operating only on some children who are predisposed to be aggressive and only in some circumstances.* It is also recognized that both the heavy viewing of violence and violent or aggressive behavior could be the joint products of some other common source. They could both be symptoms of a wider condition.

This last point confirms our own research on television and delinquency carried out in England some years before the Surgeon General's work (Halloran et al., 1970). In this research it it was also found that the television viewing patterns of the delinquents did not differ significantly from those of their nondelinquent peers from the socioeconomic background. Neither were any significant differences in television viewing and preferences discovered when the media behavior of aggressive and nonaggressive teenagers in the North East of England were compared (Howett and Dembo, 1974).

These and other studies led us to state some years ago that no case had been made where television (or the other media) could be legitimately regarded as a causal, or even as a major contributory factor of any form of violent behavior. A more recent conclusion following a survey of work in this country and elsewhere (including research from the U.S.A.) is that it has still not been established that the mass media have any significant effect on the level of violence in society (Howitt and Cumberbatch, 1975). In fact, the whole weight of research and theory in this field would suggest that the mass media, except just possibly in the case of a small number of pathological individuals, are never the sole cause of such behavior. At most they play a contributory role and that a minor one.

We should not be surprised at this, rather we should be surprised at the persistence with which researchers will look for simple cause and effect relationships. In the strict sense, we really should not be asking questions about the effect of television. We rarely ask such questions about other institiutions such as the family, religion, or education.

Two points need to be made with regard to the above comments. First, they refer mainly to studies which conceptualize the problem in terms of initiation, increased aggression, attitude change, and so on. These represent what may be termed the conventional approach which, so it is argued here, is based on àn inadequate understanding of the media, of violence, of the communication process, and of the nature of society. As we shall see later, the media do have influence, but not primarily in this way.

Secondly, most of the conventional research—the results of which are often used to support the causal argument—has been carried out in the

U.S.A. The U.S.A. is different from Britain and other countries in a variety of ways, particularly with regard to the nature and amount of violence both on the screen and in society at large. What obtains in one country need not obtain in another.

More to the point, however, is the possibility that this work, or at least certain interpretations of it, does not even hold in the U.S.A. It has been criticized on several grounds (theoretically, conceptually, and methodologically), particularly for the lack of clarity and consistency in the use of such concepts as violence and aggression. In many cases the operationalization of the concepts is also very questionable. There is likely to be a substantial gap between behavioral, verbal, and attitudinal responses in a laboratory and antisocial aggression or violence in the home or street. The major weaknesses in the experimental laboratory work are the artificiality in the setting, the type and time of the measurements, and the nature of the "victim" (e.g., dolls, balloons, recipients of electric shocks, etc.). Moreover, it is by no means always clear what is really being measured. Validity is low. Generalization to antisocial behavior in real-life situations must be very suspect indeed. Survey work—the results of which, so it is claimed, point in the same directions as those from the laboratory work—is more realistic, but it is not susceptible to causal explanation.

Perhaps the last word on this highly controversial topic should be given to George Comstock, who is thoroughly familiar with the work and who has been closely and supportively associated with the Surgeon General's research and its follow-up over the last few years. Comstock (1976:10), fully aware of the convergence of the different research approaches, reports as follows:

> It is tempting to conclude that television violence makes viewers more anti-socially aggressive, somewhat callous, and generally more fearful of the society in which they live. It may, but the social and behavioral science evidence does not support such a broad indictment.
>
> The evidence on desensitization and fearfulness is too limited for such broad conclusions at this time. The evidence on aggressiveness is much more extensive, but it does not support a conclusion on increased anti-social aggression. Such a concluion rests on the willingness of the person who chooses to sit in judgment to extrapolate from the findings on interpersonal aggression to more serious, non-legal acts.
>
> Most important the evidence does not tell us anything about the degree of social harm or criminal anti-social violence that may be attributable to television. It may be great, negligible, or nil.

The media are certainly not without influence, but it is the process of influence which is more complex and probably more far-reaching than is commonly realized. For example, the way the media report violence and deviant behavior plays a part in defining problems and gives focus to public concern. Violence and deviant behavior, particularly in their extreme forms, are extensively covered by the media in most western societies. There is nothing new about this practice, or about the style or manner of presentation, except that it may not be quite as sensational as it once was. Yet possibly because of the nature of our fragmented, pluralistic, industrial society, in which many believe mediated culture plays an increasingly prominent part in shaping our values and behavior, media portrayals of violence and deviance may have more important social repercussions today than they had in the past.

Some years ago in American sociologist, Marshall Clinard (1963:177), writing on "The Newpaper and Crime," argued that:

> The press has been charged with generally promoting and glorifying crime because of the volume of its news items. . . . The amount and prominence of space devoted to crime in the newpapers and the amount of conversation based on these stories present a bewildering picture of immorality in our society. By continually playing up crime, it is likely that newspapers are important in making us a crime centered culture. As a result crime often seems more frequent than it is.

Although this claim and others like it are rarely accompanied by hard supporting evidence, it is not unreasonable to hypothesize that what people read in the papers, hear on the radio, and see on television might influence their views *about the nature and extent of violence in our society*. Some years ago studies carried out in the U.S. indicated that public estimates of the amount and type of crime in the community were more closely related to newspaper reports than to the actual amounts of crime as recorded by the police. Although other studies have been more ambiguous, there is no need here to argue the pros and cons of conflicting research results. The main point is to draw attention to one of the ways in which the media may be related to public perceptions of violent behavior (Halloran, 1976; Croll, 1976).

The media help to set the social/political agenda. They select, organize, emphasize, define, and amplify. They convey meanings and perspectives, offer solutions, associate certain groups with certain types of values and behavior, create anxiety, and legitimate or justify the status quo and the prevailing systems of social control. They structure "the pictures of the world" that are available to us and, in turn, these pictures may structure our beliefs and possible modes of action. It is in these complex and difficult ways that we must examine the influence of the media.

The media, of course, do not work in isolation. What we should really study is the mix, the interaction or interrelationship between media experiences on the one hand, and nonmedia or situational experiences on the other. These will differ from issue to issue, from person to person, from country to country, and so on. For example, we know from our research on race relations and racial conflict that the media may have a disproportionate influence in conveying meanings and perspectives where personal experience is lacking. Our work on the media and race showed that, over a seven-year period, the media portrayed non-white people essentially as a threat and a problem, and that this was reflected in public attitudes (Hartmann et al., 1974; Hartmann and Husband, 1974). Here we have a clear example of the media exacerbating conflict and reinforcing if not actually creating social problems. Our research also show that the coverage by the British media of the hostilities in Northern Ireland is another example of conflict exacerbation (Elliott, 1977:263-376).

There are, then, several questions we might ask. For example, what kind of pictures are being presented to us? Are they false pictures in which the extent of violence and deviance is exaggerated and its nature distorted? Is it true that by designating violence as news (the more violent, the more newsworthy) a climate of alarm is created, and fears, anticipations, and expectations about violent behavior are built up?

These questions bring us to the even more fundamental ones of: What is news? Do the mass media create new "facts" by making non-news news? Must the negative, deviant, violent, or sensational always predominate? There are other questions that need not be detailed here, but one point we can make at this stage is that, on the whole, the way the news about violence and related issues is presented by the media makes it unlikely that the facts will be placed in a meaningful context or that the issues behind the story with regard to offense, offender, victim, or official agency will be adequately covered.

It is often argued by those working in the media that when events are reported it is natural to focus on the immediate case. That is where the drama lies, where the action is, and what the public wants to know about. This may be true, but it provides a poor base from which an adequate understanding of the problem can be developed.

The formation of sound social policy typically depends on knowledge of changes in the development rate and distribution of the relevant events, but policies are formed more frequently in reaction to certain extreme cases. The media deal in extreme cases, and we know they are widely used as the main source of information and are regarded by many as highly credible.

One reason why the media portray situations as they do is because they operate within a socio-economic system where readers and viewers have to be won and kept. The presentation of violence and related phenomena have become vital in this connection.

For the daily news media, persons, events, and happenings (particularly negative ones) are the basic units of news. One reason for the concentration on events is the "publication frequency" of the media themselves. Events are more likely to be picked up by the media working to a daily publication cycle if they occur within the space of one day. For example, a demonstration is a possible news event, but the development of a political movement over several years does not have the correct "frequency."

The concentration on events itself makes some aspects of the a story more likely to be regarded as newsworthy than others. The issue of violence, for example, is directly related to the visible forms of events on the streets. But this preoccupation with events and incidents tends to exclude consideration of background development and the issues involved.

One of our research projects, which focused on the media coverage of a large political demonstration, provides a good illustration of some of the foregoing points. It also raises several important questions about the influence of this form of presentation on the general public's assessment of the events going on in the world and its consequences for social action (Halloran, 1977).

In this research, differences between the various media in the treatment of the demonstration were obviously detected, but we were also able to show a more important and fundamental *similarity* between practically all branches of the media. In all but one case the story was interpreted in terms of the same basic issue which had originally made it news. Viewers and readers were not presented with various interpretations focusing on different aspects of the same event, but with basically the same interpretation which focused on the same limited aspect, namely the issue of violence. Yet violence need not have been central; in fact, in reality it was not central. The "set" of violence was used because, together with the other implications of news values, it was the logical outcome of the existing organization of the new process, and of the assumptions on which it rested.

As indicated earlier, these news values are an integral part of professional news selection and presentation as this has developed within our particular socio-economic system. No matter what lofty ideals are claimed, numbers of readers, listeners and viewers, and the economics of advertising play an important part in shaping these values and the news which they underlie.

It is also important to note that the images created in this way may endure and be capable of being extended to related areas. The coverage of student demonstrations against the visiting South African rugby team are but two of many examples of the apparent pervasiveness and durability of the image of violent confrontation and other related negative stereotypes.

But, argues the media man, we know what the public wants and we provide it. The public likes what it is familiar with, what it has been given over the years, what it has come to accept and expect. Supply influences demand. It is of course clear that many people like their news to be action-packed and incident-oriented, lively, entertaining, even sensational and violent. This sort of material may meet different needs for different people, but the emphasis on action, visual attractiveness, and immediacy (rather than on what is socially significant) does not stem solely from some basic human need. It receives plenty of help and reinforcement from the media.

What, then, are the results of this form of news presentation? One interpretation is that the way the media deal with these situations may lead to labelling, to the association—perhaps unjustifiable—of certain groups with violent behavior, and possibly to the acceptance of violence as a legitimate way of dealing with problems or as a necessary form of retaliation.

In the case of the demonstration projects, given the climate of public opinion at the time of the research, the largely negative presentation was almost bound to devalue the case of the protesters. Moreover, in the long run, this might increase rather than reduce the risk of violent behavior. Because of the way the media operate, a minority group may have to be violent before there is any chance of its case being presented to the general public.

It would also appear from this and related research that whether we are dealing with student demands for reform in the universities, antiapartheid marches, anti-war demonstrations, drug taking, alchoholics, homosexuals, prisoners' unions, racial questions, or strikes, there is a very good chance the news story will center on violence and confrontation. The account will be largely isolated from antecedent conditions, and convey little understanding of either root causes or aims. In fact, the whole presentation is likely to be fragmented and out of context.

Research has shown that in reporting violence and deviance the media exaggerate, sensationalize, and stereotype, and that public perceptions derived from these presentations may modify or even create the behavior in question. For example, the images of drug use obtained from the media, so it is claimed, have influenced court and police behavior and, in turn, this has influenced the behavior in such a way as to make it conform with the stereotypes. The stereotypes were fulfilled, the behavior—previously marginal—became more central and frequent, and this was followed by further (reinforcing) social reaction. The problem was confirmed at a redefined level, and all sides behaved as they were "expected" to behave.

At a different level, the overall effect of this type of presentation of deviance and social problems could be to eliminate or play down alternative conceptions of social order. The news selection process, therefore, may have an ideological significance for the maintenance of the status quo of power and interest by managing conflict and dissent in the interest of the establishment.

This represents a more complex and indirect approach to media influence than is normally postulated, but surely the study of the media in this way is much more valid and rewarding than the relatively simple-minded causal stimulus-response approaches which have been frequently if unproductively utilized in the past.

But these newer approaches do not provide all the answers. For example, the labelling-amplification approach mentioned earlier, although useful and interesting, does not account for deviant behavior and still less for the initial deviation. It also has a limited application because it does not apply equally to all forms of deviant behavior some of which are clearly visible.

The importance of public definitions and expectations about violence as contributory factors to the processes by which the behavior is publicly defined, labelled or stereotyped, and even on occasions amplified, should always be borne in mind, without exaggerating the possibilities. People do have experiences other than media experiences and, although the agenda may be set by the media, the ability of the public to selectively use and interpret what the media make available should not be underestimated. The media may inform public perceptions and beliefs about violence, but there are other sources of information even though in many societies most of the population have little or no personal experience of violence.

Generally, media violence is viewed negatively and is criticized or condemned because of its alleged disruptive effects. But we have already referred to the possibility that the media may serve a "positive function in their portrayal of violence and deviance by acting as an instrument of social control and by maintaining the status quo. The function may be regarded as positive from the standpoint of the establishment although not necessarily from the standpoint of other groups in society who are seeking change. (Coser, 1966).

The media may reinforce the status quo by maintaining a "cultural consensus." It is possible that the media coverage of violence could enhance normative consensus and community integration. Where people have little firsthand knowledge of violent crime, they are likely to depend on the media for most of their information. The media inform, bring to light, create awareness, redefine the boundaries of what is acceptable and what is not, and structure perceptions of the nature and extent of violence. In doing this they bring people together in opposition to disorder, reinforce a belief in common values, facilitate the imposition of sanctions, and strengthen social control. In order to do this, however, the violence must be made visible throughout society—hence the importance of the media.

Although many of the hypotheses stemming from this approach have still to be put to the test, there is nothing new in the view that regards violence as a catalyst. Marx, Durkheim, and Mead all stressed the unanticipated functions of crime in creating a sense of solidarity within the community by arousing the moral and aesthetic sentiments of the public. More recently, Lewis Coser developed a related idea when he argued that not only criminals, but also law-enforcing agents may call forth a sense of solidarity against their behavior. In certain circumstances the use of extra-legal violence, particularly when exhibited under the glare of television cameras, and made highly visible to the public at large, could lead to awareness, indignation, and revulsion, which might result in the rejection of a hitherto accepted practice. Many questionable things that we no not know abour—or at least do not intrude too much into our everyday lives—are done in our name and in the name of social order and justice. However, passivity and acquiescence become more difficult with an increase in visibility. It has been suggested that the media coverage of racial disturbances in the southern states in the U.S.A. in the early 1960s is a case in point.

The media coverage of racial disturbances in the U.S.A., as well as drawing attention once more to the different definitions of violence and to its functional or dysfunctional consequences, also shows the complexity of this whole problem in a heterogeneous, pluralistic, stratified society. After seeing racial disturbances in the streets on their television sets, some people may reach for their guns in the name of law and order, others may learn a lesson or two that they will put into practical use when their time comes, and still others—as the hitherto invisible or partly visible becomes clearly visible—may be jolted out of their apathy and stirred into social action directed at the roots of the problem. Here, as in other situations, different people take different things from the same message. There are no easy decisions for the responsible broadcaster in deciding what to present and how to present it in situations like this. In reminding broadcasters of their responsibilities, we must also recognize their difficulties and try to understand their problems.

In the last few pages we have been dealing with nonfictional media material, but George Gerbner, one of the most prominent mass communication researchers in the U.S.A., is much more concered with fictional material (Gerbner and Gross, 1976). He would agree with some of the criticisms made above about the inadequacies of the conventional research approaches, particularly those which focus of attitude and behavioral change and the stimulation of aggression. He is also critical of studies based on selectively used media, which in part stems from his firm conviction that television is essentially different from the other media, and that research on television requires an entirely new approach.

> The essential differences between television and the other media are more crucial than the similarities . . . the reach, scope, ritualization, organic connectedness and non-selective use of mainstream television makes it different from other media of mass communications.

Gerbner argues that television should not be isolated from the mainstream of modern culture because "it *is* the mainstream." It is "the central cultural aim of American society," a "major force for enculturation—(which permeates)—both the initial and final years of life as well as the years between." His interest is not so much in individual programs or specific messages as in "whole systems of messages" and their consequences for "Common consciousness."

He sees little point in making the conventional distinction between information and entertainment. He regards entertainment, particularly television drama, as highly informative—"the most broadly effective educational fare in any culture"—and maintains that all of us, whatever our status or educational background, obtain much of our knowldge of the real world from fictional representations. Television entertainment provides common ground for all sections of the populations as it offers a continuous stream of "facts" and impressions about the many aspects of life and society. "Never before have all classes and groups (as well as ages) shared so much of the same culture and the same perspectives."

This is not just a speculative exercise on Gerbner's part, for he supports at least part of his case with some of the most impressive systematic analysis of television content ever carried out. Naturally, he recognizes and accepts that content analysis by itself tells us nothing definitive about the viewing public's reactions to the content. He claims, however, that his studies of the public, although as yet in their early stages, demonstrate quite clearly the ability of television to cultivate its own "reality." In all the cases studied, heavier viewers had versions of social reality which squared more with "the television world" than did the versions of the lighter viewers.

Gerbner's work, then, provides some support for the main themes of this chapter. Namely that television is not without influence (Gerbner would put it much more strongly than this), but that the nature and directions of the influence are not as commonly supposed or of the kind that conventional researchers seem anxious to trace and identify. He also supports the view that the concern about media violence, based on the possibilities of disruption that threaten the established norms of belief, behavior and morality, is ill-conceived and badly directed.

Gerbner, then is certainly worried about television's portrayal of violence, but this is not because of its potential for disruption or even change, but because it might function to legitimate and maintain the power and authority of the establishment. Change is more likely to be impeded than facilitated as television demonstrates the values of society and the rules of the game "by dramatic stories of their symbolic violations." In this way it serves the social order of the industrial system. "The system is the message" and the system works well—perhaps "too well in cultivating uniform assumptions, exploitable fears, acquiescence to power and resistance to meaningful change."

Gerbner sees television violence as the simplest and cheapest dramatic means available to demonstrate the rules of the game of power, to reinforce social control, and to maintain the existing social order. He supports this view with data from his research, suggesting that the maintenance mechanism seems to work through cultivating a sense of danger, risk, and insecurity. This leads, especially for the less powerful groups in the community, to acquiescence to and dependence upon established authority. It also facilitates the legitimation of the use of force by the authorities in order to keep their position.

As far as the influence of television is concerned, this reinforcement or maintenance function is considered to be far more important than any threat to the social order which might stem from television-induced imitation, attitude change, or increased aggressive drives. In fact, Gerbner states that:

Media-incited criminal violence may be a price industrial cultures extract from some citizens for the general pacification of most others. . . . Television—the established religion of the industrial order—appears to cultivate assumptions that fit its socially functional myths.

Violence and its portrayal by the media clearly serve specific social functions, although these will differ from country to country, as will the nature and extent of media violence. Veikko Pietila (1976), the Finnish scholar, in comparing television violence in the U.S.A. and U.S.S.R., shows that in the two countries it is presented in different contexts and serves different functions.

In the U.S.S.R., televised violence tends to be presented in historical, societal, and collective contests, while in the U.S.A. the emphasis is on individually oriented aggression which is frequently linked to personal success, achievement, and private property. In the U.S.A., one of the main aims is to create excitement and attract and keep an audience in a fiercely competitive system where profits have to be made. In the U.S.S.R., according to Pietila, the purposes are more often propagandistic and educational.

Pietila comments on both the commodity (box office) and ideological functions of televised violence in the U.S.A., and asks a question not unlike some of those already posed here. He asks if television violence represents a vital aspect of the essential nature of this society, because a core element in its history and development has been individual success by means of violence or aggression. This form of violence is deeply rooted in the society, and the media portrayal of violence is a manifestation of this state of affairs, which should not surprise us. It is also suggested that the constant emphasis on this theme by reinforcement, diversion, or some other process helps to preserve the existing order.

Pietela confines this type of speculative analysis to capitalist societies and refers to television content contributing "to the directing and regulating of social process in such a way that the existing order and form of these societies is protected." We say that Pietila's research indicated that televised violence in socialist societies is different in content and context from that in capitalist societies. Not surprisingly he argues that media violence functions in different ways in the two countries. However, at another level it serves both systems by reinforcing the existing order. At this level the system is the message in both countries.

This and similar topics could be pursued much further and at greater depth, but enough has been written to illustrate one of the main aims of the chapter, which is to suggest some of the social and political consequences which may possibly stem from the ways in which the media deal with violence and related phenomena—ways which do not figure prominently either in the general debate or in the research programs of most mass communications researchers.

It must be emphasized, however, that at this stage we are mainly theorizing and talking in terms of possibilities and hypotheses. We are not in a position to make clear definitive statements, supported by evidence, on the precise role of the media in the areas and directions outlined here. The necessary research has not been carried out. Moreover, even if the recommended research were carried out, the neat, simple, packaged, convenient, unequivocal answers sought by so many are still not likely to be forthcoming. The nature of the problem is not susceptible to this type of answer. The process is too complex.

Of course, new research is required—it always will be if we are to have informed policies. To accept that research by itself is unable to provide an answer to all our questions, like a catechism, is not to reject its usefulness. We must not be unrealistic in our expectations, but there is no doubt that research has a substantial contribution to make to our understanding of social institutions and social processes. I am writing, of course, about a particular type of research.

I am convinced it will be more profitable to explore the avenues of enquiry outlined in this chapter, difficult though it may be—even just to speculate on these approaches—than to persist in the much simpler conventional search which attempts to establish causal links between media violence and real life violence.

One final point needs to be made. As far as research is concerned, although a great deal remains to be done, we are not entirely ignorant, as I hope the references to the results from quite a number of projects will have established. We have enough information now to know where to start if we wish to reduce violent behavior in our societies. The final report of the National Commission on the Causes and Prevention of Violence called in 1969 for "a reordering of national priorities and for a greater investment of resources—to establish justice and to ensure domestic tranquillity." The emphasis was on social reform and increased expenditure to facilitate the achievement of essential social goals. The needs and the priorities are still the same, and are likely to remain that way for some time.

NOTES

1. This does not apply by any means to all those who at some time or other have expressed concern about the media protrayal of violence.

REFERENCES

CLINARD, M.B. (1963). Sociology of deviant behavior. New York: Holt, Rinehart, and Winston.

COMSTOCK, G. (9176). The evidence of television violence. Santa Monica, Cal.: Rand.

COSER, L.A. (1966). "Some social functions of violence." Annals of the American Academy of Political and Social Science, 374:8-18.

CROLL, P. (1976). The nature of public concern with television with particular reference to violence. Leicester: Center for Mass Communications Research.

ELLIOTT, P. (1977). Reporting northern Ireland, in ethnicity and the media. Paris: UNESCO.

GERBNER, G., and GROSS, L. (1976). "Living with television: A violence profile." Journal of Communications, 26(2):173-200.

GRAHAM, H.D., and GURR, T.R. (1969). The history of violence in America: A report to the National Commission on the Causes and Prevention of Violence. New York: Bantam.

HALLORAN, J.D. (1976). Probleme der berichterstattung in den massenmedien vber kriminelles verhalten. Leicester: Center for Mass Communications Research.

_____ (1977). Demonstrations and communication. Harmondsworth, England: Penguin.

HALLORAN, J.D. et al. (1970). Television and delinquency. Leicester: Leicester University Press.

HARTMANN, P. et al. (1974). Race as news: A study in the handling of race in the British national press from 1963 to 1970. Paris: UNESCO.

HARTMANN, P., and HUSBAND, C. (1974). Racism and the mass media. London. Davis-Poynter.

HOWITT, D., and CUMBERBATCH, G. (1975). Mass media violence and society. London: Elek.

HOWITT, D., and DEMBO, R. (1974). "A subcultural account of media effects." Human Relations, 27(1):2541.

National Commission on the Causes and Prevention of Violence (1969). Final report, Appendix 2. Washington, D.C.:U.S. Government Printing Office.

PIETILA, V. (1976). "Notes on violence in the mass media." Instant Research on Peace and Violence, Tampere Peace Research Institute/Finland, 4:195-197.

Surgeon General's Scientific Advisory Committee (1972). Television and growing up: The impact of televised violence. Washington, D.C.: Department of Health, Education and Welfare.

ABOUT THE CONTRIBUTORS

PETER ARVIDSSON is a lecturer in communication at the University of Lund, Lund, Sweden.

GERALD CROMER, Lecturer in the Department of Criminology at Bar Ilan University and Institute of Criminology at Hebrew University of Jerusalem, has published articles on the generation gap, politicization of deviance, and self-help groups. He is currently engaged in research on character assassination and violence and corruption in sport.

ROBERT G. DELISLE is Director of the Graduate Program in Reading at Herbert H. Lehman College, CUNY. He is President of the Bronx Reading Council.

JOSEPH R. DOMINICK is an associate professor in the Grady School of Journalism and Mass Communication at the University of Georgia.

GILBERT GEIS, a member of the Social Ecology Program at the University of California, Irvine, is the author of many monographs and articles on juvenile justice, mass media, drug abuse, and social control. Among his many books are *Not the Law's Business?* and *Man, Crime, and Society.*

GEORGE GERBNER is Dean of the Annenberg School of Communications, University of Pennsylvania, and editor of the Journal of Communication. Creator of the Violence Index and the Cultural Indicators Project, his content analyses have been widely discussed and currently represent the most influential empirical studies in the field of mass communications.

JAMES D. HALLORAN, Director of the Center for Mass Communications Research at the University of Leicester, in England, is President of the International Association for Mass Communications Research.

ANDREW KARMEN is an assistant professor of sociology at John Jay College of Criminal Justice in New York City. He has taught at Boston State College, University of Lowell, and City College of New York. He is author of articles on heroin addiction, police practices, and other social problems.

PHILIP J. LEONHARD-SPARK is assistant professor of sociology and Director of the Social Sciences Computer Laboratory at City College, CUNY, where he teaches courses in methods of social research. He has been Lecturer in Nutrition at Teachers College, Columbia University.

JOAN LIEBMANN-SMITH is a member of the Medical Sociology Program of the City University of New York and the Mt. Sinai School of Medicine. She has done extensive research in the field of drug abuse.

HAROLD MENDELSOHN, professor and chairman, Department of Mass Communications, University of Denver, is also Director of the University's Communication Arts Center. As a member of the Surgeon General's Scientific Advisory Committee on Television and Social Behavior, he was a co-author of the Committee's monograph report, *Television and Growing Up: The Impact of Televised Violence.* He is the author of *Mass Entertainment* and co-author of *Polls, Television, and the New Politics, Minorities and the Police,* and *The People Choose a President: Influences on Voter Decision Making.*

GARRETT J. O'KEEFE, associate professor in the Department of Mass Communications at the University of Denver, holds the Ph.D. in mass communication from the University of Wisconsin-Madison. He has published a variety of studies on relationships among mass communication, interpersonal communication, and political and social behavior. He is co-author of *The People Choose a President: Influences on Voter Decision Making.*

SHARON L. ROSEN is a member of the Medical Sociology Program at the City University of New York and the Mt. Sinai School of Medicine. She is currently doing research on the socialization of medical students.

KARL ERIK ROSENGREN is Associate Professor and Senior Lecturer at the University of Lund, Sweden, and Research Fellow of the Swedish Council for Research in the Humanities and Social Sciences. He has been a Research Fellow of the Swedish Social Science Council and has published widely in mass communications and the theory of social science.

EDWARD SAGARIN is professor of sociology at City College and the Graduate Center, CUNY. He is author of *Deviants and Deviance, Okk Man In,* and co-author of *Sex, Crime and the Law* and editor of *Deviance and Social Change.* He has been president of the American Soceity of Criminology and editor of *Criminology.*

SANFORD SHERIZEN, associate professor of sociology at Boston University, spend five years at the Research Department of the Chicago Urban League and previously taught in the Department of Criminal Justice at the University of Illinois, Chicago Circle. During the 1973-1974 academic year, he investigated European alternatives to imprisonment.

DAHN STURESSON is a Lecturer in Communication at the College of Vaxjo in Sweden.

CHARLES WINICK is coordinator of the Mass Communications Sequence and the Program in Deviance, CUNY Graduate Center, Department of Sociology, and professor of sociology at City College, CUNY. Formerly a faculty member at University of Rochester, MIT, and Columbia, he is author or editor of 20 books.

ABIGAIL STAHL WOODS is Acting Director, Program in Early Childhood Education, Herbert H. Lehman College, CUNY. She is directing a program of research into children's perceptions of illness and death.